## DATE DUE

| | | | |
|---|---|---|---|
| | | | |
| | | | |
| | | | |
| | | | |
| | | | |
| | | | |
| | | | |
| | | | |
| | | | |
| | | | |
| | | | |
| | | | |
| | | | |
| | | | |
| | | | |
| | | | |
| | | | |
| | | | |
| | | | PRINTED IN U.S.A. |
| | | | |

# FROM
# THE TABLES
# OF
# TUSCAN WOMEN

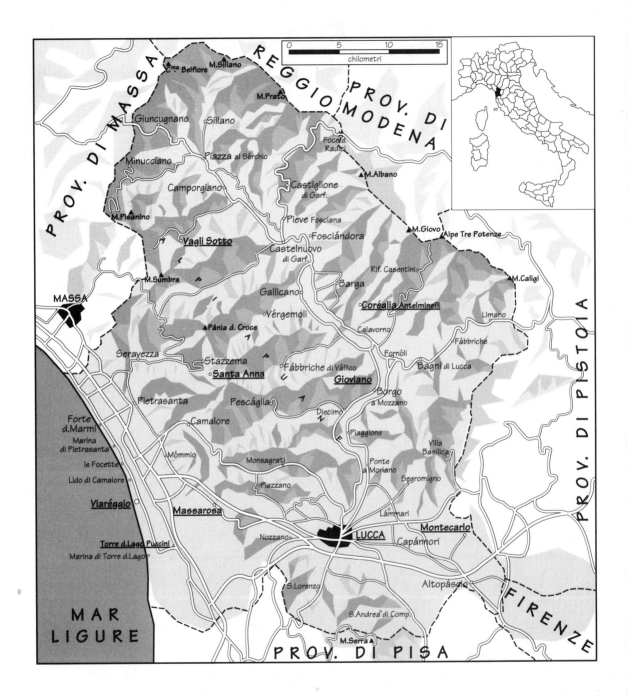

# FROM THE TABLES OF TUSCAN WOMEN

*Recipes and Traditions*

ANNE BIANCHI

Photographs by Douglas Hatschek

THE ECCO PRESS

THE ECCO PRESS
100 West Broad Street
Hopewell, New Jersey 08525
Published simultaneously in Canada by
Penguin Books Canada Ltd., Ontario
Printed in the United States of America

Library of Congress Cataloging-in-Publication Data
Bianchi, Anne.
    From the tables of Tuscan women : recipes and traditions / by Anne
Bianchi.
        p.    cm.
    Includes index.
    ISBN 0-88001-425-3
    1. Cookery, Italian—Tuscan style.  2. Tuscany (Italy)—Social
life and customs.    I. Title.
TX723.2.T86B53    1995
641.5945'5—dc20                95-10075

Designed by Barbara Cohen Aronica
The text of this book is set in Bembo

10  9  8  7  6  5  4  3  2  1

FIRST EDITION

*To my mother, the original Signora, with love and thanks.*

# Contents

$\mathcal{W}$hen you take a look around your average bookstore, you see a great many books about Tuscany in general, and even more about the *cuisine* of Tuscany. Whether specifically mentioned or not, however, the geographical focus of such books is generally on the *eastern* part of Tuscany —on the provinces of either Florence or Siena. Talk to your average cookbook reader about San Gemignano, Chianti, Montepuleiano, or Orvieto, and chances are the person either already *has* a book about that area's cuisine or plans to purchase one in the near future.

But Tuscany has eight other provinces besides Florence and Siena, each with its own set of individual charms and—most certainly—its own distinct style of cooking. From Livorno to Pisa to Massa to Carrara to Lucca to Arezzo to Grosseto to Pistota to the aforementioned Firenze and Siena, one province's *foccacia* is another province's *schiacchetta*.

This book turns its gaze *westward* and somewhat to the north of Florence—to the province of Lucca, with its fascinating blend of natural beauty, exciting nightlife, and ancient culture. Lucca's western border is the Tyrrhenian Sea, fronted by twenty kilometers of pristine white sand beaches, and referred to in geographical terms as the Versilia. On the north are the forests of the Garfagnana, dotted with tiny villages and filled with hundreds of thousands of chestnut trees. The *east* is a maze of scattered hill towns, each surrounded by olive groves and magnificently terraced vineyards. And the south is where you'll find the provincial seal—Lucca, an eleventh-century walled enclave that is both perfectly preserved and impeccably maintained.

While the province of Lucca (the Lucchesía) is, comparatively speaking, largely undiscovered by foreign travelers, those fortunate few who *do* venture onto its soil end up describing it as the richest and most diverse of all Tuscan provinces. Its cuisine, in fact, is linked to this diversity—to this blend of mountain and coast that creates a wealth of ingredients not otherwise available.

From *fritto misto di pesce,* a mixed assortment of fish, battered and fried in olive oil, to *cacciucco,* a soup made entirely of fish and served on thick slices of toasted bread rubbed with garlic, to *castagnaccio,* a sweet cake made from chestnut flour, the cooking style of the Lucchesía depends, to a large extent, on foods that can either be fished from the sea or—like mushrooms and chestnuts—can be retrieved from the forest floor.

In addition to its unique blend of culinary ingredients, however, Lucca's cuisine is also dependent on factors having nothing to do with food—on, for example, a uniquely Mediterranean lifestyle that mixes marvelous climate, a relaxed attitude, and an unrelenting passion for sitting down at the table. The end result? A gastronomic excellence not easily rivaled.

Judge for yourself: Baby clams sautéed with garlic and fresh parsley . . . scampi basted with olive oil and grilled over hot coals . . . sage dipped in batter and fried to a golden crispness . . . fresh shell beans placed in a flask with olive oil and rosemary and cooked over an open fire . . . artichokes roasted with baby lamb and fresh tomatoes . . . rabbit with polenta and porcini mushrooms—these are the components of an everyday meal in the province of Lucca.

But there is also another factor that is less widely discussed, and that is the people of the province. Having spent a great part of my life in this part of Tuscany, I can say (along with every other writer who has, at one point or another, turned an eye toward this area) that no people anywhere in the world are more dramatic, outspoken, or riotously arrogant than the people of the Lucchesía. In the words of Dante, they "have Paradise in their eyes, and Inferno in their mouths."

The evidence is everywhere. Spend a few minutes standing in any piazza in the Lucchesía discussing something as banal as the weather, and in ten minutes time, you will be treated to a hilariously caustic assessment of: hunters, local politicians, the cardinals in the Vatican, banktellers, the butcher's new son-in-law who comes from Sardinia, the state of olive oil pressing in twentieth-century Tuscany, wine growers, and Pavarotti's chance of lasting another six months. All accompanied by theatrical gestures, exaggerated inflections, and a highly conspiratorial I-know-you-know-exactly-what-I-mean attitude.

It is this particular blend of factors—the geography, the people, and the recipes—that I have chosen to bring together to illustrate the cuisine of the Lucchesía. To my way of thinking, the recipes alone—while they might have produced a wonderful meal—would always leave the food wanting. Missing would be the spirit, the attitude, the conviction, the carriage.

And so, on the following pages, you will meet nine amazing women, hear their stories, stroll through their towns, and sample the best of their recipes. My hope is that you will be infused with the spirit of the Lucchesía, and that the food at your table will, as a result, sparkle.

One more thing. When preparing these recipes, remember that the end result has more to do with your *feel* for the food than on any strict adherence to either the ingredients or the directions. If you think the dish would be better served by a little more rosemary or a little less oil, listen to your instincts. Tuscans are nothing if not magnificent individualists cooking-wise; each person does things just a little bit differently. Ada Boni, the great Italian cookbook author, puts it like this: "Nowhere does the cooking of food make as much of a political statement as it does in Tuscany; there are no masses in this part of the country; only masters."

It is now time to begin your journey through the traditions and rituals of the Lucchesía. I raise my glass in your honor. *Buon viaggio,* and *buon appetito*!

## Acknowledgments

*T*his book would not have been possible without the following people to whom I give my wholehearted thanks:

My mother, Maria Valleroni, who lives in Tuscany and not only put up with my living in her house during the writing of this book but fed me—royally; Douglas Hatschek, for both his outstanding photography and consistent spiritual support ("Send it out *again*," he'd say when the initial proposal would come back, rejected, from yet another publisher); Sandra Lotti, who provided the main body of research and technical support *(Grazie Bellezza, sensa di te, che avrei fatto?)*; Tom Gelinne ("un capo cuoco") for his generous and invaluable technical assistance in reviewing the recipes; Judith Lamb for retouching photographs; Amerina Castiglia, for the generous use of her private library and for her extensive contacts in Tuscany; my Tuscan relatives and friends—Umbretta Lotti, Santi Bianchi, Reno Bicicchi, Alessandra Orlandi, and Paolo Lotti—who chauffeured me from village to village in search of material; Susan Etkind for sparking the original inspiration; Norma Venturi for the loan of her mother's ancient cookbook; my editors and copyeditors at Ecco Press—Ellen, Dan, and Phyllis; and, of course, the women themselves whose magnificent spirits floated effortlessly onto the pages of this book.

*Signora Iris Redini*

*Chapter One*

# THE ESSENCE
# OF ARROGANCE

## APPETIZERS

*W*hen one stops to contemplate the history of Tuscany's occupation by foreigners, it's not the occupied who warrant pity; it's the *occupiers*. Because in the end—whether they were forced by virtue of their pride to remain for a few years and keep up the *appearance* of victory, or whether they quickly left with their tails between their legs—every conquering hero eventually came to the same realization: that he had conquered a people who, unfortunately, viewed *themselves* as masters, and all others as, well, somewhat less.

So you can imagine the plight of those great warriors who, after the trumpets and the chariots and the blaring declarations of victory, found themselves feeling not only like subjugants but subjugants who—learning of their decrepit status—were instantly relegated to seeing themselves as ridiculous, both for having dreamt of victory in the first place and, worse, for having imposed their presence on a people so obviously more exalted than they.

And so it is that foreigners stumbling onto Tuscan soil have always continued on their way rather than tarrying in a place that reduced them to such shoddiness.

Witness Hannibal, certainly among the greatest generals of all times. According to legend, not one city in Tuscany offered him so much as a passing glance. At town after town, village after village, his arrival always generated the same response: pure and visible scorn. There he would stand, this great Carthaginian leader, trumpeting his arrival outside the village walls. Eventually, it would become quite clear that no one was looking in his direction, the people of the town just going about their business with those grand Tuscan noses thrust into the air, refusing to acknowledge his existence. And soon, any thought Hannibal had ever entertained of invasion and conquest would dissolve completely. If he wanted food, he had to pick it from the hillsides; if he wanted wine, he had to buy it. So he journeyed through Tuscany step by step, passing from the hill towns of the Garfagnana to the open plains of the Maremma, vowing with each footfall never to return to this accursed region, preferring instead to conquer the southern towns of Abbruzze and Calabria where the people had a proper understanding of the respect due a hero of his caliber.

But, to Signora Iris Redini, it's incredible that Hannibal could not have foreseen his ultimate fate. "He was in Tuscany after all! What did he think—that we would simply prostrate ourselves before the majesty of his elephants like all the others?"

She waves her arms to take in the panorama of the distant hills. "Look far and wide. What you see up here are not people who are so easily impressed. Judges are what you see, not spectators. Not witnesses without opinion. Ask anyone in the world and they will tell you that Tuscans are ebullient people always willing to engage in conversation. But why is that so? Because we're by nature outgoing and enthusiastic? Certainly not! It is because we are gathering information to use as the basis for our judgments. That's why we want to know so much about you—what you eat, what you drink, how many pairs of pants you have in your closet, what you and your husband say to each other before going to bed at night. No, no, no," she concludes. "Tuscans are nothing if not good judges."

I ask the Signora why she thinks Tuscans are like this. Her answer is given without the slightest hesitation. "It's the air," she says conclusively. "The climate. Tuscans, after all, live much of their lives outside. How can you help but pass judgment with everyone so constantly in view!"

Then she gets down to the fine details. "When you walk down the street in Tuscany, you are looked at from top to bottom," she says. "Up and down, the people take you in. At their most blatant, they stop cold a few feet from your side, hands on hips to watch you squirm by. And squirm by you do, knowing that even as you did your best to dress well that morning and pluck the breakfast crumbs from your teeth, you might as well not have bothered.

"Look at how we treated Mussolini, who came to Tuscany only on a very few occasions, preferring instead to spend his time in places where the same three planes parading down four different streets could be sold to the people as a fleet of twelve. Il Duce was *furbo* [shrewd],"the Signora asserts. "And his *furbízia* seemed so highly evolved that Tuscans (who would know such a thing, being, themselves, the shrewdest of the world's people) initially judged it as worthy of further investigation.

"Beh," she continues, "the love affair faded quickly as Mussolini showed himself to be less of a *furbo* and more *il fesso* [the fool], a transformation not universally accepted by Italians-at-large, particularly those who, even today—*especially* today," she adds under her breath—"continue to maintain shrines in his honor. Occasionally," the Signora adds, "you might even find a Tuscan among that group, although, if you do, you can be sure their admiration has more to do with his genius for putting on a good show than for any true leadership ability."

She forces herself back to the topic at hand. "But if you *really* want to understand our penchant for judging, let's talk about the day the allied forces came to the town, those poor tired soldiers, *poverini,* who came to Tuscany fresh from having routed the Germans in the South where, for the next three days, they were paraded through the town and treated as the heroes they had shown themselves to be. But then they came marching down *our* streets. And I won't tell you we didn't also treat them like heroes. What I *will* say is that we generally prefer to decide for ourselves about such matters and not be handed our heroes on a plate.

"Beh," she says shaking her head. "It was immediately apparent that the soldiers were used to overflowing adulation. You could see it on their faces, the childlike smiles as they rounded the main *corso,* walking five or six abreast into the brilliant summer sunshine. And then, suddenly, they became aware of something that made them hesitate, if only for the slightest second. Their smiles were not being returned. And worse, the candy bars they tossed randomly into the crowd brought forth—instead of cheers—simply a quiet acknowledgment that these strange confections called *Milky Ways* were, indeed, quite good."

She purses her lips together and shakes her head sadly. "I think, however, that what caused the greatest tension was that we had the audacity to look *at* them—not with our eyes down like other Italians, not in unadulterated acceptance, but in scrutiny. 'After all,' many of us were thinking, 'we could eventually have done this ourselves, what with the growing strength of our partisans.'

"And so it happened that, for that one awkward second, the GIs slowed their pace, thinking perhaps they had sauntered into one of the many German enclaves that still existed throughout these hills. But only for a second. Then the crowd made up its mind. The *Yankis* were all right—not the goliaths they had been made out to be, and certainly not the caliber of, say, the *Garibaldini,* but for now, they would do. And besides, it was clear that we had all arrived at a clear understanding of who, exactly, were the Masters, and who the invited guests."

We stroll into the Signora's kitchen, and our discussion regarding dinner makes me realize that, in the Redini household, "mastery" is a concept that applies as much to the preparation of food as to the essence of being Tuscan. Nobody, according to the Signora, cooks like the Tuscans. In other provinces, they merely *play* in the kitchen, she says.

"And France! Well, what can I say about a cuisine that describes its ingredients in hushed, reverential whispers?"

"But is French cooking not just an advanced form of mastery?" I ask. Instantly I know I've said the wrong thing.

"If you are talking about the mastery of the few, then you are quite correct, *cara.* But if you are talking about mastery-at-large, mastery by an entire people—mastery that celebrates nature and family and exhilaration—then you can only talk about the cuisine of Tuscany."

Signora Redini lives in Coreglia Antelminelli, a small hill town on the left bank of the Serchio River that was built in 1300 by the Antelminelli, a wealthy family banished from Lucca after a fierce battle with the black Guelphs of the Obizzi. In 1314, Castruccio Castracani, a member of the Antelminelli family, used it as a base to conquer not only Lucca but also most of Tuscany. He died of malaria, however, while attempting to add Florence to his empire.

Coreglia's churches contain many works of art, among them a magnificent thirteenth-century processional cross which belonged to Barone Berlinghieri di Lucca. For lovers of the idiosyncratic, there's the Museo della Figurina, devoted to Coreglia's traditional manufacture of religious figurines made of gesso. At one time during the 1960s, a few dozen of Coreglia's current residents—members of Signora Redini's family included—moved to Union City, New Jersey, where they started successful businesses making these gesso saints. "I, too, am in the museum," she says proudly, referring to a picture taken of her in the 1950s, before she left for America, where she lived for fifteen years. That she and her husband returned to Coreglia after all that time serves as testimony, she says, to the town's many lures.

Signora Redini lives in a wonderful little house whose third-floor balcony offers a magnificent view of the Apuan Alps. To get to her front door, you must leave your car in the parking lot outside the town and walk through a maze of cobbled streets that climb and descend with challenging regularity. This morning, when I arrived, her husband Balíla was just returning from the *panifício* with a hearty loaf of *schiacchétto,* a typical bread of this region.

As we sit down to lunch, the Signora gives me an impromptu lesson in cooking, Tuscan style. Control is everything, she explains. That, and the innate sense possessed by every Tuscan concerning which ingredients go well together and which do not. The Umbrians, she says, do not understand this. They use butter in everything, even when it is clear that certain dishes are better prepared with olive oil. The Lombards drench their food in sauces, serving their polentas in plates overflowing with tomatoes and oils.

The secret, she tells me, is to imagine yourself as an artist, to see the food before you as one of your many elegant creations. She compares the process to that of creating a beautiful painting. To start, you need some knowledge of the chemical composition of each paint on your palette. But, if that is the sum total of your learning, you will never create a work of art. What you need, she maintains, is to free yourself from academic knowledge, to embody the information in such a way that it becomes part of your skin, part of your soul, part of the very lining of your veins. You need a sense of pride, hubris, the arrogance to assume control of your ingredients, to reduce them to subservience, to rob them of their individuality. Conceit makes good cooks, she declares, not humility.

She points, as an example, to the person who presents you with a terrine of risotto and accompanies it by saying: *Spero che ti piacerá*—I hope you will like it. That person, she says, should instead have gone to the local *rosticerría* for a carry-out order of fried fish.

"When you cook, you must *know* it will be good. You must assume the authority to *make* it good. You must command. Only then can you sense whether your ingredients are in balance, whether, in fact, sage should go with the rabbit, or whether you should use a little more of the tiny, prickly leaved thyme."

# CROCCETTE DI PATATE
## *Potato Croquettes*

*The Signora's recipe for potato croquettes illustrates perfectly the principles of balance and control. In making them, she says, you must be astute enough to enrich their flavor without masking their inherent delicacy. You must also have enough control of the process to keep the insides moist and tender while cooking the outsides to a crispy, golden crust. Note that in Tuscany, croquettes are traditionally oblong in shape.*

6 medium-size red potatoes
2 tablespoons extra-virgin olive oil
2 medium-size onions, finely minced
3 cloves of garlic, finely minced
1 large handful of fresh parsley, finely minced
4 ounces ground sirloin of beef
2 teaspoons fresh thyme, minced (or ¼ tablespoon dried)
1 egg, well beaten
3 ounces Parmigiano Reggiano, grated
1 cup unflavored breadcrumbs, dry
Olive oil for frying (vegetable oil can also be used)

1. Boil the potatoes in their skins until soft in the center; remove skins when slightly cooled.

2. Pass the potatoes through a sieve until of a pastelike consistency.

3. Heat 2 tablespoons of the oil in a skillet. Sauté the onions over medium heat until almost browned; add the garlic and sauté for one more minute.

4. To the potatoes add the onion and garlic mixture, parsley, meat, thyme, egg, and cheese.

5. Mix well with your hands until all ingredients are thoroughly blended.

6. Place the breadcrumbs on a dinner plate.

7. With your hands, scoop out enough of the potato mixture to form an oblong ball approximately 1½ inches in width and 2½ to 3 inches in length.

8. Roll the croquettes in the bread crumbs; continue until all the mixture has been used.

9. In a heavy skillet heat ½ inch of oil for frying.

10. Place the croquettes in the hot oil, a few at a time, making sure to leave enough room between them to turn.

11. Brown the croquettes on one side, then turn; continue until all sides are browned, approximately 20 minutes total.

12. Repeat steps 9 to 11 until all the croquettes are cooked.

13. Serve either hot, or cold with lemon wedges.

*Makes approximately 10–15 croquettes*

*A view from the Signora's balcony.*

Of all the appetizers made in this part of Tuscany, *crostini* offer the greatest possibility for variety. Essentially slices of toast on which is spread a topping, *crostini* can be made with fish, meat, cheese, vegetables, or any combination thereof.

In making *crostini,* one needs first to decide which kind of bread to use. Here there is no set dictum. Bread choices range from *pane rustico*—rustic or peasant bread—to *pane al latte*—bread made with milk, which is a softer, more refined type.

The most famous recipe for *crostini* in the province of Lucca uses chicken livers as a topping. Following is an excellent recipe for *Crostini di fegatini,* Crostini with Chicken Livers, as well as four other options for you to sample.

*The pouring of the "gesso" into the molds.*

# CROSTINI DI FEGATINI
*Crostini with Chicken Livers*

*If there is enough time to make this dish two hours or so in advance of serving, a bay leaf added to the chicken liver after pureeing results in a very nice taste. Make sure to remove the bay leaf before spreading on the toasts.*

3 tablespoons extra-virgin olive oil
1 medium red onion, minced
1¼ pound uncooked chicken livers, minced
1 medium red apple (neither too sweet nor too tart—Rome or
    MacIntosh would do nicely), chopped
6 ounces dry red wine
4 tablespoons sweet butter
Salt and pepper to taste
8 slices good-quality bread

1. Heat the oil in a medium-size skillet and sauté the onion slowly, about 10 minutes, over very low heat without allowing it to brown.

2. Add the chicken livers and blend thoroughly with a wooden spoon; cook 10 minutes longer.

3. Add the apple and the wine; cook until all ingredients have softened.

4. Place the mixture in a food processor along with the butter and blend on high speed to pastelike consistency. Add salt and pepper, and blend again on high speed for a few seconds.

5. Toast both sides of the bread in the oven broiler. Cut into 4 sections each.

6. Spread the bread with the chicken liver mixture.

7. Serve at room temperature.

*Serves 4*

# CROSTINI CON ARSELLE
*Crostini with Baby Clams*

*Although this recipe works best with baby clams, any clam will do in a pinch.*

2 pounds baby clams
3 plum tomatoes
5 tablespoons extra-virgin olive oil
2 cloves garlic, sliced in half, plus 2 cloves garlic, crushed
¼ teaspoon crushed chili pepper (optional)
½ cup dry white wine
8 slices good-quality bread
3 tablespoons of finely minced fresh parsley
Salt and pepper to taste

1. Wash the clams in several changes of water; shake dry. Place them in a heavy sauce pot either dry or with a little bit of water and cook, covered, over medium heat until the shells open after a few minutes. Remove the clams from the pot and strain the water through a filter, reserving 1 cup of the resulting "juice."

2. Remove the clams from the shells and chop coarsely.

3. Place the tomatoes in boiling water for 10 seconds, and then immediately run them under cold water. Remove the skins and mince the peeled tomatoes coarsely.

4. Heat the oil in a heavy skillet and sauté the garlic without allowing it to brown.

5. Add the chili pepper; stir.

6. Add the clams, stirring the mixture for 30 seconds. Salt and pepper to taste.

7. Turn the heat to the highest setting; add the wine, stirring constantly until the wine has evaporated.

8. Add the minced tomatoes and enough filtered clam juice to prevent the mixture from sticking to the pan; cover and cook for 10 minutes.

9. While the clam mixture is cooking, rub the bread sections with the garlic halves until all the garlic is used up.

10. Toast both sides of the bread in the oven broiler. Cut into 4 sections each.

11. Add the parsley to the clam mixture and spread on the toasted bread.

12. Serve hot.

*Serves 4*

# CROSTINI AL FUNGHI
*Crostini with Mushrooms*

*Portobellos or other wild mushrooms will do if you are absolutely unable to find porcinis. See also page 43, "All About Mushrooms."*

> 4 tablespoons extra-virgin olive oil
> 1 clove garlic, crushed
> 3 tablespoons dry white wine
> 3 tablespoons lemon juice
> 3 tablespoons of finely minced fresh parsley
> Salt and pepper to taste
> 8 slices rustic-type bread

1. Heat the oil in a heavy skillet and sauté the garlic for 30 seconds without allowing it to brown.

2. Add the mushrooms and stir the mixture for one minute.

3. Add the white wine and stir until the wine has evaporated.

4. Add the lemon juice, parsley, salt, and pepper.

5. Toast both sides of the bread in the oven broiler, cut into 4 sections each, and spread with the mushroom mixture.

6. Serve at room temperature.

*Serves 4*

# CROSTINI CON STRACCHINO E SALSICCIA
*Crostini with Stracchino Cheese and Sausage*

*If you are unable to find stracchino, you can use any white, salty cheese that is soft enough to spread, but not cream cheese.*

8 ounces stracchino cheese
2 links of sweet Italian pork sausage, removed from the casing
8 slices good-quality bread, cut into 4 sections each

1. Place the cheese in a large bowl; mash with a fork until of a creamy consistency.

2. Add the sausage and blend well.

3. Spread the sausage-and-cheese mixture on the bread sections.

4. Place the bread sections under the oven broiler until the tops are slightly browned and the cheese is bubbly.

5. Serve hot.

*Serves 4*

# MUSCOLI RIPIENI
## *Stuffed Mussels*

*Since the Ligurian Sea forms the western border of the province of Lucca, it stands to reason that many of the best* antipasti *emanating from this province involve fish. The following recipe uses the blue mussels that are plentiful in the waters off the Versilian coast. Any mussel, however, will do for this flavorful and substantial dish.*

> *For the stuffing*:
>    2 dozen mussels
>    3 tablespoons extra-virgin olive oil
>    2 cloves garlic, crushed
>    ¼ teaspoon crushed chili pepper
>    4 ounces chopped sirloin
>    2 eggs, thoroughly beaten
>    1 ounce mortadella or prosciutto, minced
>    3 tablespoons of finely minced fresh parsley
>    ½ cup unflavored dry bread crumbs
>    1 ounce Parmigiano Reggiano, grated
> *For the sauce*:
>    2 cloves garlic, crushed
>    3 tablespoons extra-virgin olive oil
>    1 cup dry white wine
>    1 large can peeled plum tomatoes (29 or 32 ounces)
>    3 tablespoons finely minced fresh parsley

1. Clean the mussels by slicing them open with a knife and removing the beard. (Do not cut all the way through the shell; leave the two halves attached.) Scrub the shells in several changes of water.

2. Remove the raw mussels to a cutting board and mince them finely.

3. Begin the stuffing by heating the oil and sautéing the garlic until browned.

4. Add the chili and stir for 30 seconds; remove garlic mixture from heat and place in a medium-size bowl.

5.  Add remaining stuffing ingredients to the bowl along with the chopped mussels, stirring mixture with a wooden spoon until thoroughly blended.

6.  Using a teaspoon, fill the shells with just enough stuffing so that the shell halves close completely; discard any stuffing that remains, or use for another recipe.

7.  Place the stuffed mussels in one layer in a large soup pot.

8.  Add all the ingredients for the sauce except the parsley.

9.  Cook over medium heat for 15 minutes; turn mussels carefully and cook for another 15 minutes.

10.  Remove the mussels to a serving dish.

11.  Add the parsley to the sauce and stir for 1 minute.

12.  Pour the sauce over the mussels and serve.

*Serves 4*

*To some, the magic of Tuscan cuisine lies in its full-bodied, complex flavors and fresh ingredients; to others, the ease with which most recipes are prepared. And yet, how can both exist simultaneously?*

*The answer lies in three simple words that serve as the quintessential basis for a cuisine hailed by gastronomes far and wide as being among the world's finest. Three words that, when understood and mastered in the same way as even the lowliest of Tuscan cooks, can transform the most ordinary of ingredients into an extraordinary meal worthy of the likes of Lorenzo the Magnificent:* sofritto, *the Italian equivalent of "sauté,"* insaporire, *which means "to give flavor to the food," and* odori, *which are the vegetables and herbs used in making the* sofritto.

***Odori:*** *A blend of vegetables and herbs that—diced and sautéed in extra-virgin olive oil—serve as the flavor base for ninety percent of Tuscan recipes. Generally, the term is understood to mean celery, carrots, onions, parsley, and other herbs (rosemary, sage, thyme, bay leaves, or any combinations thereof). So essential are they to the cuisine that most vendors of fresh produce give them away for the asking. Make a purchase at any outdoor Tuscan market, for example, and you'll inevitably be asked if you'd like some* odori. *If you say yes (and sometimes even if you say no), the vendor will go to a crate filled with what would generally be considered "waste"—the outer leaves of celery, broken pieces of carrots, and parsley or rosemary sprigs too large to be sold in bundles, and place a few of each in your bag.*

***Sofritto:*** *This is what you do with* l'odori *once you have them home. Most Tuscan recipes start with a basic* sofritto *(a sauté) consisting of 1 small carrot, 1 small onion, and a celery stalk—all diced—and a sprig or two of rosemary, sage, parsley, or all three. Some recipes also call for a clove or two of crushed garlic. These ingredients are then cooked in hot olive oil (or, more rarely, butter) over a medium flame for 10 minutes or until they are somewhat softened. For recipes requiring a more pungent taste, the ingredients will be cooked for an additional 5 to 10 minutes or until they are lightly browned. Pancetta (smoked bacon) or prosciutto can then be added for recipes requiring a more complex flavor.*

**Insaporire:** *At the base of almost every Tuscan recipe lies the concept of* insaporire, *the infusion of the main ingredients with a flavor base made up of vegetables, herbs, and/or cured meats, which are sauteéd in olive oil until the individual aromas have blended around each other. The rest of the ingredients are then added and cooked for as long as it takes to soak up the basic flavor of the* sofritto, *the sauté.*

# TOTANO RIPIENO
*Stuffed Cuttlefish*

*Here is one of Signora Redini's favorite recipes for an* antipasto *involving fish, this time, cuttlefish, which are baby squids. One of the very best things about this recipe, she says ("apart from its exquisite taste"), is that while it results in a very elegant end product, the preparation is relatively simple and requires few kitchen implements.*

> *For the stuffing*:
>   8 cuttlefish
>   8 ounces tuna fish, packed in olive oil
>   2 cloves garlic
>   3 tablespoons of finely minced fresh parsley
>   ¼ cup unflavored bread crumbs
>   2 eggs
>   1 ounce mortadella or prosciutto, minced
>   1 ounce Parmigiano Reggiano, grated
> *For the sauce*:
>   Juice of 2 lemons
>   3 tablespoons extra-virgin olive oil
>   2 sprigs of finely minced fresh parsley

1. Remove the tentacles from the cuttlefish.

2. Place the tentacles in the food processor with the remaining stuffing ingredients (including the olive oil in which the tuna was packed) except the actual bodies of the cuttlefish.

3. Blend to form a medium-grind paste.

4. Stuff the cuttlefish and sew up the ends using needle and thread.

5. Place 2 quarts of water in a large soup pot; arrange the 8 cuttlefish in one layer.

6. Heat the water to boiling, and boil for 10 minutes.

7. Leave the water and the cuttlefish in the pot until cool.

8. Remove the 8 cuttlefish and cut off the ends with the stitches.

9. Slice each of the cuttlefish into pieces that are approximately 1 inch thick.

10. Arrange in a circular pattern on a serving plate.

11. Make the sauce by blending the lemon juice, oil, and parsley in a small container.

12. Pour over the cuttlefish and serve at room temperature.

*Serves 4*

# INSALATA DI MARE
*Cold Seafood Salad*

*In spring and summer, cold seafood salads become very popular with the people of the Lucchesía. Any number of fish varieties can be used as well as any number of vegetables. The important thing is that all ingredients be absolutely fresh, and that the resulting creation be as beautiful in appearance as it is sublime in taste. This recipe calls for cuttlefish or baby squid, shrimp, and blue mussels. You can also use scallops, crayfish, clams, or oysters.*

> 2 small cuttlefish or baby squid
> 8 ounces shrimp (any size)
> 8 ounces blue mussels (or any type of mussel), scrubbed under
>   running water
> 3 medium red potatoes
> ¼ cup sweet red peppers packed in olive oil, drained
> 2 teaspoons capers
> Juice of 2 large lemons
> 1 clove garlic, minced
> 2 tablespoons of finely minced fresh parsley
> ⅓ cup extra-virgin olive oil

1. Boil the cuttlefish for 5 minutes; remove from pot and slice thinly.

2. In a separate pot, boil the shrimp in 1 quart of water for 3 minutes; remove shells and devein.

3. In a third pot, boil the mussels in a small amount of water, covered, until they open; remove from the shells and discard.

4. Boil the potatoes until they are tender throughout, approximately 15 minutes. Allow to cool slightly and peel; cut into very small chunks.

5. Cut the peppers into thin slices.

6. Place the cuttlefish, shrimp, mussels, potatoes, peppers, and capers in a large bowl.

7. In a smaller bowl, whisk together the lemon juice, garlic, parsley, and olive oil. Add the salt and pepper to taste.

8. Pour dressing over the salad, mix thoroughly, and serve.

*Serves 4*

# PINZIMONIO
## *Vegetables in Olive Oil and Salt*

*A very popular appetizer with Tuscans in the province of Lucca is called* Pinzimonio, *which is nothing more than an assortment of beautifully sliced and assembled vegetables, served with individual ramekins of olive oil and tiny individual whisks or forks with which guests create their own dressing. According to the Signora, the key is to achieve as much variety as possible when choosing the vegetables and to make sure that the presentation is elegant while maintaining the informality implied by offering guests the opportunity to suit their own tastes.*

*The vegetables*:
  1 large fennel
  2 medium red peppers
  1 large leek
  3 carrots
  2 small zucchini
  5 celery stalks (those closest to the heart)
  1 cucumber, peeled
  2 tomatoes
  12 very thin scallions
  16 radishes
  8 ounces haricot beans
  8 ounces very thin asparagus
*The dressing*:
  1 cup extra-virgin olive oil (absolutely the best quality available)
  Salt
  A cruet of red wine vinegar (optional)

1. Cut the fennel, peppers, leek, carrots, zucchini, celery stalks, cucumber, and tomatoes into very thin slices (julienne).

2. Steam the beans over boiling water for 2 minutes; when cool, slice in half widthwise.

3. Steam the asparagus over boiling water for 2 minutes; remove from heat.

4. Arrange all the vegetables on a serving platter so that each is displayed to its maximum advantage.

5. For each guest supply a small bowl filled with 7 or 8 tablespoons of the oil, a tiny whisk or fork, and, if possible, an individual salt shaker or container of salt. Guests may whisk the salt into the oil (some prefer to add a bit of vinegar) and use it as a dip for the vegetables.

*Serves 4*

# POLPETTINE ALLA SALVIA
*Sage Croquettes*

*Among Tuscans, certain herbs are more popular than others. One that is on top of everyone's list is sage, which thrives in this warm, sunny climate. Use this wonderful herb as the basis for a type of meat croquette that is also a local favorite.*

    12 ounces lean sirloin, ground
    6 leaves fresh sage, finely chopped
    1 egg, lightly beaten
    ⅛ teaspoon salt
    1 ounce Parmigiano Reggiano, grated
    Flour for dusting
    Olive oil for frying
    3 tablespoons olive oil
    ¼ cup Marsala

1. Using your hands or a sturdy fork, mix the sirloin, sage, egg, salt, and cheese until all ingredients are thoroughly blended.

2. With floured hands, break off approximately a tablespoonful of the mixture, and roll into a ball; flatten slightly. Dust with flour.

3. Fry the croquettes in oil, 5 to 7 minutes per side, until both sides are a golden color; drain on paper towels.

4. When all the croquettes are done, heat 3 tablespoons of oil in a skillet large enough to hold the croquettes in one layer.

5. Place the croquettes in the pan, sprinkle with the Marsala, and allow the liquid to reduce, approximately 2 minutes.

6. Serve the croquettes hot with the Marsala drizzled over the tops.

*Serves 4*

# FRITTATA CON ARSELLE
## *Omelette with Baby Clams*

*When sitting down to an informal type of meal, says the Signora, Tuscans will often serve a cold* frittata—*an omelette—as an* antipasto. *Having already spoken of the affection for fish exhibited by the people of the region, she offers this recipe for a simple and wonderful* frittata *made with baby clams.*

> 1½ pounds baby clams (if unavailable, use any kind of clam)
> 5 tablespoons extra-virgin olive oil
> 6 eggs
> 2 tablespoons of finely minced fresh parsley
> Salt and pepper to taste

1. Wash the clams in several changes of water. Shake dry and put them into a large soup pot with half the olive oil. Cover and cook until the shells open. Remove the clams from the shells and put them into a bowl (if using large clams, slice them into thin slivers).

2. Beat the eggs lightly with a fork. Add the parsley, salt, and pepper, and pour the mixture over the clams.

3. Heat the remaining oil in a heavy skillet; add the egg and clam mixture and cook over low heat until the underside of the *frittata* is set. (You can tell if it's set by lifting one end with a spatula. If it lifts, it's set; if not, wait another minute or so.)

4. Turn the *frittata* by placing a dish over the top of the pan, turning the pan so that the *frittata* comes to rest on the dish, and then sliding the whole thing back into the pan to cook and brown the other side.

5. Serve hot.

*Serves 4*

For those who have always heard that Italians eat pasta every day, the Signora hastens to declare that, generally, it's true. However, she says, in Tuscany there is also another food staple: polenta. For the uninitiated, this wonderful dish consists of corn meal stirred into water until it thickens to a porridgelike consistency, a process which, depending on the grind—polenta can be bought coarse, medium, or fine—should take approximately 20 to 30 minutes of continuous stirring. Like pasta, it is then topped with any of a variety of sauces and a sprinkling of grated cheese.

Polenta can also be used as an appetizer. One cooks it in the same way as for a first course, but it is then allowed to cool, cut into squares, fried, and spread with a topping. See chapter 4 for more information on polenta.

*Museo della Figurina*

# POLENTA FRITTA CON FORMAGGIO
*Fried Polenta with Cheese*

*Leftover polenta makes a wonderful appetizer, but this recipe assumes you'll be starting fresh. For those who would rather bake than fry the polenta, brush both sides of the slices with olive oil and place on a baking sheet in a 350-degree oven for approximately 15 minutes or until the edges are golden brown in color; turn, and bake 15 minutes on the other side.*

¼ teaspoon salt

2 quarts of water plus another half quart

2½ cups of polenta (coarse grind)

Olive oil for frying

12 ounces stracchino cheese (or any cheese of spreadable consistency)

1. Add the salt to the 2 quarts of water and bring to a hearty boil; lower the heat to a medium boil. Boil the remaining half quart by itself and reserve.

2. Pour the polenta in a steady stream into the boiling water, stirring constantly with a wooden spoon until the consistency is such that the spoon stands by itself in the middle and the polenta pulls away cleanly from the sides of the pan; add reserved water if necessary.

3. Place a clean cotton dishtowel on the counter; pour the polenta onto the towel and allow to cool. (This should take approximately one hour, at which time the polenta will have hardened considerably.)

4. Cut the polenta into 1-inch-thick slices.

5. Fry the slices a few at a time in the hot oil until the edges are a golden brown.

6. Drain the polenta on paper towels for a few seconds, and spread with the cheese; serve immediately.

*Serves 4*

# PANZEROTTI
*Fried Bread Squares*

*This recipe comes from Tuscany's days of poverty, when families made bread and, on special occasions, snipped off a little of the yeasting dough to make panze-rotti—fried squares of dough either topped with plain salt or spread with cheese. Today, the Signora says with a bemused look, this "peasant" recipe is served at weddings, cocktail parties, and formal dinner events. Here are the essential steps for making plain panzerotti sprinkled with salt. Try them this way or spread with cheese (stracchino, bel paese, and taleggio go especially well).*

½ cup warm water
¼ teaspoon yeast
¼ teaspoon honey or sugar
1 tablespoon extra-virgin olive oil
Pinch of salt
1 cup unbleached flour plus flour for kneading
Olive oil for frying

1. Pour ½ cup warm water in a measuring cup; dissolve the yeast in the water by stirring briskly with a fork. Add the honey (or sugar), 1 table-spoon oil, and salt, blend thoroughly.

2. Place the cup in the center of a small saucepan; pour enough very warm (but not boiling) water into the pan so that it rises around the cup to the ½-cup mark. Let sit for 20 minutes or until the contents of the cup are frothy.

3. Pour the cup of flour into a large bowl or food-processor container.

4. Add the liquid in the measuring cup, pouring in a steady stream.

5. Blend thoroughly with hands or a fork, or process, until a ball is formed.

6. Dust a pastry board with the extra flour; place the ball on the floured board and knead with hands, taking in flour as needed until the ball is dry and takes up no more flour.

7. Place in an oiled bowl. Roll the ball until all sides are coated with oil, cover, and let rise in a warm place for 2 hours.

8. When the dough has risen to twice its size, place it on a large board and, using a rolling pin, roll it into a sheet that is approximately ½ inch thick.

9. Cut the sheet into squares approximately 3 inches to a side.

10. Heat oil in a heavy skillet to a depth of 1 inch.

11. Fry the squares a few at a time until golden brown; turn and fry until golden brown on the other side.

12. Drain on paper towels for a few seconds, sprinkle with salt, and serve hot.

*Serves 4*

# PAN DI ROSMARINO
*Rosemary Buns*

*As antipasti, many Tuscans serve various plates of vegetables preserved either in oil or vinegar or both. (Mushrooms, artichokes, peppers, and small white onions are typical.) According to the Signora, however, one should not even contemplate serving such an appetizer without access to good-quality bread. This recipe is for those inclined to make the bread themselves. It is for a type of small roll flavored with rosemary that is very popular throughout the province of Lucca where it was once served on Easter Sunday along with eggs that had been blessed by the local priest.*

1 pound bread dough (ingredients for *Panzerotti*, page 27, doubled,
    except omit olive oil for frying)
½ cup extra-virgin olive oil
2 tablespoons fresh minced rosemary
½ cup seedless golden raisins, soaked in warm water for 15
    minutes
flour

1. Follow directions for *Panzerotti*, steps 1 through 6.

2. Heat the oil over medium heat and sauté the rosemary for 3 minutes; do not allow it to turn black.

3. Strain the oil and discard the rosemary.

4. Put the dough on a floured board and make a hollow in the middle; add the rosemary-flavored oil and work it through the dough thoroughly, kneading for approximately five minutes.

5. Pat the raisins dry, add them to the dough, and knead for another 2 to 3 minutes.

6. Grease the hands with oil and shape the dough into small buns.

7. Arrange them, spaced well apart, on a floured baking sheet; with a knife, make a cross on each bun.

8. Cover and leave in a warm place until doubled in bulk.

9. Bake in a preheated 400 degree oven for 15 minutes; lower the temperature to 350 degrees and continue baking until the tops are golden, approximately 10 minutes.

*Makes approximately 12 buns*

# FOCACCIA

In recent years, trendy Tuscans have turned to the preparation of foods once considered the simple fare of peasants. One such food, *focaccia,* has surfaced as a particular favorite. Essentially, *focaccia* is a flat bread brushed with olive oil and topped with either herbs (rosemary is favored in this part of Tuscany), vegetables (such as sliced onions), or—in more modern preparations—any number of ingredients ranging from roasted peppers to sautéed squid. Served plain, with olive oil and salt, *focaccia* can be eaten alone, or it can be sliced and used for sandwiches. Served with a topping, it is generally eaten as a snack or, when cut into small squares, as an appetizer.

# FOCACCIA AL FORMAGGIO
*Focaccia Stuffed with Cheese*

*This tasty dish is a particular type of stuffed focaccia that can be a meal in itself, or, when cut into squares, serves as a substantial appetizer course.*

> 1 pound bread dough (ingredients for *Panzerotti*, page 27, doubled, except omit olive oil for frying)
> 4 ounces Parmigiano Reggiano, grated
> 4 ounces Pecorino cheese, grated
> 1 cup milk
> ¼ cup extra-virgin olive oil
> ½ teaspoon salt

1. Follow directions for *Panzerotti*, steps 1 through 7.

2. Blend both cheeses and the milk in a small saucepan; place over low heat and stir constantly until of a creamy consistency. Add more milk if necessary.

3. Divide the dough into two equal sections; place the first section on an oiled board. Using a rolling pin, create a round large enough to cover the bottom of a baking pan, 11 x 17 inches. Place the dough in the pan.

4. Spoon the cheese mixture across the top of the dough, spreading it evenly to within ½ inch of the border.

5. Place the second section of dough on an oiled board; using a rolling pin, create a round equal in size to the first one.

6. Cover the first round with the second, being careful not to disturb the cheese mixture; seal the edges by pressing with fingertips.

7. Brush the top with oil, sprinkle with the salt, and bake in a pre-heated 500 degree oven for 10 to 15 minutes or until both top and bottom are golden brown. (Check the bottom by lifting it with a spatula.)

8. Slice into small squares and serve hot.

*Serves 6*

# Pizza

In Tuscany, pizza can be a very different dish from the one found in America, which the Signora remembers as "good, but slightly greasy." For starters, its crust is always thin. And when it is served topped with mozzarella, the mozzarella is made from buffalo milk and tends to be both whiter and softer than the cow's-milk variety known by most Americans.

Served as a meal, Tuscan pizza appears as a 10-inch round on a plate where it is cut with fork and knife. Served as an appetizer, it is cut into small squares and served with any variety of toppings, seafood and prosciutto being among the most popular throughout the Lucchesía.

# PIZZA DI PATATE
*Potato Pizza*

*This is yet another pizza variation, made mainly with potatoes. Sliced in small squares and served with a dry white wine, it makes a very fine appetizer.*

8 ounces potatoes (any type, although new potatoes are best)
1 cup unbleached flour, sifted
½ cup canned Italian tomatoes, drained and chopped
½ teaspoon oregano
¼ cup extra-virgin olive oil
Salt and pepper to taste
8 ounces fresh buffalo mozzarella, cut into small cubes

1. Boil the potatoes; when slightly cool, peel them and pass through a sieve.

2. Add the flour and work it through with your hands until it is a ball of dough.

3. Spread the dough in a baking pan, 11 x 17 inches, using your hands and a spatula.

4. Mix the tomatoes, oregano, two-thirds of the oil, salt, and pepper in a small bowl.

5. Spread the tomato mixture over the pizza.

6. Spread the mozzarella cubes evenly over the tomatoes.

7. Drizzle with the remaining olive oil and place in a preheated 400 degree oven for 15 minutes.

8. Slice into small squares and serve hot.

*Serves 4*

# MELANZANE MARINATE
*Marinated Eggplant*

*Marinated vegetables are a very popular appetizer in this part of Tuscany where they are served with crusty bread and a dry white wine. Each vegetable has its own preparation. Some, like mushrooms, are marinated raw; others, like onions, are first blanched. For this recipe, the eggplant must first be fried.*

> 2 small eggplants
> Salt
> Olive oil for frying
> 2 teaspoons finely chopped fresh oregano
> 1 cup red wine vinegar
> 1 clove garlic, peeled and sliced

1. Peel the eggplants, cut them into ¼-inch slices, and salt heavily on both sides. Place in a colander over a bowl and cover with a heavy weight; let sit for an hour to drain.

2. Wash the eggplant under running water to remove the salt and dry thoroughly.

3. Fry the eggplant, a few slices at a time, in hot oil on both sides until slices are a golden color; reserve the oil.

4. Drain the slices on paper towels for a few seconds, and then place in a pan large enough to hold them in one layer; sprinkle the oregano evenly over the tops.

5. Make the marinade by blending together the vinegar and garlic; cook the mixture in a saucepan over high heat for approximately 1 minute.

6. Add 3 tablespoons of the reserved oil.

7. Pour the boiling liquid evenly over the eggplant, cover with a cloth, and let sit for 24 hours.

8. Serve at room temperature.

*Serves 4*

*Signora Bianca Pieri*

# Chapter Two

# AN UNRELENTING LOVE AFFAIR WITH NATURE

## MUSHROOMS AND CHESTNUTS

*I*t is a Sunday morning in late autumn. I am lying on a huge feather bed in the uppermost room of an ancient turret in Santa Anna. All I want is to go back to sleep. Last night—again—I was regaled until three in the morning by the roar of voices from the cafe across the piazza. The name of the cafe is "Da Beppe," and within the confines of its open-air patio, men gather in groups of every size and age for discussions about sports, politics, people, politics, food, politics—politics, politics, politics.

I am not to get my wish. Beginning some time after ten, when church lets out, the men are back, this time over endless cups of *doppio* (double espressos). A few, bowing now to the health mania sweeping even this country of unrepentant culinarians, order *decafeinato*. And there they sit, for the next two or three hours, until their wives and mothers are finished with the preparations for lunch, talking in voices loud enough to be heard even above the roar of teenagers racing through the village on double-barreled Vespas.

*"Ma che discorsi shemi sono questi? A un punto o l'altro, qualcosa si dovra' fare con queste pensione. Il soldi non ci sono piu; quello e chiaro."* ("What kind of ridiculous talk is this? At a certain point we're going to have to do *something* about these pensions. The money's just not there any longer; that's a fact.")

*"Eh beh, ma quei politicanti, con tutte le loro palanche, dovevano venire propio a prenderle nelle mie tasche? Perche non infilano le mani prima nelle loro?"* ("That's all well and good, but those politicians with all their money, had to come sticking their hands in *my* pockets? Why don't they first search through their own?")

In the middle of deciding whether or not to try stuffing my ears with cotton, I am jolted by the downstairs ringing of the phone.

*"Signorina Bianchi! Telefono!"*

It is Mauro Cotrelli, the village dentist and an old friend, calling to see if I want to go with him and his mother-in-law on an afternoon trek through the woods. "It's mushroom season," he tells me. "With the heavy rains of the last few weeks and the recent two days of sunshine, the forest floor should be covered with many kinds of *funghi*. If we're lucky, we'll also find a few chestnuts, although by now, the tour buses will undoubtedly have taken them all."

In the hill towns of northern Tuscany, the gathering of chestnuts and wild mushrooms is a national sport. The mushroom season starts in late September—with the advent of the postsummer rains—and continues until the weather turns cold enough to inhibit the spores. Sometimes, if the weather remains warm enough, the season can last all winter. Chestnut gathering, on the other hand, takes place in October and lasts approximately three weeks.

Of the 150 edible varieties of mushrooms that grow freely in the surrounding forests of the Garfagnana, only six or seven are widely recognized and used. These include the *porcini* (little pigs), a reference to their fat, round stems, and mammoth size) in both its black and white form; the *ovole,* which has a bland, gentle taste; the *chiodini* (little nails), pretty, cinnamon-colored, small mushrooms that grow in bunches on old wood; the *biete,* which ranges in color from a subtle purple-pink to a clear, pale persimmon and has a distinctive, rather bitter taste; and the *guatelli* (chanterelles), which are delightfully golden in color and have firm yellow flesh.

This being Tuscany, where nothing preempts the noonday meal, we start out after lunch, meeting in the piazza outside the church that, in recent years, has been transformed into an evergreen garden. Santa Anna is a quiet mountain village of 126 people. From the central piazza, you look out over a series of undulating hillsides covered with chestnut trees. In culinary circles, this tiny village is known mainly for its potato bread, which is made by the Signora and her husband, Carlo, in a small rustic hut, using two-hundred-year-old yeast. Throughout all of Tuscany, it can only be found here.

There is another side to Santa Anna, however, a side that stands in stunning opposition to its quaint beauty. For it has here, on August 12,

1944, that 560 men, women, and children were massacred by the Germans on the eve of the liberation. Among the slaughtered were hundreds of children under the age of fourteen whose bones lie, along with all the others, at the base of the Ostuary of Col di Cava, which is a five-minute walk through the woods. The ostuary is a tower, thirty feet tall, which stands out against the bright blue sky of the Apuan Alps, and can be seen from as far away as the Versilian coast. Alongside the tower is a marble wall engraved with the names of those who were killed on that tragic morning.

On a previous trip to Santa Anna, I'd visited the wall along with Mauro and his mother-in-law, Signora Bianca Pieri. As we walked together up the hill, the Signora spoke of Don Innocenzo, the heroic village priest, who, although spared by the Germans because of his vocation, offered his life in exchange for those of the area's children. "Quel vigliacchi [those cowards]," she says, "they killed him, too, but first they made him watch, along with all the parents, as they murdered each little boy and girl."

We wind our way out of town, queuing up in certain places behind dozens of other motorists in search of mushrooms. Above us, visible through the open roof of Mauro's little *cinquecento,* we can see the undulating peaks of the Alpi Apuane, the Apuan Alps. In the distance is Monte Piglione, master of the horizon at 1232 meters.

"Just look at that view," says Mauro pointing proudly. "All the colors of the Italian flag—white from the snow, green from the trees, and red from the chestnuts." This last, the red of the chestnuts, seems somewhat of a metaphorical stretch, but I keep my judgment to myself.

At a certain point, we come upon a large tract of hillside terraced with thousands of olive trees. Across each terrace, a continuous swath of orange netting has been placed to catch the olives as they fall. "It's almost time," Mauro says, referring to the fact that, soon, it will be time to cart the olives to the *frantoio* and turn them into oil.

The business of bringing olives to the *frantoio* used to be a local one, with each household carting its own olives in barrels marked with the family name. Today, however, the presses cater mostly to large concerns, and individual households are reduced to hauling their olives to the press during a few select hours in the middle of the night.

"If you *really* want to experience what it means to be Tuscan," says Mauro, "you should visit a press at two or three in the morning during olive season. There you'll find an assortment of people, most of whom know each other, with nothing to do but sit and wait their turn. But make sure you haven't eaten for a few hours, because you'll undoubtedly be offered all manner of bread and prosciutto and wine and cheese, and more than your share of impassioned conversation."

We are startled out of our leisurely pace by a sudden burst of horn blowing. *"Avanti!"* The car behind us is filled with teenagers overly anxious to reach their destination. *"Spingirti dalla parte!"* They want us to let them pass. If we do not, they will attempt an illegal *sorpasso,* even though the road is constantly curving and too narrow for one lane, much less the two that have been carved.

*"Brigandi,"* says Signora Pieri. "And with the Sacred Host not yet digested in their stomachs!"

We stop finally at a spot where Mauro says he has previously been very successful. But instead of entering the woods there and then, we walk a few hundred yards down the road, the Signora—his mother—trundling along behind us in her navy-blue wool skirt and low-heeled pumps. At a certain point, Mauro pauses in front of a chestnut tree whose trunk has been sliced in half by lightning, and I see him glancing furtively from side to side.

Has he forgotten the actual location, I wonder. But he stops my thought in midsentence, pressing his index finger tightly against his lips. *"Zita!"* he chides.

He looks around once more and then whispers an explanation. "We don't want anyone following us," he hisses. "In Tuscany, if you see an auto stopped on a road this time of year, you naturally suspect they know something you don't."

"But how could that be?" I inquire. "Wouldn't seeing our car only prompt people to go farther down the road? After all, if we're already here, wouldn't we have taken whatever mushrooms exist?"

"You are too much an American," he sighs. "Americans always want to find their *own* way, their *own* vein of gold. We in Italy are different. Why do you think our landscapes are so beautiful? Because if one person builds a house in a certain location, we *all* do. We're not like you, one person here, the other ten kilometers away, so that the horizon is blurred with endless dots of houses."

We make our way through the dense forest, each carrying a wicker basket and a *bastone*—a pointed stick that will supposedly protect us against the dreaded *vipre*—snakes—which Tuscans fear nearly as much as they do the loss of their socialized healthcare.

Despite our best efforts to secure this spot for ourselves, however, we soon hear voices coming through the trees and before long, there we are face to face with another set of gatherers. The "trespassers" consist of what is presumably a father, two small children in sweatshirts that say "Georgetown," a mother in hightop Nikes carrying a Sony video camera, and a mother in a pink jogging suit.

*"Come va?"* Mauro asks in a dejected voice. How's it going? His eyes are glued to the four hefty string bags in their possession. (When picking mushrooms in Italy, it is illegal to use anything but a container open to the air so that, as one moves around the forest, spores can fall freely from the caps and repopulate the earth. Plastic bags should never be used regardless of the law; the substances in plastic provoke a chemical reaction in the mushrooms that causes them to lose some of their crispness.)

*"Eh, bene abastanza,"* the man answers warily. Okay.

They keep walking, and so do we, but at the fork up ahead, we swerve to the left.

Two hours later, we are back in the car. Our catch consists of two or so pounds of chestnuts, four large porcini, a few guatelli, and a large variety of smaller mushrooms with which I am not familiar, but which Signora Cotrelli says will make *"una cena favolosa"*—a wonderful dinner.

This *cena* will be cooked by both the Signora and by Carla, Mauro's wife, who stayed home this afternoon to watch the season finale of "Beautiful" (BYOO-tee-fool), a hugely popular American-made soap about a family in Washington, D.C. "It's more famous than 'Dynasty,' " Carla had told me.

Tonight's meal will consist entirely of funghi and chestnuts, the five of us (Mauro, Carla, the Signora, her husband, Carlo, and I) sitting down to a wonderful dinner that is extraordinary both for its atmosphere and exquisite flavors, and yet ordinary in that it is no more noteworthy than any other dinner previously prepared in this house.

This desire for, and celebration of, "sameness" is what makes eating, for both the Pieri family and for Tuscans at large, such a gratifying experience. Food here is not for experimentation; it is for "feasting," for enjoying a daily festa, which, like other festas, is keenly anticipated and bound by the rules of tradition.

"It is very sad, how you Americans treat food," a visitor from Italy, a Tuscan friend, once told me. "In Tuscany, we see food as a vehicle for restoring us to a place of harmony. In your country, you see it as more of a necessity—a time-consuming ritual that should be made more efficient either through the use of fast foods or by eating out or both. That, of course, when you're not analyzing the food for fat content or chemical intoxication.

"When we Tuscans prepare a meal, we do so with the understanding that we will be presenting nature at its best. And when we sit down at the table, we take our time, celebrating the delicious taste of the meal we're eating as well as the taste of delicious meals past and delicious meals in the future. The table is where we are happiest, where we feel most in harmony—with ourselves, our families, and our beautiful land."

As Carla works in the kitchen, Signora Pieri prepares the chestnuts for roasting. She notches each of the shiny brown nuts with a hunting knife to prevent unwanted explosions, and then places them in a *briscia,* a huge iron pan with a yard-long handle and a bowl pierced with dozens of round holes.

At dinner's end, she will place the *briscia* over the open flames of the hearth and roast the chestnuts, occasionally sprinkling them with a *spremuta*—a dash—of white wine to make them tender. When they finally achieve the appearance of burnt coals, she will wrap them in a dishcloth and roll the cloth on the table, pressing with her full weight to separate the skin from the flesh.

The liberated chestnuts will then be accompanied by small glasses of dark, red wine, or by *vin santo,* a wine made from grapes stored for months before pressing, and then kept in small oak barrels for four or five years. Usually a very sweet wine (in Signora Pieri's house, the vin santo is made by her brothers, and is very sweet indeed), vin santo can also be quite dry, like a sherry.

An alternate use for vin santo is to serve it with *cantucci,* small, very dry biscuits with almonds. (In America, these common biscuits are now packaged in gourmet wrappings and labeled *biscotti*).

One of the favorite autumnal pastimes for people living in and around the province of Lucca is sauntering through the forested hillside of the Garfagnana in search of mushrooms. Finding them however, is not as easy as it sounds. Each mushroom grows in a particular habitat determined by climate and weather conditions.

Mushrooms are saprophytes which grow in humus that is rich in organic substance, or on tree trunks. They produce neither flower nor fruit, and reproduce via their spores—minuscule organisms that are invisible to the naked eye. Factors which influence growth include: type of terrain, vegetation, climatic conditions, and season. Of these, the most important is temperature—of both the terrain, and the air. Ideal conditions include dark, humid soil, and an autumnal weather pattern consisting of heavy rain followed by a few days of sun and warm, wind-free nights.

In Italy, mushroom picking is regulated by law, with each region having different powers. In the Lucchesía, for example, mushrooms can only be carted off in containers that are open to the air—baskets or string bags. This is done in order to allow the spores from the freshly picked mushrooms to fall back to the ground and repopulate.

There are at least 37,000 different kinds of mushrooms in Italy, and these are divided into two categories: edible and inedible. Within the first category, the mushrooms are further divided according to whether they are: "excellent" (especially good); "good" (with a pleasant taste); or "mediocre" (not particularly interesting from an eating point of view).

Inedible mushrooms are divided into "harmless," "poisonous," and "deadly." About 10,000 cases of poisoning occur each year in Europe due to consumption of mushrooms from either the second or third category. Symptoms range from gastro-enteritis to irritation of the nervous system, paralysis, convulsions, vomiting, hallucinations, and hemorrhaging. Most symptoms appear within 30 hours of consuming the poison.

Mushrooms have only recently come to be valued as a source of food. Previously, their use have been restricted to the production of fermented cheese, antibiotics, vitamins, and chemicals (i.e. citric acid, gallic acid, and enzymes). They have also been used to ferment alcohol, and in the production of sugar and fats. In some places, it has long been known that mushrooms can be utilized—along with bacteria—to break down organic waste.

There are many different ways of preserving mushrooms. They can be dried, put under oil or vinegar, and—in some cases—frozen.

Fresh mushrooms are a different story. Since the chemical composition of fresh mushrooms tends to break down quickly, they must be cooked as soon as possible after picking (or buying). Once cooked, however, mushrooms last longer than many other vegetables—3 or 4 days refrigerated—and lend themselves well to reheating.

When cleaning mushrooms of any kind, do not soak or place under running water. Mushroom caps are like sponges, and tend to absorb liquid very quickly. Best to use a mushroom brush to dust off any surface dirt, or a coarse sponge. If the mushrooms are large, you might want to salt them before using to force out any little worms housed in the caps. Use ½ teaspoon salt sprinkled on the cap, and let sit for 15 to 20 minutes. Brush off any worms emitted.

Mushrooms should always be cooked uncovered to prevent their becoming too watery. If a recipe does call for a cover, it should only be employed after the liquid from mushrooms has already evaporated. Cooking time is approximately ½ hour for the larger variety wild mushrooms.

Dried mushrooms should always be soaked for at least ½ hour before cooking.

According to Signora Pieri, the porcini's popularity among Tuscans has neither to do with its flavor nor with the lush whiteness of its imposing crown, but with the sly deception surrounding its initial act of generosity.

A porcini, she says, thinks nothing of giving away its liquid during the first phase of cooking; in that free and unquestioning gesture of generosity, it resembles all other mushrooms. But unlike other mushrooms, porcinis do not then consider the matter closed and go about the rest of their lives content simply to have given. A porcini sits shrewdly in the middle of its juices, waiting, watching, the liquid quietly encircling the herbs and spices that simmer at its side. Then, when the juices are fully blended, and the dish has become what seems like a perfect mixture of mushroom and seasoning, the porcini tugs on its heartstrings, sucking back its now-enhanced liquid to re-create itself as the plump, succulent star of the show.

"When you are given something by a Tuscan," says the Signora, "look for the invisible elastic cord that is invariably attached to its side. In the middle of the night, open one eye, and you will see the gift that was delivered to you being dragged slowly across the floor, on its way back to its owner."

# PORCINI TRIFOLATI
*Braised Porcini Mushrooms*

4 medium porcini mushrooms (approximately 1½ pounds)
5 tablespoons extra-virgin olive oil
1 clove garlic, cut in half
1 small onion, minced
1 small red chili pepper, minced (fresh is better but dry will also
   work well)
1 tablespoon tomato paste
Salt and pepper to taste
2 tablespoons of finely chopped fresh parsley

1. Clean the porcinis (see "All About Mushrooms," page 43) and slice
the caps into slivers, each approximately ¼ inch in width; reserve the
stems for a future soup.

2. Place the olive oil in a skillet over medium heat; cook the garlic until it is lightly browned and then discard.

3. Sauté the onion and chili in the same oil as the garlic, until the onions are slightly browned; place in a bowl and cover.

4. Place the porcini slices in a clean skillet and cook over high heat,
stirring occasionally, until the mushrooms begin to give up their liquid,
approximately 5 minutes.

5. Return the onion and chili mixture to the skillet and add the tomato
paste, salt, and pepper; turn heat to medium and cook for approximately 10 minutes, or until most of the liquid has been reabsorbed by
the mushrooms.

6. Sprinkle with parsley and serve.

*Serves 6 as a side dish*

# CACCIUCCO DI FUNGHI

*Mushroom Stew*

*Most people who are familiar with Tuscan cooking have heard of cacciucco, the famous fish stew popular on the coast. Very few, however, have tried a cacciucco made entirely of mushrooms. As with the fishstew, this one depends for its excellence on using as many varieties of fresh, wild mushrooms as can be had. Porcinis are a must; others can include whatever is available that day at your local store. This recipe also includes the liberal use of fresh mint, which, contrary to what most people would think, is a widely used herb in the Lucchesía.*

3 tablespoons extra-virgin olive oil
1 medium onion, chopped
2 cloves garlic, minced
Salt and pepper to taste
2 pounds wild mushrooms (at least ¾ pound should be porcinis),
   cleaned and sliced thin
1 35-ounce can Italian tomatoes, drained and chopped
¼ teaspoon crushed chili pepper
2 tablespoons finely chopped fresh mint
4 slices thick, crusty bread
2 cloves garlic, sliced in half

1. Heat the oil in a skillet over medium heat; add the onion, minced garlic, salt, and pepper. Cook until the onion and garlic are just beginning to turn brown.

2. Add the mushrooms; cook for 5 minutes, stirring often.

3. Add the tomatoes, chili, and mint; cook for 5 minutes longer.

4. Rub each of the bread slices with halved garlic cloves; toast in the oven on both sides. Place slices in individual bowls.

5. Pour the mushroom mixture on top of the bread.

6. Serve hot with large glasses of red wine.

*Serves 4*

"If I had to name the five dishes most characteristic of the cuisine of the Lucchesía, I would have to include *Polenta con funghi*," says Signora Pieri when I ask her for just such a listing. She follows with two of her own recipes for this culinary delight, one using fresh porcini and one using dried. Which is better? "When you have tramped through the woods and come home with one or two of the fresh, of course, the fresh is better. But when dried is all you have, you savor it with such satisfaction that you can't even imagine liking any other type better."

*The Garfagnana; Treasure House of Mushrooms and Chestnuts.*

# POLENTA CON SALSA
# DI FUNGHI FRESCHI
*Polenta with Fresh Mushrooms*

*To make* Polenta con Salsa di Funghi Secchi, *Polenta with Dried Mushrooms, soak 4 ounces dried mushrooms in warm water for 2 hours; drain and chop the mushrooms. (Reserve the water for another use.) Proceed with the recipe, substituting the dried mushrooms for the fresh.*

  3 cups polenta (coarse grind)
  3 tablespoons extra-virgin olive oil
  2 cloves garlic, chopped coarsely
  1 pound fresh porcini mushrooms, cleaned and sliced thin
  1 cup peeled canned plum tomatoes, drained
  ½ cup water
  Salt and pepper to taste
  2 tablespoons finely chopped fresh parsley

1. Cook the polenta (see directions, page 127).

2. Heat the oil in a skillet over medium heat. Sauté the garlic until lightly browned; discard the garlic.

3. Add the mushrooms to the garlic-flavored oil; sauté for 10 minutes, stirring constantly with a wooden spoon.

4. Add the tomatoes and water; simmer over medium heat for 10 minutes.

5. Add the salt and pepper and simmer for 5 minutes more.

6. Just before serving, add the parsley, stir for 1 minute, and remove from heat.

7. Place a hefty serving of polenta in each bowl; top with mushroom sauce and serve hot.

*Serves 4*

# RISOTTO CON FUNGHI FRESCHI
*Rice with Fresh Mushrooms*

*The province of Lucca exhibits greater variety in its* primi piatti, *or first courses, than any other region in Italy. Here you'll find equal importance given to broths, soups, pastas, and rice dishes. This recipe fits into the last category, rice dishes or risottos, and is an excellent vehicle for sampling, yet again, the wonders of fresh porcini mushrooms. In a pinch, you can try using portobello, shitake, or other types of wild mushrooms although the taste will not be as sharp.*

*For the mushrooms:*
　1¼ pound fresh porcini mushrooms, cleaned and sliced
　3 tablespoons extra-virgin olive oil
　1 small onion, minced
　2 cloves garlic, chopped
　3 tablespoons fresh parsley, chopped
　Salt and pepper, to taste
*For the rice:*
　1 small onion, minced
　3 tablespoons extra-virgin olive oil
　2½ cups arborio rice
　1 quart chicken broth (homemade is best, but very good quality
　　canned may be used)
　1 cup dry white wine
　1 quart boiling water

1. To make the mushrooms, place the oil in a skillet; sauté the onion and garlic over medium heat until both are slightly browned.

2. Add the mushrooms and cook, uncovered, for 40 minutes.

3. In the meantime make the risotto. Using a large, thick saucepan, sauté the onion in the oil over medium heat. Stir constantly until the onion is slightly brown around the edges.

4. Add the rice and stir, making sure to coat each grain with the onion and olive oil.

5. Add the wine and stir until it has completely evaporated.

6. Add the broth a little at a time, making sure that each addition is completely absorbed before adding more.

7. When the rice is still somewhat hard, add a large spoonful of the mushroom mixture; stir with a wooden spoon until the mushrooms are completely blended into the rice.

8. When the broth is completely absorbed, check the rice. The kernels should be tender and the consistency somewhat soupy. If not, add a little more water. Total cooking time should be approximately 25 minutes.

9. When the mushrooms are in the last few minutes of cooking, add the parsley, salt and pepper and stir thoroughly.

10. When the rice is done, assemble the risotto. Place a portion of rice in the middle of a large plate, hollow out the center and fill with mushrooms; serve hot.

*Serves 4*

There are stuffed mushrooms and then there are stuffed mushrooms. In Santa Anna, however, stuffed mushrooms can mean only one thing: stuffed porcini. When I explained to the Signora that it is moderately difficult to find porcinis in American markets, she softened somewhat, allowing that other wild mushrooms could be used to good result. But she *did* insist on using wild mushrooms "and not those small, white, *prefabricated* mushrooms you find all over France."

# FUNGHI PORCINI RIPIENI
*Stuffed Porcini Mushrooms*

*The Signora wishes to add that if you were to pair this recipe with a serving of polenta topped with mushroom sauce, you would truly find yourself in Paradise.*

½ pound porcini mushrooms of any shape plus 4 medium, same-size porcini mushrooms
2 cloves garlic
1 tablespoon fresh marjoram (¼ teaspoon dried)
2 tablespoons finely chopped fresh parsley
3 ounces Parmigiano Reggiano, grated
¼ cup unflavored dry breadcrumbs
Salt and pepper to taste
1 egg, slightly beaten
Extra-virgin olive oil

1. Clean and chop the ½ pound mushrooms and place in a bowl; add the garlic, marjoram, parsley, cheese, breadcrumbs, salt, and pepper, and mix well.

2. Add the egg and blend thoroughly until of a thick, homogeneous consistency.

3. Separate the stems from the caps of the 4 mushrooms; hollow out just enough of the cap to form somewhat of a bowl in which to place the filling. Chop what you have removed from the hollow and add to the filling, blending thoroughly.

4. Fill the mushroom caps with the filling, spreading it carefully so that it creates an even layer across the cap.

5. Sprinkle the caps with oil, and place in a 400 degree oven for 20 minutes.

6. Serve hot.

*Serves 4*

# ZUPPA DI FUNGHI
*Mushroom Soup*

*When I tell the Signora that mushroom soup is somewhat of a staple among Americans, she asks me about its preparation. I give her a standard recipe and then add that it is also one of the most popular soups made by a company famous for its canned soups. At that, she gives a hearty laugh. She says she was once given a can by a visiting friend, and decided to try it. She cooked it according to the directions and when it was ready she smelled it. And that was enough. "You ate this in America? Beata te—God bless you." Here then, is the Signora's recipe for what she calls* la vera zuppa di funghi—*the real mushroom soup.*

> 1 medium stalk of celery, chopped
> 1 medium onion, minced
> 3 tablespoons extra-virgin olive oil
> 1½ pounds fresh wild mushrooms (porcinis are best, but a wide
>     variety of other fresh mushrooms work well)
> 5 plum tomatoes, peeled, seeded and chopped
> ½ fresh, red chili pepper (or ¼ teaspoon dried)
> 6 leaves fresh mint, chopped
> Salt to taste
> 4 slices thick, crusty bread

1. Using a sturdy, thick-walled soup pot, sauté the celery and onion in the oil over medium heat for 10 minutes or until the onion is lightly browned.

2. Clean the mushrooms; chop both caps and stems into small pieces. Add them to the celery and onion mixture.

3. Cook over low heat for 30 minutes, by which time you should have a goodly amount of liquid. Stir every so often with a wooden spoon.

4. Add tomatoes, chili, and mint to the mushroom mixture. Cook for 10 minutes; add salt and mix well.

5. Place a slice of the bread in each of 4 soup bowls; pour the soup over the bread.

6. Serve hot with young red wine.

*Serves 4*

# ZUPPA DI CECI CON FUNGHI PORCINI
*Chick Pea Soup with Porcini Mushrooms*

*A few years back, Signora Pieri remembers being invited to dinner at the home of a friend who made a delicious soup from chick peas and porcini mushrooms. At the table was a gentleman from Pisa who, when the friend declared proudly that she'd invented this recipe herself, remarked, "So big deal, what does it take to put together chick peas and mushrooms?" To the Signora's great joy the friend answered, "Not much, but great cooking is made of just these small, simple advances." When you taste this dish, you'll know what she meant.*

½ cup extra-virgin olive oil

1 small onion, minced

1 medium stalk celery, diced

7 tablespoons chopped fresh parsley

12 ounces young porcini mushrooms (or other wild mushrooms, such as portabello, shitake, and oyster, cleaned and sliced into thin slices

12 ounces dried chick peas, soaked overnight

Salt and pepper to taste

1 cup white wine

4 very ripe plum tomatoes, peeled, seeded, and sliced

1½ quarts Basic Meat Broth (page 95) or a good-quality, canned meat broth, heated to boiling

4 slices thick, crusty bread

2 tablespoons chopped fresh marjoram (½ teaspoon dried)

1. Drain the chick peas, and rinse under cold, running water. Place in a soup pot, cover with water, and cook over medium heat for 30 minutes or until tender. Drain.

2. Heat ¼ cup of the oil over medium heat in a skillet; add the onion, celery, and parsley and cook until the onion is lightly browned.

3. Add the mushrooms, chick peas, salt, and pepper; cook for 3 minutes, stirring often with a wooden spoon.

4. Add the wine and allow it to evaporate completely.

5. Add the tomatoes and the hot broth; cook over medium heat, covered, for 15 minutes.

6. Place the bread in separate bowls; add the soup, drizzle with the remaining oil, sprinkle with marjoram, and serve hot.

*Serves 4*

# FUNGHI PORCINI IN PADELLA
*Skillet Porcini Mushrooms*

*This is a good recipe to serve with fish, and in fact, it, itself, incorporates fish—anchovies, which Tuscans are used to eating fresh, but which can also be canned. The important thing here is to use fresh, young, wild mushrooms; any kind will do although porcinis should certainly be your first choice.*

> 3 tablespoons extra-virgin olive oil
> 3 anchovy fillets, cleaned and deboned (if canned, washed well to remove the salt)
> 2 pounds fresh, young porcini or other wild mushrooms, cleaned and sliced thickly
> 2 cloves garlic, halved
> 3 or 4 very ripe peeled plum tomatoes, chopped & seeded
> 1 tablespoon minced fresh mint
> Salt and pepper to taste

1. Heat the oil in a large skillet over low heat; add the anchovies and cook for 3 minutes, pressing the anchovies with a wooden spoon until they are reduced to pastelike consistency.

2. Add the remaining ingredients and cook over medium heat, uncovered, for 1 hour, stirring occasionally.

3. Just before serving, remove the garlic.

4. Place the mushrooms on a heated platter and serve hot.

*Serves 4*

# FUNGHI CON MOZZARELLA
*Mushrooms with Fresh Mozzarella*

*Dried porcini mushrooms are every bit as good as their fresh counterparts except, of course, in mushroom season when no Tuscan would be caught dead eating anything other than those that had just been yanked from the ground. And yet, there is nothing quite like the taste of a dried mushroom with all its earthiness and concentrated zest. This recipe combines the delectable flavor of dried porcinis with the subtle taste and gentle texture of fresh mozzarella to produce a dish substantial enough to stand ably on its own as an entree.*

4 ounces dried porcini mushrooms
2 tablespoons extra-virgin olive oil
1 clove garlic, sliced in half
12 ounces plum tomatoes, peeled, seeded and diced
Salt and pepper to taste
1 fresh one-pound buffalo mozzarella, cubed (either plain or
   salted)
¼ cup unbleached white flour for dredging
2 tablespoons unsalted butter

1. Soak the mushrooms in warm water for 2 hours; drain, rinse, and slice in small pieces. (Reserve the soaking liquid for another use.)

2. Heat the oil in a pan over medium heat; add the mushrooms and garlic and sauté for 3 minutes or until the garlic is lightly browned. Remove the garlic and discard.

3. Add the tomatoes, salt, and pepper; cook for 5 minutes or until the tomatoes are soft. Keep mixture very hot.

4. In the meantime, dredge the mozzarella in the flour and sauté in the butter until the mozzarella is just beginning to ooze.

5. Pour the mushroom mixture over the mozzarella and serve immediately.

*Serves 4*

# VELLUTATA AL FUNGHI
*Mushroom Velvet*

*Cooking with heavy cream is very popular in northern Tuscany, and its use is called for in a great many recipes using mushrooms, such as this dish. Its name cannot be literally translated—at best,* vellutata *means "kind of velvety," a description that comes from coating the mushrooms with an addictive blend of butter and heavy cream.*

8 ounces fresh wild mushrooms (any type), cleaned and chopped
    into small pieces
Juice of 1 lemon
1 medium onion, chopped
3 tablespoons unsalted butter
¼ cup chicken broth (homemade or canned)
1 tablespoon chopped fresh mint (or ⅛ teaspoon dried)
1 tablespoon chopped fresh marjoram (or ⅛ teaspoon dried)
Small pinch grated nutmeg
Salt and pepper to taste
1 cup heavy cream
1 egg yolk
Pinch paprika
2 tablespoons chopped fresh parsley

1. Toss the mushroom pieces with half of the lemon juice.

2. Sauté the onion in the butter over medium heat for 3 minutes; do not allow to brown.

3. Add the mushrooms and the remaining lemon juice; cook for 5 minutes, stirring often with a wooden spoon.

4. Add the chicken broth, mint, marjoram, nutmeg, salt, and pepper; cook for 15 minutes, uncovered.

5. Pass the mushroom mixture through a food mill and replace in pan, adding half the heavy cream; bring to boiling point, stirring often.

6. In the meantime, beat together the remaining cream, the egg yolk, paprika, and parsley until well blended.

7. Add to the mushroom mixture, stir thoroughly being careful not to boil again to avoid curdling the egg, and serve hot as a side dish.

*Serves 4*

# PIZZA DI CARCIOFI E FUNGHI
## *Pizza with Artichokes and Mushrooms*

*Pizza comes in many varieties in the province of Lucca, and this is one of the most popular—a wonderful blend of mushrooms, artichokes, and grated cheese placed on a crust that is somewhat different from the traditional, yeasted pizza crusts.*

*The dough:*
  2 cups unbleached flour, sifted
  1 egg, lightly beaten
  ¼ teaspoon salt
  1 stick of unsalted butter, softened to room temperature
  ½ cup water
*The toppings:*
  8 ounces champignon mushrooms, cleaned and sliced
  4 tablespoons extra-virgin olive oil
  4 artichoke heart sections preserved in olive oil, sliced in half
  4 eggs, hard cooked, peeled, and sliced
  ¼ cup Parmigiano Reggiano, grated
  6 tablespoons dry unflavored breadcrumbs
*The sauce:*
  2 ounces unsalted butter
  ¼ cup white flour
  ½ cup milk
  ⅛ teaspoon salt

1. Mix together the flour, beaten egg, salt, softened butter, and water to form a ball. Place in a bowl, covered, for 30 minutes.

2. Sauté the mushrooms in half the oil until they are soft; leave in pan and reserve.

3. Now make the sauce by heating the remaining butter in a skillet over medium heat; add the remaining flour and the milk, stirring constantly with a fork or whisk until of a creamy consistency. Add the salt and blend thoroughly.

4. Assemble the pizza by rolling out the dough to the size of either a 12-inch round pan, or a 10 x 10 square pan, or 11 x 17 inches. Place

the dough in the pan and fold over the edges until they form a nice rolled crust around the perimeter.

5.  Drizzle the remaining oil over the crust; evenly arrange the mushrooms, artichokes, and sliced eggs on the surface.

6.  Pour the sauce over the top, sprinkle with the cheese and breadcrumbs, and bake in a preheated 400 degree oven for 30 minutes.

*Serves 4*

# BALDINO DI CASTAGNA
## *Sweet Chestnut Cake*

*This is a type of sweet bread made by mixing chestnut flour—which is softer and sweeter than that made from wheat—with water, olive oil, and a variety of dried fruits and nuts. When the paste is well mixed, it can be topped with scattered sprigs of rosemary or grated lemon peel. In Signora Pieri's house, it is still made the old way—by placing the cake tin on top of a few embers beside the fire, covering it with an old sauce lid, and putting more embers on top of the lid, thus creating a very primitive kind of convection oven. It can, however, be made using a modern oven. It is very good as a not-too-sweet dessert, or as an appetizer served with a dry white wine, or even as an accompaniment to soup on a dark, rainy day.*

> 3 cups chestnut flour
> Water
> 2 tablespoons extra-virgin olive oil
> ⅛ teaspoon salt
> 4 ounces currants
> 2 ounces raisins
> 4 ounces pine nuts, crushed
> Olive oil for greasing the pan
> 2 tablespoons finely minced fresh rosemary
> 1 teaspoon grated lemon rind

1. Place the flour in a mixing bowl; stirring constantly with a wooden spoon, slowly add enough water to convert the mixture into a rather liquid dough.

2. When the dough is of a consistency that can easily be poured, add the olive oil and salt, and mix thoroughly.

3. Add the currants, raisins, and pine nuts, and mix well enough to create an even distribution.

4. Oil a round, shallow, 8-inch cake tin, making sure to cover both the sides and the bottom; preheat the oven to 350 degrees.

5. Pour the mixture into the pan to a depth of about ½ inch; sprinkle the rosemary and lemon rind over the top.

6. Bake approximately 30 minutes or until the top is a deep, crusty brown.

*Serves 8 as a dessert, 10 as an appetizer, thinly sliced*

# GNOCCHI DI CASTAGNE
*Chestnut Gnocchi*

*Finding chestnut flour in northern Tuscany is like finding butter—every store has it. Americans are not as lucky. If you look in specialty stores, however, you might just have some luck, and the Signora heartily hopes you do, for this recipe is one she readily admits she would not be prepared to do without. For the uninitiated, gnocchi (pronounced NEEO-kee) are small potato and flour dumplings that are boiled and then served with sauce, like pasta (more on gnocchi on page 134).*

> The gnocchi:
>> 2 pounds potatoes (any kind except red which absorbs too much water), boiled until soft throughout, then peeled
>> 3 cups chestnut flour plus ½ cup
>> 2 eggs, lightly beaten
>> Salt and pepper to taste
>
> The sauce:
>> 2 cloves garlic, minced
>> 2 tablespoons extra-virgin olive oil
>> 1 35-ounce can Italian tomatoes, drained and chopped
>> 3 leaves fresh basil
>> Salt to taste
>> Parmigiano Reggiano, grated

1. Mash the potatoes with a hand masher; add 2 cups of the flour and the eggs. Add the salt and pepper. Mix by hand until thoroughly blended and of a sticky consistency.

2. Divide and shape the dough into a series of balls approximately 2 inches in diameter, or the size of baseballs.

3. Spread some flour across a large pastry board or counter. Working with one "baseball" at a time, roll on the counter with the palms of your hands working from the center out until you have a long rope approximately 1-inch in diameter.

4. Cut each "rope" into small sections that resemble wine corks; continue until all the dough has been rolled and cut.

5. Now make the sauce. Sauté the garlic in the hot oil until it is very lightly browned; add the tomatoes, basil, and salt, and cook, covered, over low heat for 15 minutes.

6. While the sauce is simmering, cook the gnocchi. Boil 3 quarts of water in a large pasta pot; when the water is boiling, add one-fourth of the gnocchi, tossing them in a few at a time. The gnocchi are cooked as soon as they float to the top. Continue until all have been cooked.

7. Remove each batch of gnocchi with a slotted spoon as soon as they are cooked; place in a large serving bowl. Top with a layer of sauce and a sprinkle of cheese. Continue layering in this manner until all the gnocchi have been used.

8. Serve hot with a young red wine.

*Serves 4*

# INSALATA DI FUNGHI
*Mushroom Salad*

*Sometimes, on Sunday evenings, Signora Pieri desires nothing more than a nice salad with cheese, bread, and wine. Here is a favorite for such occasions, a well-seasoned salad made with ordinary small, white mushrooms. Add to this a generous wedge of fresh pecorino cheese, a bottle of Chianti, and—as the Signora says—you dine with the angels! Note that this salad can also be made with wild mushrooms, in which case do not add the chives; they would compromise the mushrooms' strong taste.*

> 1½ pounds small white champignon mushrooms, cleaned and
>    thinly sliced
> Juice of 1 lemon
> 6 tablespoons extra-virgin olive oil
> Salt and pepper to taste
> 1 small bunch young chives, diced
> 2 tablespoons finely chopped fresh parsley

1. Toss the mushroom slices with the lemon juice.

2. Add the oil, salt, and pepper; blend until each mushroom slice is well coated in the juices.

3. Refrigerate for 30 minutes.

4. Just before serving add the chives and parsley, and toss well to blend together all the flavors.

*Serves 4*

# CASTAGNACCIO
## Chestnut Cake

*This is, without doubt, the most common and most characteristic cake recipe in the entire Versilia-Garfagnana area. That's not to say you won't find Castagnaccio anywhere else in northern Tuscany, but in the mountains and on the coast, when it's chestnut season, you will unquestionably find it on every table—whether in restaurants or private homes.*

4 cups chestnut flour
¼ cup water
4 tablespoons sugar
2 tablespoons grated orange rind
¼ cup pine nuts
¼ cup golden raisins
1 tablespoon finely chopped fresh rosemary
2 ounces chopped walnuts
2 tablespoons extra-virgin olive oil
1 tablespoon butter for greasing, plus 2 tablespoons, cut into pats, for the cake's surface

1. Place the chestnut flour in a large bowl; add ¼ cup water and mix with a fork. Continue to add water, 1 tablespoon at a time, mixing constantly with a fork until the dough is soft and almost creamy.

2. Add the remaining ingredients except the butter, and blend well with a fork or a wooden spoon.

3. Butter a round baking pan, 8 or 9 inches in diameter and not more than 3 inches high.

4. Preheat the oven to 400 degrees; pour the dough into the pan and place the pats of butter here and there on the cake's surface.

5. Bake for 1 hour or until the surface is crusty and golden brown.

*Serves 6*

# FRITELLE DI CASTAGNE CON RICOTTA
*Ricotta-topped Chestnut Fritters*

*When peasants worked the fields of northern Tuscany, the following treat was eaten without regard for fats or calories. Today, however, things have changed. But not so much, says the Signora, that we have to do away completely with the foods we love best. This recipe for chestnut fritters topped with ricotta is, indeed, a food loved by the people of the Lucchesía. Be wise, advises Signora Pieri. Eat only a few. But under no circumstances should you entirely deprive yourself of this extraordinary culinary delight.*

> 2 cups chestnut flour
> ⅛ teaspoon salt
> Water
> 2 tablespoons grated orange rind
> Olive oil for frying
> 8 ounces fresh ricotta

1. Place the flour in a mixing bowl; add the salt and just enough water, one tablespoon at a time, to create a somewhat creamy dough.

2. Add the orange rind and blend into the dough.

3. Place the olive oil in a frying pan to the 1-inch mark; heat.

4. Drop the fritters into the hot oil, 1 tablespoon at a time; fry until golden brown on one side. Turn and fry on the reverse side. Drain on paper towels; keep warm.

5. Continue until all the batter has been fried.

6. Spread the ricotta over the fritters, and serve hot.

*Makes approximately 10 fritters*

# CASTAGNE LESSATE
*Boiled Chestnuts*

*Chestnuts form the basis for more than desserts; they also work very well as side dishes—especially accompanying pork—and as a stuffing for goose and turkey. This and the next are two quick and wonderful recipes for preparing chestnut contorni—side dishes that one would serve as an accompaniment to roast pork or pan-fried pork cutlets, or even a pork stew.*

> 1½ pounds chestnuts or, to avoid peeling, 1 pound dried chestnuts
> ½ teaspoon salt
> 1 celery stalk
> 1 bay leaf

1. Place the chestnuts in a pot filled with cold water; add the salt, celery stalk, and bay leaf.

2. Cook over medium heat, covered, for 1 hour.

3. Peel, if necessary, and serve as a side dish for pork along with sautéed greens.

*Serves 4*


# PURE DI CASTAGNE
*Chestnut Puree*

> 1½ pounds chestnuts in the skins, or 1 pound dried chestnuts
> ½ teaspoon salt
> 1 celery stalk
> ½ cup milk or, for a saltier taste, ½ cup chicken broth
> 2 tablespoons butter

1. Place the chestnuts in a pot filled with cold water; add the salt and celery stalk.

2. Cook over medium heat for approximately one hour.

3. Puree the chestnuts by passing them through a food mill.

4. Add the milk (or broth) and butter; blend well.

5. Serve as an accompaniment to roast pork.

*Serves 4*

# MONDINE QUASI CARAMELLATE
*Quasi-caramelized Chestnuts*

*Here is an ancient recipe for caramelized chestnuts from the hill towns of northern Tuscany. This was a dish served on cold winter nights when everyone would gather around the fire with a glass of* vin santo. *Although you may still be lucky enough to have a hearth and can therefore cook the chestnuts in the "old" way, you can also roast them in a covered pot on the stove.*

    1½ pounds fresh chestnuts
    1 cup dry white wine
    2 tablespoons sugar
    ½ cup rum

1. Place the chestnuts in a heavy skillet; cook, covered, over low heat for 45 minutes, shaking the skillet every 5 minutes or so, to turn the chestnuts.

2. When the chestnut skins are crisp, remove from the heat and wrap them, still in their skins, in an old dishcloth.

3. Roll the cloth once or twice over a hard surface to loosen the skins just a bit.

4. Place the chestnuts in a bowl and cover with the wine; let them sit for 5 minutes or so to absorb the essence of the liquid.

5. Peel the chestnuts and place them in an oven-proof dish with the sugar and rum; toss until the chestnuts are well coated with the sweet mixture.

6. Using a long match, ignite the surface of the chestnuts and stir them during burning until the sugar melts and forms a caramelized surface.

7. Serve hot with plenty of vin santo or red wine.

*Serves 4*

# CROCCHETTINE DI CASTAGNE
*Chestnut Croquettes*

*"When I was young," says the Signora, "I was always fed crocchettine di castagne—chestnut croquettes—as a midmorning or midafternoon snack. My mother would bring them to school. In those days, parents brought hot snacks at 10 a.m. and 3 p.m. right into the classroom so that their darling children—us— would not starve. Then I grew older and eventually married, but I often found myself craving this wonderful treat. So, in addition to serving it to my own children as a* merenda, *a snack, I began serving it as a dessert, and still do."*

1 pound chestnuts, peeled
2 cups milk
1 tablespoon vanilla
4 tablespoons butter
¾ cup sugar
2 egg yolks, slightly beaten
Vegetable oil for frying
Rum

1. Place the chestnuts in a saucepan with the milk and vanilla. Cook over medium heat, covered, for 25 minutes.

2. Pass the chestnut mixture through a food mill, or place in a food processor and blend until it takes on a paste-like consistency.

3. Add the butter, sugar, and egg yolks; blend thoroughly.

4. Place the mixture in a saucepan and cook over low heat for 2 minutes or just long enough to dry the mixture somewhat; cool.

5. Form into balls approximately 1½ inches in diameter and fry in hot oil until all sides are a golden-brown color.

6. Drain on paper towels, sprinkle with rum (or, if serving to children, powdered sugar), and serve.

*Makes approximately 20 croquettes*

*Signora Velia Giannini*

# Chapter Three

# RIVALRY FOREVER

## BEANS AND SOUPS

To go from Pisa to Lucca, there's only one main road. And on that road there is a mountain pass, Passo di San Giuliano, which effectively separates the two provinces from each other. The pass has been a fact of life for eight decades, but a few years back, the *Pisani* proposed to their regional congress that it be closed. Not temporarily. Not until another road could be built. Just closed. Period.

Officially, they cited reasons of public safety—a few small rocks had supposedly "catapulted" onto the road earlier that week. But the people of Lucca knew better. *E un altra di quelle Pisanata*, they told each other— another of those uniquely Pisan snubs.

Their conviction is rooted in the ongoing rivalry that has existed between the Lucchese and the Pisani for centuries. *Meglio un morto in casa che un Pisano a l'uscio*, goes the old Lucchese proverb—better a dead person in the house than a Pisano at the door. So longstanding is the conflict that it has even insinuated itself into Tuscan literature. *Le Poesie di Geppe* is a book of poetry written in the Lucchese vernacular by Gino Custer De Nobili in 1906. In it you'll find a poem entitled "*Tra Lucchesi e Pisani*," "Between the People of Lucca and the People of Pisa," which gives a humorous account of the ongoing bitterness. One stanza, written in the voice of a Pisano, reads "*O gentaccia di Lucca peorona, é l'ora di fonilla*"—"O ye whining scum of Lucca, it's time to end this nonsense once and for all."

Originally the two provinces fought about feudal duchies and who would hold the seat of power. Today the debate is more a fussy stereotyping of character, fierce enough, however, to incite restaurant chefs in Lucca to unload their culinary faux pas on unsuspecting Pisani. "The mouths of the Pisani are lined with cotton," a Lucchese chef is likely to tell you. "So what if I send to their table a dish of pasta that cooked a little too long?"

The character assaults reach into every facet of life. "You can always tell when the Pisani are on the road because they're the ones trying to pass you on the right," goes one. "You can always spot the Pisani in a bar because they're the ones ordering an aperitif *after* a meal." "The Pisani strut." "The Pisani are arrogant." "The Pisani brood." "The Pisani have long pointy chins." *Un vero pasticcio,* as they say in Tuscany. A fine mess.

But if you think that's as bad as it gets, then you know nothing about Tuscany and its people. Even worse than the rivalry between the provinces is the feuding between cities and towns in the *same* province. Take Viareggio and Lucca for example, a rivalry so fierce that, on occasion, Florence (the capital city) has had to come in to mediate. At issue is the fact that the Viareggini see themselves as a completely different species from the Lucchese. For each of the last three years, in fact, Viareggio has requested the right to secede from Lucca in order to form a province of their own. Thus far, they have been refused. The main point of contention between the two lies in the area of cultural differences. The Lucchesi are too stuffy, claim the Viareggini. "All they talk about is their collection of artistic treasures. But when people want to enjoy themselves—when they want to eat well or go to the beach or go out dancing—they come here, to Viareggio."

Talk is only the beginning. There's also the never-to-be-forgotten incident of the *Burlamacco del Carnivale.* The *Burlamacco* is a huge, stuffed, puppet-character that has always served as the mascot of Viareggio's annual carnival. Traditionally, it is erected at the end of the town, facing the carnival route. But that also means that its rear end faces the city of Lucca. Two years ago, a Lucchese newspaper featured an article venting the supposed "anger felt by the people of Lucca" over this slight. "Why should we, the proud people of Lucca, have to wake up each morning facing an ass?" The article generated a minifrenzy, and before long, the Lucchese were threatening to boycott the carnival. So last year, the *Burlamacco* was scrapped in favor of a new mascot, *Il Re del Carnivale,* the Carnival King, which was erected on the beach so that nobody but the Sardinians could complain of being snubbed.

And then there's the annual *Canzonette,* a theatrical revue held in Viareggio satirizing the various Tuscan rivalries. One spoof from last year's event featured a character symbolizing Lucca (whose citizens are known throughout the province for their "fiscal restraint") sitting in a cafe, waving his arms as if snatching at the air. The Viareggino at the next table watches for a while and then asks *"Che prendi?"* which can mean both "What are you trying to catch?" and "What will you have?" To which the Lucchese promptly responds, "A brioche and a cappuccino, thanks."

Signora Velia Giannini laughs over these rivalries as if they were nothing more than an amusing sketch. "This is the way we are," she says, throwing up her hands. "What can we do? It must be that we are blessed with too much—a wonderful climate, the beauty of our hills, our culture. Perhaps we must instigate these rivalries merely to keep our blood active."

The Signora lives in Massarosa, which has its own share of rivalries. "The people of Bozzano (a tiny village two miles to the east)—their beans are without equal, but must their men always come serenading after *our* women?"

Massarosa, a small hill town surrounded by olive groves, lies halfway between Lucca and Viareggio. Its charms are many, from the seventeenth-century homes built along tree-lined cobbled lanes, to the remnants of a Roman bath built on Lake Massacciuccoli, to the eleventh-century Church of San Pantaleone in Pieve a Elici, to scores of scenic views—the Apuan Alps on one side, the beaches of Viareggio on the other.

The Signora's home is directly across from the Church of San Iacopo and San Andrea. Her balcony faces the Piazza Vittorio Veneto, in whose center is found a curious little construction referred to rather grandly as *Il Monumento,* dedicated as it is to those who died in World War I. The last time I visited Massarosa I was awakened at 7:30 in the morning by a band of six men—all more than 80—trumpeting and drumming in front of this monument. It was the anniversary of The Surrender, I was told later, and they had come to lay a commemorative wreath. I caught them just as they were finishing their task, and as I watched groggily from my window, they hobbled away down the main street, trumpets and drums in full review. The "parade" lasted all of about five minutes.

This time I have come to Massarosa to accompany the Signora on a procession honoring the sixtieth anniversary of the construction of an enormous cross dominating the hillside behind the church. The procession will start at another church, that of San Rocco, a tiny vaultlike structure at the end of the main road, which houses a number of important works, among them, a thirteenth-century silver cross and a beautiful fifteenth-century marble shrine. The Signora was one of the Massarosa's original residents. In 1934, she and a group of friends each carried one stone up to the top of Monte Iacopo in order to build the platform underlying the giant cross. When we get to the top tonight, Don Fausto, the town's *proposto* (parish priest), will pay tribute to all the elders who were part of the original procession, and especially those who were still able to manage the hike.

We leave San Rocco at 9 p.m. on a chilly Saturday night, a group of approximately two hundred people—men, women, children, and many teenagers—and make our way holding long white candles cupped at the tips by colored paper to block the wind. Every hundred feet or so we come to a set of white lights strung across the path by the young people of this town as a tribute to its elders. The view of Massarosa becomes more magnificent with each curve. With each one also comes an increasing doubt on the part of the Signora that she will, in fact, make it to the top. *"Un bastone, Signora?"* a young boy asks at one point. He offers her the branch of a tree. She declines, preferring to lean on my arm.

Everyone knows each other. Everyone also knows I am a visitor, and people make a point of walking alongside the Signora for a few seconds until she has made the necessary introductions. Their initial appraisal is critical, wary. I am looked at from head to toe. But it is only for a second because, after all, I am with Signora Giannini, and so there is no need to cast me as a rival. There are no rivals here. Just a group of Massarosini struggling together to reach the top of a mountain. Along the way, we pause often to listen to tributes written and recited by the children of the town.

The last hundred feet are very steep and slippery due to yesterday's rains. I walk behind the Signora, propping her as best I can, my efforts supported by those of many others—Duilio, Marco, Mauro, Anna, the woman from the pharmacy. They're all there, hands outstretched. *Ecco Signora, ora ci siamo.* Just a little further Signora, we're almost there. When we finally reach the top, the Signora is congratulated by nearly everybody. One by one they hug her, kiss her, ask for a few recollections. She beams.

On the way down, she squeezes my arm. I squeeze back, and when I look at her, I see tears in her eyes. "Beh, even this time, I have made it," she says.

The next day we begin to search for recipes. "What you need for a successful book are preparations from as many Tuscan towns as possible," she says, culling through her collection. I am awed by the magnanimity of her gesture. But in the next minute, she has pulled out a yellowed, crumbling index card written in her own script, indicating a minestrone recipe from the town of Livorno, "Look here," she says, pointing to the ingredients. "This calls for the use of white beans." She shakes her head sadly. "Those Livornese, they have no sense of what it means to eat well."

*The cross atop Mount Iacopo.*

When using fresh shell beans, avoid those whose outside casings have black spots. Discard any beans from inside the shell that are yellowed or dried, and calculate approximately ¼ pound per person. Dried beans must always be soaked before cooking, preferably for 12 hours in lukewarm water with a pinch of bicarbonate of soda added. While cooking dried beans, discard any that float to the top of the water. Do not add salt until near the end of the cooking time or dried beans will become hard and bitter.

**How to Cook Fresh Shell Beans:** *Shell the beans and place them in a pot filled with cold water to the level of 3 or 4 inches above that of the beans. Add 1 celery stalk, 1 tablespoon of fresh sage, and 1 clove of garlic. Cook over medium heat, uncovered, and as soon as the water begins to boil, lower the flame. The secret to cooking fresh shell beans is never to interrupt the boil. Have on hand a quart or so of boiling water so that if, in lowering the flame, the water should cool, you can resume the boil with the addition of the extra water. Cooking time depends on the type of bean; regardless all fresh shell beans should cook a minimum of 1 hour, but the long and short of it is they'll be done when they're tender. When cooked, you can drizzle with a few tablespoons of extra-virgin olive oil—never vinegar or lemon.*

**How to Cook Dried Beans:** *Soak the beans for at least 12 hours in lukewarm water. Drain and rinse well under running water. Place in a pot of cold water; add 1 clove of garlic and a sprig or two of fresh sage. Bring to a boil over low heat, covered, and then lower the flame even further so that the beans are barely boiling. Cooking time is 3 hours at a minimum. If at any time it becomes necessary to add liquid, use only water that is already at a boil.*

# FAGIOLI NEL FIASCO
*Beans Cooked in a Flask*

*This is a very old and very famous Tuscan dish in which the beans are cooked in a wine flask (or, in Garfagnana, in a terra-cotta flask created specially for this preparation) over a smoldering charcoal fire for about 3 hours, or until all the liquid has evaporated. In general, dried beans are used, or fresh white beans (haricots), shelled. The same results are achieved today by placing the flask in a double boiler or slow oven. While somewhat more cumbersome than cooking the beans in a pot, the flask method results in a degree of tenderness not otherwise attainable.*

    1 pound dried beans, or 1 pound fresh white beans, shelled
    Cold water
    ½ cup extra-virgin olive oil
    2 cloves garlic, crushed in their skin
    2 tablespoons chopped fresh sage
    ¼ teaspoon fresh peppercorns, crushed
    ½ teaspoon salt

1. Place the beans in a 1.5 liter wine flask (preferably one with a bowl-shaped bottom); add cold water until the flask is one-third full.

2. Add the oil, garlic, sage, and peppercorns.

3. Seal the flask with a cork; place in a large double boiler over water, and cook over medium heat for 3 hours or until the beans are dry.

4. Remove the cork; add the salt and cook for another 10 minutes.

5. Shake the beans out of the flask and into the bowl. Remove the sage and serve hot or cold.

*Serves 4*

# FAGIOLI ALL UCCELLETTO
*Beans Cooked like Small Birds*

*This title refers, possibly, to the use of sage, a popular ingredient in the cooking of small birds. A popular dish throughout all of northern Tuscany, Fagioli all Uccelletto is such a constant in the Versilian kitchen that Viareggio, for example, thinks of it as a local specialty. In certain towns in Versilia, it is customary to add 2 tablespoons of strong balsamic vinegar just before serving. Try it.*

1 tablespoon minced fresh thyme
1 tablespoon minced fresh rosemary
2 tablespoons chopped fresh sage
1 pound fresh white (haricot) beans (or if absolutely unavailable, 1
    pound dried cannellini beans, soaked overnight)
Water
6 tablespoons extra-virgin olive oil
2 cloves garlic, crushed
12 ounces canned Italian tomatoes, chopped and with liquid
1 cube beef bouillon
Salt (omit if bouillon is very salty)
Pepper

1. Make a package of the thyme, rosemary, and 1 sprig of the sage by tying together in a small piece of white cheesecloth.

2. Place the beans in a pot of water, add the herb packet, and cook the beans according to the instructions on page 76; remove and discard the herb package when the beans are done.

3. Heat the oil in a thick skillet (if possible, use terra-cotta); add the garlic and the remaining sprig of sage. Remove the garlic when it is slightly browned.

4. Add the tomatoes and the bouillon cube; stir until the cube is completely dissolved.

5. With the tomato mixture still at a boil, add the beans with their liquid, and salt and pepper to taste; cook for 15 minutes, stirring frequently to blend the flavors.

6. Serve hot.

*Serves 4*

# SFORMATO DI FAGIOLI
*Bean Mold*

*Sformati are vegetable "pies" cooked with besciamella—a butter, flour, and milk sauce—and flavored with grated cheese. Tuscans eat sformati of all types. Most popular are those made with cauliflower, artichokes, onions, and the following two made with beans—one using dried, the other using any type of fresh, shelled bean.*

8 ounces dried beans (cannellini beans are best)
2 cloves garlic
1 tablespoon finely chopped fresh sage
4 tablespoons unsalted butter
3 tablespoons white flour
1 cup milk
2 eggs, separated
4 tablespoons Parmigiano Reggiano, grated
3 tablespoons unflavored dry bread crumbs
Salt and pepper to taste

1. Cook the beans with the garlic and sage according to the instructions on page 76.

2. Drain and pass through a food mill, or puree in a food processor until the beans take on the consistency of a thick, creamy paste.

3. Heat the butter in a skillet over low heat. Add the flour and milk, and stir with a fork or whisk until the mixture is thick and pastelike; remove from heat.

4. Blend together the beans and the milk-and-butter mixture; add the egg yolks, the salt and pepper, and the cheese.

5. Beat the egg whites until stiff; fold the bean mixture into the egg whites.

6. Butter an 8- or 9-inch round baking pan; sprinkle with the bread crumbs.

7. Pour the bean mixture into the pan, and cook in a preheated 350 degree oven for 20 minutes or until completely set.

8. Cut into slices and serve hot.

*Serves 4*

# SFORMATO DI FAGIOLI FRESCHI AL POMODORO

*Vegetable Mold with Fresh Shell Beans and Tomatoes*

3 pounds fresh shell beans (any type will do, but fava or broad
    beans are best)
1 tablespoon finely chopped fresh sage
2 cloves garlic
2 tablespoons olive oil
1 small onion, minced
1 small carrot, diced
1 medium stalk celery, diced
1 leaf fresh basil, chopped
½ cup canned Italian tomatoes
3 tablespoons unsalted butter
4 tablespoons white flour
½ cup milk
2 eggs, separated
2 tablespoons Parmigiano Reggiano, grated
Salt and pepper to taste
2 tablespoons unflavored dry bread crumbs

1. Cook the beans with the sage and garlic according to instructions on page 76; drain and pass through a food mill, or blend in a food processor until the mixture is reduced to a thick paste.

2. Heat the oil in a skillet; add the onion, carrot, celery, and basil and cook until the onion has browned. Add the tomatoes and simmer over low heat for 15 minutes, stirring often.

3. In a separate skillet melt the butter; add the flour and milk and stir with a fork until the consistency is thick and pasty.

4. Place the beans in a large bowl; add the tomato and milk mixture. Stir until all ingredients are thoroughly blended; cool to room temperature.

5. Add the lightly beaten egg yolks, grated cheese, and salt and pepper; blend with a fork.

6. Beat the egg whites until stiff; fold into the bean mixture.

7. Butter an 8- or 9-inch round baking pan; sprinkle with the bread crumbs.

8. Pour the beans into the dish; bake in a preheated 350 degree oven for 30 minutes.

9. Slice and serve hot.

*Serves 4*

# COTECHINO CON FAGIOLI BIANCHI E FINOCCHIO
*Pork Sausage with White Beans and Fennel*

*A delectable sausage created for boiling whose name comes from* cotíca, *an Italian word for pork rind, cotechino is made from minced pork, nutmeg, cloves, salt, and pepper, and then stuffed into a rather fat little piece of pork skin. The result is an ovular shape that resembles a small blimp. It is usually cooked for 1 to 2 hours, by which time, it has developed a rich, creamy texture, and is served in glistening splendor, sliced, on a bed of white beans (or alternatively, lentils) that have been cooked with bulbs of firm, white fennel. Cotechini are readily available at Italian markets and specialty stores.*

> 8 ounces dried cannellini beans, soaked overnight
> 2 garlic cloves
> 2 tablespoons fresh sage
> 1 cotechino (1–1½ pounds)
> 2 bulbs fennel, cut in half (tops removed and discarded)
> Extra-virgin olive oil
> Salt and pepper to taste

1. Cook the beans with the garlic and sage according to the instructions on page 76.

2. Prick the skin of the cotechino with a fork in approximately 5 or 6 spots and cook separately. Place in a pot with enough cold water to cover, add the fennel, and cook, covered, over medium heat 1½ hours.

3. Remove the beans from the cooking liquid with a slotted spoon; place on a serving platter so that the beans create a "bed" for the meat.

4. Remove the fennel with a slotted spoon; arrange around the outside of the platter on top of the beans.

5. Slice the cotechino into rounds, and cut each round in half; discard the skin.

6. Arrange the pieces of cotechino in the center of the serving platter on top of the beans; serve hot drizzled with the oil.

*Serves 4*

In Italy, there are as many justifications for badmouthing people from another region as there are types of cheese. One frequent argument is over the question of who exactly created the dish *Pasta e Fagioli,* Pasta with Beans. The answer has incited more than a few word battles. To the Southern Italians, the dish is obviously of their own imagining. To those from Padua or the Veneto (people who have been referred to by one of Italy's most important modern-day poets as "self-ensconced pedestal dwellers"), it's not so much a matter of who invented it as who perfected it. To the Signora, however, the solution is so obvious that any further conversation would be simply a wasting of one's breath.

"Pasta e fagioli is clearly a Tuscan dish," she maintains. "It is we, after all, who are called the 'bean eaters of Italy.' Who else even *grows* beans? No no no, you put this recipe in your book, and rest assured that its location of origin is principled and legitimate."

# PASTA E FAGIOLI
*Pasta with Beans*

*Here, per instructions of Signora Giannini, is the one and only Tuscan recipe.*

2 pounds fresh shell beans
1 cup extra-virgin olive oil
1 thin slice prosciutto, diced
2 thin slices pancetta (cured bacon), diced
1 small onion, minced
3 cloves garlic, crushed
1 dried chili pepper, crushed
4 plum tomatoes, peeled and diced
1 tablespoon tomato paste
8 ounces tagliatelle (a type of thick spaghetti)
Salt and pepper to taste

1. Shell the beans and cook according to the instructions on page 76.

2. Pass through a food mill and return to the soup pot.

3. Heat 3 tablespoons of the oil in a skillet; add the prosciutto, pancetta, onion, garlic, chili, and salt and pepper. Cook over low heat until the onion is golden in color.

4. Add the tomatoes and the tomato paste and cook for 5 minutes longer.

5. Cook the pasta according to the directions on the package.

6. Place the pasta in a bowl; add the tomato mixture and stir with a wooden spoon until well blended.

7. Serve hot and topped with a hefty dollop of extra-virgin olive oil.

*Serves 6*

# DOLCE DI FAGIOLI
*Bean Cake*

*According to the Signora, the very best Tuscan cooking comes from a time when the people were poor and ingredients had to be used in as many ways as could be imagined. The recipe for this wonderful cake made from dried white beans is one she credits to the Garfagnini, who were not only poor but also isolated and had to create both everyday foods and specialty treats from the same few staples.*

12 ounces dried cannellini beans, soaked overnight
White flour
3 eggs, separated
1 cup sugar
4 ounces assorted candied fruit
1 teaspoon baker's yeast

1. Cook the beans according to the instructions on page 76, except omit the garlic and sage.

2. Drain and pass through a food mill, or puree in a food processor until the mixture is reduced to a thick paste; add flour if necessary to thicken the blend.

3. Beat the egg yolks and add to the bean mixture; add the sugar, candied fruit, and yeast and blend well.

4. Beat the egg whites until stiff enough to create peaks; fold into the bean mixture.

5. Butter a round baking dish, 8 or 9 inches in diameter and at least 3 inches high; pour the beans into the dish and bake in a preheated 350 degree oven for 45 minutes or until the cake is cooked throughout.

6. Cool in the pan to room temperature before serving.

*Serves 8*

Soups

The Tuscan word for soup is zuppa, but all similarity between the two
ends there. Whereas "soup" is a generic term encompassing all kinds
of "liquid meals," "zuppe" refers only to a specific kind of soup—
those that are ladled over a thick slab of bread. Minestrone, garmugia, and carabaccio are all zuppe, for example.

Zuppe are almost always simple and a little rustic, flavored with
a sauté of onions, carrots, and herbs, and blended through with the
pungent odor of extra-virgin olive oil. The slices of bread are, for the
most part, toasted and rubbed with garlic.

Minestre, on the other hand, are cooked together with some
kind of pasta, or in some cases, served plain as a puree. Broths of all
kinds are "minestre" because they are prepared with either a very thin
vermicelli or orzo or even pastina, which are tiny pieces of pasta cut
into squares or stars or the letters of the alphabet.

Minestre are generally lighter and more refined than zuppe.
While some zuppe, such as cacciucco (a soup made entirely of fish),
can serve as an entire meal, minestre are always merely a first coarse.
Zuppe are usually eaten in winter; minestre are seasonless.

Included in the category of minestre are also passate, or purees.
Passate are always made of vegetables, such as chick peas, cauliflower,
or onions, and are eaten either plain or with some kind of pasta
(Tagliarini con Ceci, for example, is a puree of chick peas in which
homemade squares of thick pasta are cooked).

Pappa is a term often used interchangeably with passate. There's
Pappa di Pomodoro, for example, and Pappa di Zucchini, which
are both vegetable purees drizzled with a few tablespoons of olive oil
before serving.

# FARINATA GARFAGNINA
*Farinata, Garfagnana Style*

*This is neither a zuppa nor a minestra but in a category all its own. Farinata, according to the Signora, is the rustic invention of poor people seeking to stretch a simple vegetable soup into an entire meal. "In Tuscany, it is made with 'black' cabbage, which Americans have yet to develop." The cabbage is cooked with other vegetables and herbs, and then thickened with corn meal to the consistency of polenta. A wonderfully hearty meal the first time around, farinata is even better reheated in a skillet that has been splashed with extra-virgin olive oil. The Signora's recipe substitutes a variety of vegetables for the missing black cabbage.*

10 tablespoons extra-virgin olive oil
1 large onion, chopped
2 medium carrots, diced
1 medium stalk celery, diced
2 quarts cold water
½ savoy cabbage, cut into chunks
2 potatoes, diced
½ pound fresh shell beans, cooked to the halfway point according
   to instructions on page 82
2 chicken bouillon cubes
1 tablespoon finely chopped fresh sage
1 tablespoon finely chopped fresh rosemary
1 tablespoon finely chopped fresh oregano
Salt and pepper to taste
2 cups polenta (coarse grind)

1. Heat 3 tablespoons of the oil in a skillet over medium heat; add the onion, carrots, and celery and cook until the onion is browned.

2. Place the onion mixture in a large soup pot and fill with 2 quarts cold water; add the remaining ingredients except the polenta and 4 tablespoons of the oil. Cook for 1 hour or until all ingredients are tender.

3. Add the polenta, pouring in a steady stream and stirring constantly with a wooden spoon; cook for 15 minutes longer.

4. Divide into 6 dishes and serve hot, drizzled with the remaining oil.

*Serves 6*

**Note**: *When cooled, farinata tends to harden, and can be sliced and reheated in extra-virgin olive oil.*

"There is no question about it," the Signora tells me one day as we sit in her kitchen discussing the origin of certain recipes. "The famous 'soupe à l'oignon gratinée,' the veritable mainstay of French cuisine, was born from the Tuscan *carabazada,* which today is known simply as *carabaccia.*"

"They"—she points above her head, presumably in the direction of France—"they think they are such gastronomes. What kind of gastronomy relies on pilfering the recipes of others? Did they think we would not notice?"

She eventually concedes, that the question of who invented onion soup is made murky by virtue of the culinary contributions of Catherine de Medici who, throughout her life, had one foot in Italy and the other in France. "But," the Signora adds, "Caterina knew who created things and who merely refined them. And if she were here today, she would tell you herself: The Tuscans—they are the true cooks, not like the French who use hundreds of implements and, in the end, come up with foods that require the addition of sauces in order to make them complete."

# CARABACCIA
*Onion Soup*

*This is the Signora's recipe for what she stridently maintains is the "real" onion soup.*

4 ounces pancetta (cured bacon), diced
1 cup extra-virgin olive oil
1 medium celery stalk, diced
2 small carrots, chopped
2 leaves fresh basil, chopped
2 pounds red onions, sliced
¼ teaspoon salt
½ cup dry white wine
1 cup chicken broth (homemade or good quality canned)
½ pound fresh green peas (or frozen)
3 ounces Parmigiano Reggiano, grated
4 slices thick crusty bread, toasted on both sides

1. Place the pancetta, oil, celery, carrots, and basil in a large earthenware pot and cook over medium heat until the carrots and celery are lightly browned.

2. Add the onions and salt, and cook for one hour over low heat.

3. Pour the wine over the onion mixture and allow to evaporate before adding the broth and the peas; cook over low heat for another hour.

4. Sprinkle with the cheese, stir, and let sit for a few minutes.

5. Place one slice of bread in each bowl, pour the soup, and serve hot.

*Serves 4*

# GARMUGIA LUCCHESE
*Garmugia Lucca-style*

*A garmugia is a* zuppa *suitable for early spring. In the Signora's household, the recipe has been handed down from her great grandmother and is a culinary staple.*

6 small artichokes, cleaned and with the outer leaves removed
2 tablespoons extra-virgin olive oil
3 small onions, sliced thinly
4 ounces lean beef, diced
4-ounce slab of pancetta (cured bacon), cut into small cubes
3 tablespoons fresh peas (or frozen)
12 asparagus tips
3 ounces fresh shell beans
1 quart beef broth
4 slices thick crusty bread

1. Slice the artichokes into sixths; remove and discard the core.

2. Heat the oil in a skillet over medium heat; sauté the onions until lightly browned.

3. Add the beef and the pancetta and cook for 10 minutes longer.

4. Add the remaining ingredients and cook for 45 minutes.

5. Toast the bread on both sides and place one slice in each of four soup plates.

6. Pour the soup over the bread, let sit for a few minutes, and serve.

*Serves 4*

# ZUPPA DI VONGOLE
## *Clam Soup*

*The Versilian Coast has as many recipes for fish soups as there are fish in the Mediterranean. Zuppe di Vongole, one of the best, is a spicy blend of clams, chili pepper, and white wine. The Signora advises having extra bread on hand, since, in her experience, the broth is good as both a soup and a dip.*

> 3 pounds clams (any size will do)
> 6 tablespoons extra-virgin olive oil
> 1 dried chili pepper, crushed
> 4 cloves garlic, minced
> Salt and pepper to taste
> ½ cup dry white wine
> 4 slices thick crusty bread, toasted on both sides
> 1 lemon

1. Wash the clams under cold running water; smell each during washing and discard any whose odor indicates a lack of freshness. Dry with paper towels.

2. Heat the oil in a large skillet; sauté the chili and garlic until the garlic is a golden brown. Add salt and pepper to taste.

3. Add the wine and cook over low heat for 3 minutes.

4. Add the clams, stirring with a wooden spoon until the shells open.

5. Place the bread in each of 4 soup bowls; arrange the clams over the bread and cover with the soup.

6. Squeeze lemon over each of the soup bowls, and serve hot.

*Serves 4*

# LA PANZANELLA DEL PRETE
*Priest's Panzanella*

*Why credited to a priest? The Signora has no idea.*

La panzanella *is often confused with* le panzanelle. *The latter are small focaccie that are fried and often served in place of bread. The former is a fabulous* zuppa *served most often in summer since it depends for its flavor on the freshest of tender vegetables. In making a* panzanella, *you will need a great many ingredients—this one has more than twenty and serves at least eight. But then, in Tuscany,* panzanella *is served in a country setting where two or three families have gathered together on a Sunday afternoon at an outdoor table overflowing with thick crusty bread, good wine, and plenty of summertime laughter.*

1 ripe tomato

2 small cucumbers

1 large head lettuce, light green and very tender, such as
    buttercrunch

8 radishes

2 stalks celery

2 carrots

1 bulb fennel, top discarded

8 slices thick, crusty bread

Extra-virgin olive oil

Balsamic vinegar

Salt and pepper to taste

½ pound slab prosciutto, cut into small cubes

8 ounces tuna canned in olive oil, drained and crumbled

3 canned anchovies, drained, rinsed to remove the salt, and
    minced

8 ounces Parmigiano Reggiano, cut into small cubes

4 ounces Gruyère, cut into small cubes

20 capers

1 large red onion, thinly sliced

4 ounces small white onions, pickled

4 ounces artichoke hearts packed in olive oil, drained and sliced

8 leaves fresh basil, chopped

1 tablespoon finely chopped fresh thyme

3 tablespoons finely chopped fresh parsley

1 clove garlic, crushed (optional)
2 hard-cooked eggs, thinly sliced
2 red peppers, cored, seeded, and cut into thin strips

1. Cut the tomato, cucumbers, lettuce, radishes, celery, carrots, and fennel into small chunks.

2. Place the slices of bread on the bottom of a large soup bowl; pour a good amount of oil and 3 or 4 tablespoons vinegar over the bread so that it is soaked in the condiment; salt and pepper to taste.

3. Add the remaining ingredients, except the eggs and the red pepper.

4. Decorate the top by alternating the slices of egg with the pepper; refrigerate and let sit for 2 to 3 hours before serving.

*Serves 8*

*The Church of San Pantaleone, in Pieve a Elici.*

# ZUPPA DI PORRI
*Leek Soup*

*In the days when most Tuscans were peasants, soups were made with any and all types of vegetables—whatever one had in the garden, says the Signora. Nowadays, many of those ancient soup recipes are no longer used. She offers this preparation, however, for a simple little soup made with leeks and served over crostoni—cubes of bread that have been coated with oil and garlic, and toasted until crisp.*

> 7–8 leeks
> 2 quarts chicken broth (homemade or very good quality canned)
> 2 tablespoons unsalted butter
> 3 cloves garlic, crushed
> 4 tablespoons extra-virgin olive oil
> 4 slices thick, crusty bread, cut into cubes
> Salt and pepper to taste

1. Clean the leeks well, cut the white part of each leek into 2-inch strips, and discard the green parts.

2. Heat the chicken broth in a large saucepan.

3. Sauté the leeks in the butter until they are golden brown in color. Add to the hot broth and cook, covered, for 30 minutes.

4. Meanwhile, make the *crostoni:* Sauté the garlic in the oil until lightly browned; remove and discard. Add the bread to the oil and toss well until each cube is coated; add the salt and pepper. Place cubes in a baking pan in one layer; bake in a 400 degree oven for 10 minutes.

5. Place a few *crostoni* in each of 4 soup bowls; pour the soup over the bread cubes, and serve hot.

*Serves 4*

# BRODO DI CARNE
*Basic Meat Broth*

*This following recipe yields approximately 2 quarts of a very good broth that can be served by itself, steaming hot in cups and with a thick slice of crusty bread, or as the basis for many of the soups and other preparations described throughout this book. Do not discard the meat after the broth is made. Sliced and topped with sauce (see Chapter 8) it makes a very fine entree.*

    2 pounds beef rump roast
    2 quarts cold water
    2 large onions, cut in half
    2 cloves garlic, sliced in half
    2 medium carrots, cut in 3 or 4 chunks
    3 stalks of celery, cut in 3 or 4 pieces
    4 plum tomatoes, sliced in half
    Salt to taste

1. Place the meat in a large pot filled with 2 quarts of cold water; add the remaining ingredients. Bring to a boil, uncovered, over medium heat, and immediately lower the heat to low.

2. Cook over low heat, covered, for 2½ hours; skim off the fat every 20 minutes or so.

3. Remove the meat and reserve. Remove the vegetables and place through a food mill or puree in a food processor; return to broth.

4. Chill the broth and refrigerate until the fat has formed a hardened layer on top; remove the fat.

5. Serve broth by itself in a cup, or as the basis for other preparations.

*Makes 2 quarts*

# MINESTRA DI FAGIOLI CON FARRO
*Bean Soup with Spelt*

*Farro—spelt—is a grain grown in Garfagnana and used in place of rice for win-ter soups. This is a wonderful bean soup made by mixing* farro *with sausage or pork loin to create a thick, hearty dish.*

> 8 ounces dried cannellini beans, soaked overnight
> 2 cloves garlic
> 2 leaves fresh sage
> 3 tablespoons extra-virgin olive oil
> 2 links pork sausage, removed from the casing and mashed, or ¼
>     pound pork loin, cubed
> Salt and pepper to taste
> 1 cup spelt, soaked overnight (or barley can be substituted)

1. Cook the beans with the garlic, sage, 1 tablespoon olive oil, and the sausage or pork loin according to the instructions on page 76, except use 1½ times the amount of water because the spelt will soak up much of the broth. Add the salt and pepper when the beans are half cooked.

2. When the beans are three-fourths cooked, remove half of them to a large bowl; puree with a potato masher and return to the soup pot, stir-ring with a wooden spoon until there is a thick broth.

3. Add the spelt and the 2 remaining tablespoons olive oil; cook for 40 minutes longer. If necessary, add boiling water to maintain consistency.

4. Serve hot.

*Serves 6*

# INTRUGLIA CON SALSICCIA
*Intruglia with Sausage*

Intruglia *is a type of* minestra *conceived in Versilia and adopted by the people of the Garfagnana with one major change in the original recipe: the addition of sausage. Eaten hot, it is a hearty soup much like the* farinata *described on page 88. When it cools, however, it thickens—like polenta or farinata—into a solid mass, and is wonderful sliced and reheated in extra-virgin olive oil.*

> 3 tablespoons extra-virgin olive oil
> 1 tablespoon chopped fresh rosemary
> 1 tablespoon chopped fresh thyme (or ¼ teaspoon dried)
> 1 tablespoon chopped fresh sage (or 3 dried leaves)
> 1 bay leaf
> 3 links pork sausage, removed from the casing
> 1 pound fresh kale, cut into thick strips
> Salt and pepper to taste
> 1 pound dried kidney beans, cooked according to the instructions
>    on page 76
> 1 cup polenta (coarse grind)

1.  Heat the oil in a large skillet, add the herbs and the sausage, mixing with a fork until the sausage is completely broken apart.

2.  Add the kale, salt, and pepper, and stir until the sausage is completely cooked.

3.  Add the beans with their cooking liquid, and as soon as the soup returns to a boil, add the polenta in a steady stream, stirring constantly; cook for 20 minutes or until of a thick, creamy consistency.

4.  Serve hot drizzled with olive oil if desired.

*Serves 6*

# MINESTRA DI CECI
## *Chick Pea Soup*

*Chick peas—ceci—are very popular in Tuscany where they are used in a variety of ways. You'll find them boiled and dressed as a* contorno *(the term used for vegetables that will be served with meat), ground into a flour used for making foccacia (cecina is a very thin, very crisp foccacia), and as the basis for an extraordinary minestra, which in Pietrasanta (a town on the Versilian coast just north of Viareggio) is cooked with* Paternostri, *a thick pasta with a ridged surface.*

*"It's funny," the Signora says, "that in Pietrasanta they have* Paternostri, *which is a rather large type of pasta,* Ave Marie, *which are medium in size, and* Gloria Patri, *which is the same pasta as the other two, but very tiny."*

> 8 ounces dried chick peas, soaked overnight and drained
> 3 quarts water
> 1 stalk celery, cut into 3 pieces
> 1 onion, halved
> 1 carrot, cut widthwise into 3 pieces
> 5 tablespoons olive oil
> 2 tablespoons tomato paste
> Salt and pepper to taste
> 8 ounces ridged ziti

1. Place the chick peas, celery, onion, carrot, and olive oil in 3 quarts water; cook for 2 hours over low heat until chick peas are tender. Add water if necessary to maintain a thin, liquid consistency.

2. Remove chick peas, celery, onion, and carrot from the liquid with a slotted spoon and pass through a food mill or puree in a food processor; return the mixture to the cooking liquid.

3. Add the tomato paste, salt, and pepper to the soup, and cook for 20 minutes over low heat.

4. Cook the pasta according to the directions on the package; add the cooked pasta to the chick pea soup and cook for 2 minutes, stirring with a wooden spoon to blend thoroughly.

5. Serve hot.

*Serves 4*

# BRODO CON POLPETTONE
*Chicken Soup with Meatloaf*

*When the chill air seeps around the edges of doors, the Tuscans warm themselves with a chicken soup in which floats both slivers of succulent chicken and a plump meatloaf made of a combination of ground meats. The meatloaf, usually accompanied by* un bollito misto—*a mixed group of boiled vegetables including green beans and potatoes drizzled with olive oil—later becomes the* secondo *to the* primo, *which is the soup, and thus creates an ancient version of a "one-pot meal."*

*The soup:*
   4 large onions, quartered, plus 1 small onion, minced
   6 medium carrots, sliced lengthwise, plus 1 small carrot, minced
   6 medium stalks of celery, cut in half, plus 1 stalk of celery,
      minced
   3 tablespoons extra-virgin olive oil
   3 quarts water
   1 pound combination chicken breasts and thighs, skinned
   1 tablespoon finely minced fresh rosemary
   1 tablespoon finely minced fresh sage
   3 leaves fresh basil
   Salt and pepper to taste
   ½ pound pastina (any very tiny pasta, such as alphabets)
*The meatloaf:*
   2 medium onions, minced
   2 tablespoons olive oil
   4 ounces each ground veal, beef, and pork
   4 ounces Parmigiano Reggiano, grated
   7 tablespoons finely minced fresh parsley
   4 ounces unflavored dry breadcrumbs
   1 egg, lightly beaten
   Salt and pepper to taste

1. For the broth sauté the minced onion, carrot, and celery in the oil until all are lightly browned.

2. Place the water in a soup pot; add the sauté and the remaining soup ingredients except the pastina. Cover and cook over medium heat for 2 hours.

3. Meanwhile prepare the meatloaf: Sauté the onions in the oil until golden.

4. Place the sautéed onions and the remaining loaf ingredients in a large bowl; using your hands, mix thoroughly until all the ingredients have blended together. Shape into a plump oval resembling a football.

5. Forty-five minutes before the soup is done, place the meatloaf carefully in the pot.

6. At the end of the cooking time, remove the meatloaf with a slotted spoon; slice into ½-inch-thick slices. Place slices on a serving platter and keep warm.

7. Using the same slotted spoon, remove the pieces of chicken from the pot and allow to cool. Remove the onions, carrots, and celery, and discard.

8. When the chicken is cool enough to touch, remove and discard the bones, and shred the meat into tiny slivers; arrange on the serving platter with the meatloaf.

9. Reboil the soup and add the pastina; cook for 7 minutes.

10. Serve the soup as a first course and the meatloaf and chicken as a second course, accompanied by a *bollito misto* consisting of boiled string beans, potatoes, and zucchini, all sliced and arranged and drizzled with extra-virgin olive oil.

*Serves 6*

# PAPPA DI ZUCCHINI
*Thick Zucchini Soup*

*When I tell the Signora that* Pappa al Pomodoro, *Thick Tomato Soup, has become somewhat of a staple in America, she waves away my words.* Via, via, alloro si mette la Pappa di Zucchini, *she says. All right, all right, so then let's use this recipe for Thick Zucchini Soup. I tell her I've never heard of* Pappa di Zucchini. *It was absolutely the right thing to say, because in the next few minutes she was off, with me in tow—the two of us heading to the market to buy the ingredients with which she then created the most delectable soup imaginable.*

    1¼ pounds small young zucchini with a few flowers attached
    4 tablespoons extra-virgin olive oil
    2 onions, diced
    Salt and pepper to taste
    1 quart good-quality vegetable broth

1. Slice the zucchini into rounds no larger that ¼ inch thick; reserve the flowers.

2. Place the oil in a large skillet over medium heat and brown the zucchini and onions; add salt while browning to keep the green of the zucchini alive. Add pepper.

3. Add the zucchini flowers and let cook for a few minutes; total cooking time for the zucchini and the flowers should be no longer than 10 minutes.

4. Add the broth and heat through.

5. Place in a blender or food processor and reduce to a thick, creamy soup.

6. Return to flame long enough to heat through, and serve with a drizzle of olive oil across the top.

*Serves 4*

# MINESTRONE FREDDO DI VERDURA
*Cold Vegetable Minestrone*

*For hundreds of years, the marble that came from the Apuan Alps was mined by the men of Massa and Carrara, two seaside towns north of Viareggio. Daily they would climb to the tops of the peaks and extract the choice white marble for such clients as Michelangelo and Leonardo da Vinci. But because of the time it took them to reach their workplace, the miners were unable to return home for lunch. So they took it with them, and one of their favorite dishes was this* minestrone. *Since it is a cold zuppa, it is not served over bread. Today it is used widely for summer picnics and other outdoor meals. Its popularity is enhanced by the fact that it can be made days in advance and kept well days afterwards, if refrigerated.*

> 1 potato
> 2 small carrots
> 1 stalk celery
> 2 small zucchini
> Any other very fresh vegetables that catch your eye
> 5 cups chicken broth (homemade or good quality canned)
> 6 ounces dried kidney beans, cooked according to the instructions
>     on page 76
> 4 ounces fresh peas (or frozen)
> Extra-virgin olive oil

1. Cut the potato, carrots, celery, zucchini, and other vegetables into small cubes.

2. Heat the broth and add the cubed vegetables; cook for 15 minutes.

3. Add the cooked beans with their liquid, and the peas; cook for 15 minutes longer.

4. Cool to room temperature, and serve drizzled with olive oil.

*Serves 4*

# MINESTRA DI PATATE
# DI TUTTI I GIORNI
*Everyday Potato Soup*

*In the small town of Cardoso just north of Viareggio on the Tyrrhenian coast, the peasants of old would place this soup over a wood fire at 9 a.m. on their way to the fields, and by 12 noon when they returned, the air would be "perfumed" with the fragrance of* minestra di patate di tutti i giorni, *everyday potato soup. Today, it is also called* minestra fatta a crudo—*soup made from raw ingredients— because unlike almost every other Tuscan recipe that depends for its flavor on an initial sauté, this one adds the ingredients to the pot raw.*

3 tablespoons unsalted butter

3 cloves garlic, crushed

3 tablespoons finely chopped fresh parsley

3 leaves fresh basil, minced

1 tablespoon finely chopped fresh thyme (or ¼ teaspoon dried)

2 pounds potatoes, peeled

2 quarts cold water

4 ounces canned Italian tomatoes, drained and chopped

4 tablespoons extra-virgin olive oil

Salt and pepper to taste

8 ounces fresh lasagna, cut into large rectangles, or 8 ounces dried, broken into large chunks.

1. Make a paste of the butter, garlic, parsley, basil, and thyme.

2. Place the potatoes in a pot filled with 2 quarts cold water; add the herb paste, tomatoes, oil, salt, and pepper. Cook over low heat for 2 hours, by which time the potatoes will have crumbled and formed a thick, pasty soup.

3. Add the pasta and cook for 8 to 10 minutes, depending on type.

4. Serve hot, drizzled with olive oil.

*Serves 4*

# PALLINE DI RISO IN BRODO
*Tiny Rice Balls in Chicken Broth*

*When the Signora wants to fuss over a desired guest, she makes this soup consisting of tiny balls of rice floating in a savory chicken broth. "My neighbors who know me say they can tell how I feel about certain company by what I cook for them. If it is someone who is less close to my heart, I make a simple pasta followed by a simple roast. To them, of course, it seems fine. Only I know what they're missing." I feel compelled to note that Signora Giannini has made this particular dish for me—not once, but many times.*

1½ cups white rice
3 cups milk
2 tablespoons unsalted butter
5 tablespoons Parmigiano Reggiano, grated
Salt and pepper to taste
¼ teaspoon grated nutmeg
White flour
2 eggs, lightly beaten
Olive oil for frying
2 quarts chicken broth (very best quality)
Parmigiano Reggiano, grated

1. Cook the rice in the milk until thoroughly dry; add the butter, 5 tablespoons cheese, the salt, pepper, and nutmeg and mix well with a fork.

2. Using your hands, form the rice mixture into a series of Ping-Pong–size balls; roll each in flour and dip into the beaten egg. Fry them in hot oil until all sides are browned; drain on paper towels.

3. Heat the chicken broth to boiling.

4. Arrange from 5 to 6 rice balls per soup bowl, pour the hot broth over then, and serve hot topped with grated cheese to taste.

*Serves 4*

N. 35-1741 - **Appendistrofinacci** per cucina, in ferro smaltato e con diciture L. **4,50**

N. 35-1742 - **Tegame** con manico, in ferro smaltato, diam. cm. 12 L. **2,75**, 14 L. **3,50**, 16 L. **4,—**, 18 L. **4,75**, 20 L. **5,50**, 22 L. **7,—** 24 L. **8,50**

N. 35-1744 - **Colapasta** o verdure in ferro smaltato, diam. cm. 18 L. **12,50**, 20 L. **14,50**, 22 L. **17,50**, 24 L. **21,—**, 26 L. **24,50**, 28 L. **27,50**

# Ferro smaltato

**IMPORTANTE.**
Il nostro **ferro smaltato** è di qualità **sceltissima.**

N. 35-1743 - **Casseruola** con manico o due orecchie, in ferro smaltato, diam. cm. 14 L. **6,—**, 16 L. **8,—**, 18 L. **9,50**, 20 L. **12,25**, 22 L. **14,—**, 24 L. **16,—**

N. 35-1737 - **Graticola** di ferro smaltato, a 7 barre L. **14,50**, a 9 L. **20,50**

N. 35-1747 - **Casseruola** con becco, in ferro smaltato, diametro cm. 14 L. **5,75**, cm. 16 L. **7,—**, cm. 18 L. **8,50**, cm. 20 L. **9,50**, cm. 22 L. **12,50**, cm. 24 L. **14,50**

N. 35-1749 **Mestolo** in ferro smaltato, diam., cm. 8 L. **3,—**, cm. 9 L. **3,50**, cm. 10 L. **4,—**, cm. 11 L. **4,50**

N. 35-1750 - **Casseruola** forma ovale e con coperchio, in ferro smaltato, per arrosto, cm. 23 L. **19,50**, 26 L. **27,50**, 30 L. **32,50**

N. 35-1751 **Schiumarola** in ferro smalt. cm. 11 L. **3,50** cm. 12 L. **4,50** cm. 13 L. **5,—**

*Signora Tebe Orlandi*

# Chapter Four

# A SINGULAR RESPECT FOR THE NATURE OF AUTHORITY

## PASTA, POLENTA, GNOCCHI, AND RICE

*W*hen Signora Orlandi was very young, Lucca would come alive at least once every week with drums and trumpets and the grating sound of hooves scraping the earth. Voices shouted through bullhorns announcing the arrival of *The Great This* or *The Fabulous That,* and she and her friends would drop what they were doing and race out to the piazza.

What they saw would always be the same: a marching band, either in uniforms or suits, preceding a large float pulled by horses and strung with the banners of a particular political party—one week the Communists, next week the Fascists. In between came the smaller parties: the Unified Party, the Social Democrats, the Party of the Right—each with its own songs, its own cast of characters, and its own canvas of the future yet to be painted.

After the usual fifteen-minute oration on the benefits to be gained by supporting this particular party, the crowd would be asked to declare their intentions. "Those among you who are Fascists, step forward," a formally dressed man would shout through a bullhorn. And most of the crowd would move towards the float, their hands reaching up in one outstretched mass to receive the pictures or buttons or whatever was being given out that day. Then the band would once more begin to play, and the float would move on.

And, undoubtedly, before the images of one event could firm in your mind, the tableau would again be enacted. "Which among you are

Communists? Step forward." And the crowd—the same people, mind you—would step forward to pledge their fealty once again.

The storyteller is Tebe Orlandi, a tall, elegant woman in her eighties whose words ebb and flow with the incessant rhythm of her hands. "Italians are all anarchists," she declares. "All of us, anarchists—and Tuscans worst of all. You have only to look at Carrara [a town on the Versilian Coast north of Viareggio] to see how affectionately we nurture our anarchism. Why, fascism had barely fallen, and there we were, the people of Carrara sowing the seeds for what has today become a national organization—the Italian Federation of Anarchist [FAI].

"Anarchy is in our blood," she continues. "Take, for example, a situation in which you and I are having a discussion, and I find myself in basic agreement with what you're proposing. Chances are, I would *still* disagree with you, arguing today in favor of the same point I yesterday disputed. And in the end, none of it would matter because, with us, it is only words. Content never comes to play. Only the sounds carry import, the rising and falling of our own voices as we move from allegro to adagio, forming and reforming theories that, tomorrow, might just as well be fed to the pigs."

To illustrate her point, the Signora offers up the infamous *tesera del pane,* a card that—in the period before and during World War II—identified you as a member of the Fascist party, and without which you were unable to buy bread. "For the duration of the card's existence, all Italians, regardless of what they *really* believed, became Fascists, at least insofar as they signed their name on the bottom line of the *tesera*. I knew no one who stood his ground and said, 'No, I will not prostitute myself this way.' No one even questioned it. But we also continued attending the Socialist dances on Friday nights in the back room of the church.

"Even the Fascists were anarchists," she declares. "For the longest time, they had no firm position on anything except the desire for power. Whatever seemed to work was what they did. Then, of course, they became known internationally, and ultimately had to state *some* beliefs." Which, she says, was really the beginning of the end.

Signora Orlandi is a Communist, this despite the fact that Italian Communists have now renamed themselves the Allied Party of the Left to stem the losses incurred from the worldwide repudiation of that particular ideology. Her communism, however, is with a small "c." It prevents her neither from owning land nor from presiding over a house filled with ancient Etruscan stoneware, its walls hung with paintings by some of Tuscany's greatest artists, among them Lorenzo Vianni.

For part of the year, the Signora lives in a white stucco villetta in Lucca, an eleventh-century walled city with streets so narrow that pedestrians are forced to seek safety in the nearest doorway whenever a car passes by. Comparatively small in both size and population (approximately four square miles and 20,000 inhabitants), the Lucca that exists within the walls has both a wealth of churches—at present 172, each with its own collection of ancient art treasures—and a plethora of mysterious legends, among them the sixteenth-century Palazzo Bernardini that is supposedly haunted by the ghost of Lucida Mansi, a notorious prostitute who once resided within its walls and now flaunts her power by refusing to allow the right flank of the Palazzo's doorway to remain fixed in place. Despite three hundred years' worth of attempts by various and sundry masons, the flank continues, to this day, to jut out from the building as if it had been yanked from its pilings by a bionic presence.

With its hundreds of cobblestoned piazzas and ubiquitous eighteenth-century gas lamps (most now electrified), Lucca has managed—more so than most any other city in Tuscany—to retain the precise flavor of its ancient past. Of all its outstanding features, however, the most defining is the continuous stone wall that surrounds the town's perimeter. Perfectly preserved and more than fifteen feet in width, the wall serves as a lovely tree-lined walkway for those who want to view the city from above.

To Signora Orlandi, who can often be seen from atop the walls sitting in her lovely garden surrounded by rosemary hedges and climbing bougainvillea, the wall also serves as a perfect metaphor for the character of Lucca's resident population. "The Lucchesini are a very self-contained, self-sufficient people," she says. "We enjoy our own company more than we enjoy the company of others. Yes, we are happy to host visitors, but we're even happier when our streets are so deserted as to resound with the echo of our own voices."

But now the Signora realizes she has meandered into another topic completely, and so she hurries back to her original point. "What we Italians need is a strong, honest government," she says. "Instead, for forty years we have had nothing but an endless succession of goats, all bleating over compromises and concessions, all afraid to confront the real problem, which is the innate character of the Italian himself. Until Italians can be brought into line, harnessed toward a point of view that is constant, that is unified, that holds for longer than it takes to cook pasta, we might just as well not have a government.

"Italy is like a woman," she continues. "We change our mind constantly. Just look at what happened during the war. First we were part of the Axis, then we became Allies. Who ever heard of such a thing? But for us, it made sense, because, like women everywhere, we are pragmatists. The world thinks we are Catholics, but in truth, our only religion is that which works.

"Pacifism is, in fact, a very Italian characteristic—not because we do not relish a good fight. In fact, nobody loves a good fight more than an Italian. The Italian word for 'discussion,' after all, is *argumento*. But we stay away from formalized fighting. Why? Because we cannot come together on one position and stay with that position for as long as it takes to reach a conclusion. Somewhere along the line, it occurs to us either that the position is a ridiculous one and merits abandonment, or that it was conceived by somebody else in the first place and so let him deal with it, or—even worse—that, in view of the brilliant sunshine, our time could be better spent sitting outside with a good *cacciucco* and a flask of wine."

That night, the Signora takes me to a symphonic concert held outdoors in the Piazza del Amfiteatro, a wonderful circular piazza completely bordered on all sides by houses, and which can be entered only through one archway. The concert is an annual event, a competition among Lucca's orchestra and the orchestras of a few neighboring towns. It is a free event, she tells me, and there will be open seating.

Along the way, we meet two of the Signora's friends who are also en route to the concert. I have heard much about these women; they, like the Signora, are descended from the aristocracy that once ruled Lucca—if not by governance, then by commerce.

We arrive at the Piazza a few minutes before the start of the concert. Most seats are already filled. The first two rows are empty, however, and, as I hesitate, pondering the protocol of placement, I see the Signora and her friends sliding into front-row seats. "I thought you said it was open seating," I say to the Signora once I am seated beside her. "Why are these rows empty?"

She answers my question with one of her own. "Why should they not be empty?" she asks dismissively. "It is a sign of respect."

Later I find out from the neighborhood fruit vendor that during many of the social events sponsored by the town of Lucca, the first two rows are often left empty in deference to the descendants of the old aristocrats. "No one makes them do it," he says when I ask if there is some leftover rule, still adhered to out of habit. "It is just our way."

Today at lunchtime, the Signora and I sit on opposite sides of a large wooden table in her garden. We are eating *tagliatelle* with fresh mushrooms. In theory, the dish is made by Amelia, an old woman who comes in twice a day to cook for the Signora. In practice, however, the dish is merely *carried out* by Amelia, the Signora having hovered over her shoulder throughout its entire preparation, suggesting a little more sage, a little less salt, a few extra tablespoons of oil.

"You do not make *Tagliatelle al funghi* with sage," Amelia says to the Signora, who is busy crushing leaves of the herb into the skillet. "You use *nepitella* [a type of mint]."

"*You* use *nepitella*. I will make it with sage."

"Why pay me to make it in the first place if every day you come into the kitchen to improve on my cooking?"

"If you prefer, I will not pay you."

"I will not cook another meal in this kitchen unless you stop adding and subtracting ingredients."

"What comes from this kitchen could not even be categorized as a *meal* if I did not give it some of my attention."

Amelia, I was told by the neighbors, has been cooking for the Signora for fifteen years. "Never does a meal come to the table without the two of them squabbling over it for the entirety of its preparation," said Fulvia, the proprietess of the flower shop just down the street. "It is just the way they are."

As we savor the tagliatelle, whose condiment contains both nepitella *and* sage, the Signora asks about my life in America.

"Ah, New York," she says at one point. "I visited once that great city. What stayed most in my mind was the patience of your people, the respect they have for the written laws." She rings the bell for Amelia to bring more bread. It arrives just as she has risen to her feet, about to get it herself. She continues her narrative, recalling a ride in a taxi down Fifth Avenue. It was late at night and the sidewalks were empty, but cars clogged the streets, one behind the other in a solemn procession. "Traffic," she recalls the driver answering when she inquired about the source of the problem.

"'Then use the sidewalk,' I told him. We were only going another two streets, after all, and there was nobody in the way. But he continued to stay behind the other cars, waiting. At one point, he even turned off the motor!"

Another time, she remembers being on line at a bank, waiting to change money. "The lines were long, and everyone moved along at the pace of a turtle. But no one seemed to mind. In fact, there were many people reading books, turning the pages calmly as they inched patiently forward. In Tuscany, everyone would have rushed to the front, demanding to be served immediately. And the teller's attention would have gone to the person who demanded the loudest!"

Tonight, I am invited by the Signora to join the two of them for dinner in the kitchen. ("In the kitchen?" Amelia had said when I told her how much I was looking forward to it.) As we work, the Signora talks about the difference between the cooking of Tuscany and the cooking of Provence, the French province with which Tuscany is very often compared.

In Provence, she says, every recipe must be exact, each chef cooking it precisely in the same manner as every other. That, she maintains, is the main reason for the static quality of their cuisine. "In Tuscany, the food is always different. The *Taglierini al Ceci* made in Segromigno is often completely different from the one made in Camigliano, just ten minutes away by auto. Here in Tuscany, we celebrate food. We do not venerate it, judging it with stars and forks and chef hats and God knows what else."

Pasta is truly Italy's national dish. From region to region, however, there is great variety in both the types of pasta used and the accompanying sauces. Sauces can be made of meat, fish, vegetables, or even a simple blend of olive oil and garlic.

In general, Italian pasta can be either dried or fresh.

Pasta made from dried grains is the most popular and widely used of the two. By law, Italian dried pasta can be made only from semolina, which is a derivative of hard wheat obtained by "grating" the wheat kernels with purified water to a very fine, sandy consistency. The semolina is then dried in specially air-conditioned chambers until a certain firmness has been achieved. The result is the packaged product known throughout the world as distinctly "Italian" pasta.

Dried pasta can be cut into many different shapes. In the 1940s and 1950s, there were 250 types of cut pasta approved by the Italian government; today, there are, at most, fifty or sixty. Categories include long, round pastas such as vermicelli, spaghetti, capellini and ziti; long, flat, thin pastas such an linguini and tagliarellini; long, flat, thick pastas such as fettucini and lasagne; long, rectangular pastas such as tagliatelle (specialty pastas are generally included in this category); and short pastas such as penne, mostaccioli, ditali, farfalle, fusilli, canestri, etc. Pastine are tiny forms of cut dried pasta generally used in broths.

Fresh egg pasta is generally made at home, either by hand or with a pasta machine. In most cities, and towns it is also sold commercially. Fresh pasta cooks faster than its dried counterpart, and absorbs very little water during the cooking process, which means it remains roughly the same size and weight as before cooking. By law, Italian fresh pasta must be made of semolina flour and achieve a balance of 5 whole eggs for every kilo (2.2 pounds) of semolina.

Specialty pastas have small quantities of vegetables added to the ingredients. Specialty pastas can be either fresh or dried, and the most popular types are those made with either spinach or tomatoes. Sauces are generally lighter than for other pasta varieties in order to allow the taste of the pasta to emerge.

*While there are few rules governing the cooking of pasta, those rules must be strictly obeyed if the end product is to equal those delectable* primos *consumed by every Italian on a daily basis. Generally speaking, a one-to-one ratio is best: one gallon of salted water for each pound of pasta. The water must be at a hearty boil before the pasta is added and, since this will undoubtedly cause some cooling, be returned to boiling as soon as possible. Cover the pot after adding the pasta, but remove the cover as soon as the water returns to boiling.*

*A good dried pasta grows to three times its weight during cooking, and all types of pasta require frequent stirring during cooking to prevent sticking. Cooking times vary depending on the type of pasta, the mineral content and alkalinity level of the water, and altitude. The best method for determining when the pasta is done is to taste it, allowing for the fact that thin pastas or those topped by very liquid sauces will continue their "cooking" in the serving bowl. To control for this possibility, add a cup of cold water to the pasta pot immediately after removing it from the heat and before draining. Generally speaking, the better the quality of pasta, the more it will continue to absorb liquid even after it has been placed in the serving bowl.*

# LINGUETTE VERDI
*Green Linguini*

*According to the Signora, Tuscans and Ligurians are very far apart when it comes to intricate matters of the kitchen. There is one area in which they appear united, however, and that is in their mutual love of "green" pasta. I have a slight suspicion—generated by the Signora's hesitation to pinpoint the exact point of origin—that this recipe really comes from Genoa, which is in Liguria, but in her mind it is as Tuscan a dish as you'll ever find.*

  10 leaves fresh basil
  2 sprigs fresh parsley
  2 ounces roasted pignoli nuts
  ¼ teaspoon dried marjoram
  1 dried chili pepper
  4 tablespoons Parmigiano Reggiano, grated
  Salt to taste
  1 pound dried linguini (or 1½ pounds fresh)
  2 ounces unsalted butter

1. Place the basil, parsley, pignoli nuts, marjoram, pepper, cheese, and salt in a food processor; blend to pastelike consistency.

2. Cook the pasta according to instructions on page 114.

3. While the pasta is cooking, melt the butter over low heat in a skillet large enough to hold the cooked pasta.

4. Add the herb paste to the skillet and sauté over medium heat.

5. When the pasta is done, add to the skillet, and toss until well blended.

6. Serve hot, and with plenty of young red wine.

*Serves 4*

# TACCONI ALLA LUCCHESE
*Tacconi Lucca-style*

*Tacconi are simply another kind of pasta. Where did they get their name? In the Signora's mind, it is probably because, at one time when ingredients were minimal, the pasta turned out so hard as to resemble* tacchi, *or the soles of shoes. Fortunately, she says, times have changed. This is a wonderful culinary creation that starts with the delicacy of homemade pasta rectangles and tops it off with a thick, creamy sauce made from rabbit and red wine.*

The sauce:
1 small onion, quartered
1 small carrot, cut in half
2 stalks celery, cut in half
2 cloves garlic, crushed
3 whole cloves
½ bottle dry red wine
½ farm-raised rabbit (or chicken), skinned and cut into pieces
½ cup extra-virgin olive oil
1 tablespoon finely chopped fresh rosemary
1 tablespoon finely chopped fresh sage
2 leaves fresh basil, chopped
2 bay leaves
4 ounces ground beef
1 pound plum tomatoes, peeled and diced
Salt and pepper to taste
The pasta:
8 cups white flour
½ teaspoon salt
5 eggs, lightly beaten
½ cup water
2 tablespoons olive oil
Parmigiano Reggiano, grated (for the topping)

1. Add the onion, carrot, celery, garlic, and cloves to the wine and marinate the rabbit (or chicken) in the mixture, refrigerated, for 12 hours. Turn once or twice during that time.

2. Heat 2 tablespoons of the oil in a skillet; sauté the rosemary, sage, basil, bay leaves, and ground meat until the meat is slightly pink. Add the rabbit and the marinade and cook, stirring often, for 20 minutes.

3. Add the tomatoes, cover, and cook for 1½ hours.

4. Remove the rabbit from the sauce; debone and cut the meat into small slivers. Add to the sauce. Remove the bay leaves and cloves. Add the salt and pepper.

5. Meanwhile, make the pasta. Place the flour in a bowl and blend with the salt; add the remaining ingredients and mix together with a fork, or blend in a food processor, until you have formed a ball.

6. Using a rolling pin, roll out the ball on a floured surface to ¼-inch thickness; cut into rectangles approximately 2 x 3 inches.

7. Heat a gallon of salted water to boiling. Place the tacconi in the water and cook for 5 minutes; drain.

8. Using a large bowl, layer the tacconi with the sauce, topping off the dish with a heavy sprinkling of cheese; serve hot.

*Serves 6*

## PANNA

A few years back, heavy cream was the "in" ingredient in Tuscany. No matter where you went to eat—whether to a restaurant or someone's home—you could count on at least one course having been cooked with *panna*. Then there came a sort of backlash, with culinarians claiming not only that the cream was masking the taste of the ingredients (one noted gastronome went so far as to deride the "deceitfulness of chefs who use heavy cream in place of fresh ingredients"), but that the ancient recipes and traditions were being lost. And so, today, heavy cream is "out." It is still used, however, by cooks who value its ability to tie flavors together, albeit in very small quantities. It is with this introduction that the Signora presented the following dish cooked "in the style of woodcutters," and so, she says, "it could not possibly be part of that hopefully departed school of nouvelle cuisine."

# PENNETTE ALLA BOSCAIOLA
*Penne in the Woodcutter-style*

4 tablespoons extra-virgin olive oil
1 celery stalk, chopped
1 small carrot, chopped
1 onion, chopped
3 ounces fresh Porcini mushrooms, cleaned and sliced (or 2 ounces dried)
4 ounces canned Italian tomatoes, drained and chopped
2 ounces heavy cream
1 pound dried penne

1. Heat the oil in a large skillet; sauté the celery, carrot, and onion until lightly browned.

2. Add the mushrooms and continue to cook until the mushrooms give up their liquid. Add the tomatoes; cook for 5 minutes or until all ingredients are blended.

3. Lower the heat and add the cream; keep warm over a simmering flame.

4. Cook the penne according to the instructions on page 114; drain.

5. Add the penne to the skillet and toss until the pasta is well coated with the sauce; serve hot.

*Serves 4*

# TORDELLI DI CARNE
*Tordelli Stuffed with Meat*

*Of all the primos (first-course dishes) tordelli, or small, filled rounds of fresh pasta, are the most characteristic of the Versilia-Garfagnana region. This recipe uses a filling made of two kinds of meat, two kinds of cheese, vegetables, and herbs, and tops it all off with a delicious, equally complex sauce. A time-consuming recipe, but well worth it—in fact, why else would the dish be so popular if not for the ecstasy produced by its taste?*

*The sauce:*
  3 tablespoons extra-virgin olive oil
  1 small onion, diced
  1 tablespoon finely chopped fresh rosemary
  1 tablespoon finely chopped fresh sage
  2 leaves fresh basil, chopped
  8 ounces pork loin, diced
  8 ounces sirloin of beef, diced
  Salt and pepper to taste
  1 clove
  Pinch of cinnamon
  Pinch of nutmeg
  ½ cup dry white wine

*The filling:*
  3 tablespoons olive oil
  4 ounces sirloin of beef, diced
  4 ounces loin of pork, diced
  Salt and pepper to taste
  4 ounces swiss chard, boiled, drained, and chopped
  8 ounces Parmigiano Reggiano, grated
  2 ounces hard Pecorino cheese, grated
  1 cup dry unflavored breadcrumbs
  4 whole eggs, lightly beaten
  Pinch of cinnamon

*The pasta:*
  4 cups white flour
  3 whole eggs, lightly beaten
  1 tablespoon olive oil

2 tablespoons milk
Parmigiano Reggiano for the topping

1. First make the sauce: Place the oil in a skillet over medium heat; add the remaining sauce ingredients except the wine and cook until the meat is thoroughly done. Add the wine, lower the heat, and simmer, covered, until the pasta is done.

2. Make the filling: Heat the oil and add both meats, the salt, and pepper, cooking over medium heat for 7 minutes. Add the swiss chard and cook for another minute or two, stirring constantly with a wooden spoon to blend the flavors; remove from heat and place in a large bowl.

3. Add the remaining filling ingredients and blend thoroughly until of a wet, pastelike consistency (if too dry, add a tablespoon or two of milk).

4. Now make the pasta: Place the flour in a large bowl (or food processor); add the remaining pasta ingredients and blend with a fork (or process) until a ball is formed. Place the ball on a floured surface.

5. Using a rolling pin, roll out the dough to a ¼-inch thickness (the thinner the dough, the more tender the tordelli). Using the mouth of a white wine glass, cut the dough into rounds; after the initial batch is cut, roll the dough once again into a ball, roll with the rolling pin, and cut another series of rounds. Continue until all the dough is used.

6. Fill each "round" with a small amount of filling; fold the round in half and seal the rounded edge, using the tines of a fork.

7. When all the tordelli have been filled, place them in 4 quarts boiling, salted water, one at a time (do two batches if necessary), and cook for approximately 2 minutes. Taste the dough to check for doneness; do not cook longer than necessary or they will break open.

8. Remove the tordelli with a slotted spoon and place in a large serving bowl, layered with the sauce.

9. Top with grated Parmigiano Reggiano, and serve hot.

*Makes approximately 30 tordelli to serve 6*

# SPAGHETTI E ASPARAGI
*Spaghetti and Asparagus*

*When Tuscany springs into asparagus season, there is not a kitchen anywhere that turns out three meals in succession without one of them including those tender, spiky heads of green. You'll find asparagus omelettes, fried asparagus, asparagus marinated in vinaigrette and served with cold rice, asparagus soup, and—best of all, at least in the Signora's book—this recipe.*

> 3 tablespoons extra-virgin olive oil
> 16 asparagus tips, chopped
> 3 ounces slab (or sliced) prosciutto, diced
> 2 cloves garlic, crushed
> Salt and pepper to taste
> ½ cup Basic Meat Broth (page 95) or good quality canned
> 1 pound dried spaghetti or 1½ pounds fresh

1. Heat the oil in a large skillet; sauté the asparagus tips with the prosciutto and garlic for 7 minutes or until the meat is lightly browned.

2. Add the salt, pepper, and broth and cook over low heat for 10 minutes or until the liquid is somewhat thickened.

3. Cook the pasta according to the instructions on page 114; drain.

4. Add the spaghetti to the asparagus mixture; toss until well blended, and serve hot.

*Serves 4*

# FETTUCINI ALLA DISPERATA
*A Desperate Woman's Fettucini*

*According to the Signora, this pasta came to be called* alla disperata *because the woman who invented it had a lover and, one night, came home too late to buy the ingredients for the stuffed rabbit she'd intended to make for her husband. Looking over what ingredients she had and feeling rather guilty about the whole thing, she decided to toss together the best of what was on hand, and came up with this recipe for a delicious pasta with a complex sauce of capers, olives, anchovies, and tomatoes—which, incidentally, is equally good as a topping for grilled chicken or turkey.*

3 tablespoons extra-virgin olive oil
1 clove garlic, whole
6 ounces peeled fresh plum tomatoes, chopped (or canned)
1 tablespoon chopped fresh oregano (or ¼ teaspoon dried)
1 dried chili pepper, crushed
15 capers, crushed
7 or 8 small white pickled onions, chopped
3 anchovies packed in oil, mashed
1 pound dried fettucini (or 1½ pounds fresh)

1. Place the oil in a skillet and brown the garlic; remove the garlic and discard.

2. Add the tomatoes, oregano, and pepper; cook over low heat for 15 minutes.

3. Add the capers, onions, and anchovies; stir with a wooden spoon, cover, and cook over low heat for 3 to 5 minutes.

4. Cook the fettucini according to the instructions on page 114; drain.

5. Add the fettucini to the skillet; toss well to blend all ingredients, and serve hot.

*Serves 6*

# SPAGHETTI AL TONNO
## *Spaghetti with Tuna*

*Pasta with tuna fish is a Versilian specialty, generally eaten in the winter when the pungency of a dish requiring both tuna and anchovies is a welcome shift from light salads and simple tomato sauces. Take note, however, that this recipe can only be served accompanied by plenty of dark red wine if one wishes to adequately simulate the art of Being Tuscan.*

2 tablespoons extra-virgin olive oil
1 clove garlic, crushed
1 7-ounce can tuna packed in olive oil, drained
4 canned anchovy filets, drained, rinsed, and crumbled
3 tablespoons finely chopped fresh parsley
2 leaves fresh basil, chopped
Salt and pepper to taste
1 pound dried spaghetti (or 1½ pounds fresh)
10 capers, minced

1. Heat the oil in a large skillet and sauté the garlic until lightly browned.

2. Crumble the tuna and add it to the skillet; add the anchovies and cook for 5 minutes, turning often with a wooden spoon.

3. Add the parsley, basil, salt, and pepper and blend all ingredients thoroughly.

4. Meanwhile, cook the spaghetti according to the instructions on page 114; drain.

5. Add the spaghetti to the sauce, toss to coat the pasta well, sprinkle with the capers, and serve hot.

*Serves 4*

# SPAGHETTI CON
# SALSA DI PORRI AL CARTOCCIO
*Spaghetti with Leek Sauce in Parchment*

*Tuscans love to cook* al cartoccio *even if—as in this recipe—the parchment is really aluminum foil.*

> 6 leeks
> 6 tablespoons butter
> 1 chicken bouillon cube
> Salt and pepper to taste
> 1 cup milk
> 8 ounces fresh filet of sole, cleaned and dried
> 3 tablespoons heavy cream
> 4 tablespoons Parmigiano Reggiano, grated
> 1 pound dried spaghetti (or 1½ pounds fresh)

1. Peel and wash the leeks. Cut the white part only into thin slices; discard the green part.

2. Place 4 tablespoons of the butter in a large skillet; sauté the leeks over low heat until lightly browned.

3. Crush the bouillon over the skillet and add the salt, pepper, and milk; cook for 5 minutes over low heat.

4. In a separate skillet, cook the sole in the remaining butter over medium heat; when the sole is lightly browned on both sides, remove from heat, and flake into small slivers using a fork.

5. Add the sole to the skillet with the leeks; add the cream and the cheese. Cook over low heat for 3 minutes, stirring constantly with a wooden spoon.

6. Meanwhile, cook the spaghetti according to the instructions on page 114; drain.

7. Add the spaghetti to the leek mixture, toss well.

8. Preheat the oven to 350 degrees. Place the pasta in a package made of aluminum foil, seal thoroughly, and cook in the oven for 10 minutes.

9. Serve hot.

*Serves 4*

# TAGLIATELLE GRATINATE
*Fresh Tagliatelle Au Gratin*

*There are few things the Signora and Amelia agree on when it comes to cooking. This elegant pasta, however, was selected by both women as the perfect dish to serve a houseful of company during the cold days of winter. Imagine my amazement when they further revealed the details of the recipe and, even then, there was no disagreement.*

1 pound fresh tagliatelle
6 tablespoons unsalted butter
4 ounces Parmigiano Reggiano, grated
4 ounces prosciutto, sliced into slivers
4 ounces fresh unsalted buffalo mozzarella, thinly sliced
4 tablespoons dry unflavored breadcrumbs

1. Cook the tagliatelle for 4 minutes in salted boiling water; drain.

2. Toss with 3 tablespoons of the butter and half the cheese; place in an ovenproof dish.

3. Add the prosciutto and mozzarella and toss well to blend all ingredients.

4. Sprinkle the remaining cheese and the breadcrumbs over the top; dot with the remaining butter. Bake in a preheated 400 degree oven for approximately 30 minutes until browned on top; serve hot.

*Serves 4*

## Polenta

Polenta is made from corn or, more appropriately, maize, the name given to corn by the Aztecs who were among the first to include this culinary marvel in their everyday diet. While the Romans are known to have used a blend of corn flour and flax seeds (they called the mixture puls), polenta as we know it today was not widely used by the Italians until the late 1500s. Since then its popularity has grown steadily, with the result that today, polenta is surpassed only by pasta as a fitting choice for a delectable primo piatto.

Its supporters are many, chief among them Carlo Goldoni, the well-known Italian comic and gastronome, who describes his own method of preparation thusly: "I fill to the brim a beautiful terra-cotta pot, and when the water begins to murmur loudly, sprinkle across its surface a powdered ingredient as fine as gold. When it has achieved the desired thickness, I pour it on a wooden table and divide it into bowls dusted with grated Parmigiano, and—ecco!—a meal fit for an Emperor."

In preparing your own polenta, start with a pot of salted water that has been brought to a boil. Generally speaking, there should be about 3 quarts of water for every 2 cups of polenta; the exact ratio depends, to a large part, on the coarseness of the polenta grind. Pour the polenta in a steady stream over the water's surface, and stir with a wooden spoon to prevent the grains from clumping. Continue to stir until all the grains have been blended into the water; lower the heat and cover for 45 minutes, checking every ten minutes or so to see whether the polenta is too dry. If more water is necessary, it should be boiled before adding so as not to interrupt the boil. Polenta is cooked when it no longer sticks to the sides of the pot, and when a wooden spoon stands by itself in the center.

In serving polenta, the most characteristic method—a la casalinga (in the old, home style)—is to spread a clean dishcloth on the table, and pour the polenta directly onto it from the cooking pot. The polenta will begin to thicken immediately, forming a lovely round on the dishcloth. It is then sliced and served, topped with a sauce, or dinner guests can "scoop out" their own.

Leftover polenta is as desirable as the fresh-cooked variety. Having cooled to a thick, solid consistency, the polenta can be sliced, fried *in olive oil, and topped with a creamy variety of cheese, or cut into squares and baked with a mushroom sauce, or even grilled and used as "bread" for sandwiches.*

### A POLENTA STORY

The Signora tells the story of an encounter between Curzio Malaparte, the famous Tuscan writer, and Arturo Dazzi, the equally famous sculptor: "In the early 1940s, Malaparte came to Versilia—to Forti dei Marmi, in fact—to pose for a wooden bust of himself that was to be sculpted by Dazzi. The two were as well known for their art as they were for their love of good food, and as they worked, they passed the time talking about the various preparations of food, the differences in regional cuisines, and the horrors of nouvelle cuisine, which was then just beginning to rear its ugly head. At one point, Malaparte is said to have made for Dazzi *Polenta unta e incacciata* [Polenta with Olive Oil and Pecorino Cheese], which was his favorite, a choice in which Dazzi concurred.

"Beh, the bust turned out to be a fine piece, a stupendous piece. Malaparte was nude, but this only served to please him further, exhibitionist and narcissist that he was. But when it came time to settle the accounts, Malaparte refused to pay, and Dazzi took him to court. A scandal ensued, Dazzi exposing Malaparte for a thief at the Biennale di Venezia. 'Malaparte should stick to cooking,' Dazzi told a Venetian journalist. 'His polenta is far better than any of his books.' "

# POLENTA UNTA
# E INCACIATA ALLA MALAPARTE
*Polenta with Olive Oil and Pecorino Cheese
Malaparte-style*

3 cups polenta (coarse grind)
8 ounces hard Pecorino cheese, grated
½ cup extra-virgin olive oil (very best quality)

1. Cook the polenta according to the instructions on page 127; let cool for 10 minutes or until thickened somewhat.

2. Cut into thin slabs and arrange in a serving bowl, each slab of polenta topped with plenty of cheese and drizzled with oil; continue until all ingredients are used.

3. Serve hot with new red wine.

*Serves 6*

# MATUFFI ALLA GARFAGNINA
*Matuffi, Garfagnina-style*

*Of all the recipes for making polenta, this is the one that most retains the hearty characteristics of the old days. Even its name is evocative of groups of hungry peasants just in from the fields and gathered around a large wooden table on which sits a mound of golden maize. One by one (or more likely, all at the same time) they scoop out a slice, whip it onto their plates—matuffi (mah-TOO-fee)—and ladle across the top a generous slather of fragrant sauce. Parmiano Reggiano sprinkled across the surface, a sturdy glass of red wine, and—Paradise!*

The sauce:
> 4 tablespoons olive oil
> 3 tablespoons unsalted butter
> 1½ pounds lean pork loin, cubed
> 1 carrot, chopped
> 1 celery stalk, chopped
> 2 onions, chopped
> 1 clove garlic, crushed
> 2 ounces dried Porcini mushrooms, soaked for 2 hours, drained and diced
> ½ cup dry red wine
> 1 35-ounce can Italian tomatoes, with liquid
> 1 bay leaf
> 2 basil leaves, chopped
> 1 tablespoon finely chopped fresh sage
> 1 quart Basic Meat Broth (page 95) or good quality canned

The polenta:
> 4 cups polenta (coarse grind)
> 4 quarts salted water

Parmigiano Reggiano, grated (for the topping)

1. Heat the oil and butter in a large skillet; brown the pork on all sides. Add the carrot, celery, onion, and garlic; cook until the garlic is lightly browned.

2. Add the mushrooms, and cook for 3 minutes; add the wine and cook until evaporated.

3. Add the tomatoes, herbs, and broth; cover and cook over low heat for 2 to 3 hours,

4. Cook the polenta in salted water for 25 minutes according to the instructions on page 129, except that for this dish, the polenta should be less dense than usual.

5. Serve the polenta from the pot in which it was cooked, ladling it onto individual plates in small clumps; top each clump with a ladle of sauce.

6. Dust with a generous portion of Parmigiano Reggiano, and serve hot with red wine.

*Serves 6*

Gnocchi

Gnocchi (NEEO-kee) are Italian dumplings. Generally, they are made from potatoes and flour; in some cases, eggs are also added. What gives the dish its fragrance is the sauce, which can be a simple po-morola (fresh tomato sauce), a ragu (meat sauce), a ragu di funghi (mushroom sauce), or a mix of either butter and cheese, or olive oil and cheese. In some cases vegetables are added to the dough to give the gnocchi additional flavor as well as color.

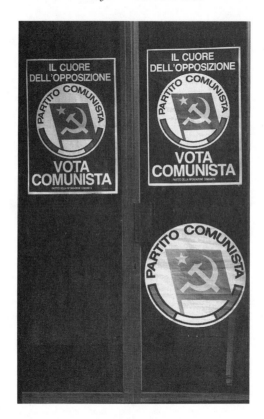

A door to the Signora's house.

# GNOCCHI VERDI
*Green Gnocchi*

*These dumplings are also good with a sauce made of fresh tomatoes and topped with Parmigiano Reggiano.*

1¾ pounds fresh spinach, washed and dried
2 pounds white potatoes, cooked, peeled, and mashed
1 cup white flour
2 egg yolks, lightly beaten
8 tablespoons unsalted butter
4 ounces Parmigiano Reggiano, grated
Salt to taste

1. Boil the spinach in a small quantity of water and drain thoroughly; while still hot pass through a food mill, or place in a food processor and reduce to a pastelike consistency.

2. Blend together the potatoes, spinach, flour, and egg yolks and mix with your hands until the dough is thick (work with the dough as little as possible).

3. On a floured surface, form the dough into a series of long cylinders approximately 1 inch in width; cut the cylinders into individual cork-size gnocchi, approximately 1 inch in length.

4. Bring to a boil 4 quarts of salted water; drop the gnocchi one by one into the water. When they float on the top they are done, approximately 8 minutes.

5. Remove with a slotted spoon and place on a serving platter, alternating a layer of gnocchi with a layer of butter pats and grated cheese; serve hot.

*Makes approximately 60-80 gnocchi to serve 4*

# GNOCCHI DI ZUCCA ALLA VERSILIESE
*Butternut Squash Gnocchi Versilia-style*

*This wonderful gnocchi recipe calls for* zucca gialla, butternut squash, *which is less watery than other squashes and, thus, ideally suited to mixing with potatoes and flour. It is an ancient recipe from the Versilian Coast and still in use among older residents, especially those in the region of Pietrasanta, a coastal town slightly north of Viareggio.*

3 pounds butternut squash, peeled, seeded, and cubed
1 cup water
1 teaspoon salt
4 eggs, lightly beaten
1 cup white flour (or as much as necessary to create a thick dough)
1 35-ounce can Italian tomatoes, drained and chopped
3 leaves fresh basil
2 cloves garlic, crushed
4 tablespoons extra-virgin olive oil
Parmigiano Reggiano, grated

1. Cook the cubed squash in 1 cup water until soft enough to mash; drain and pass through a food mill, or blend in a food processor.

2. Add the salt, eggs, and flour and work with your hands until a ball of dough is formed.

3. Roll the dough on a floured surface into a series of long cylinders approximately 1 inch in width; cut each cylinder into individual cork-size gnocchi, approximately 1 inch in length.

4. For the sauce heat the oil in a large skillet; cook the garlic until golden. Add the tomatoes and the basil, cover, and cook for 20 minutes.

5. Meanwhile, cook the gnocchi in plenty of salted boiling water; drop them one by one into the water. They are cooked when they float to the surface, approximately 6 minutes.

6. Remove with a slotted spoon and place in a serving bowl, alternating a layer of gnocchi with a layer of sauce topped with grated cheese; serve hot.

*Makes approximately 60-80 gnocchi to serve 4*

*Tuscans consume great quantities of rice; risotto, in fact, is one of the region's foremost* primi piatti, *first courses. A creamy blend of rice cooked slowly with wine, bouillon and herbs—there are almost as many different types of* risotti *as there are pastas. In general, Arborio rice—a semifine, highly polished white variety of rice—is used for* risotti, *although other types can also be employed.*

*When selecting a rice, it is important to choose one with grains consistent in both shape and color. If the grains are varied, it means that the rice is a blend, and since different types of rice require different cooking times, chances are that the finished product will not be cooked appropriately. The individual grains should be checked to make sure there are no broken ones, since broken grains turn into mush when cooked.*

*In terms of appearance, the grains should be white and shiny; opaque grains have not reached full maturity and dissolve during cooking. Avoid any grains that are yellow since this signifies that they have entered into a process of fermentation created by humidity. Ultimately, the best way to tell if rice is fresh is to submerge your hand in a sackful. If it comes out clean, the rice is young and dry; if it comes out dusted with white flour, the rice is old.*

*Rice should be stored in glass containers that are airtight. It should also be stored away from substances emitting a strong odor since rice grains are porous and easily absorb odors. Rice should also be stored in cool places (not refrigerated, however) since it tends to harbor small insects if the temperature rises above 80 degrees.*

*When making risottos, it is important to keep the rice simmering in the broth; liquids added to the pot during cooking should always first be boiled.*

## RISOTTO AND THE TUSCAN CHARACTER

Following are five recipes for risottos, each one symbolic, in a way, of a different aspect of the Tuscan character. *Risotto alla Contadina* represents the peasant side of Tuscans; *Risotto al Cognac,* the elegant side; *Risotto con Spinaci,* the strong connection between Tuscans and fresh vegetables; *Risotto con la Zucca,* the Tuscan of venerated traditions; and *Risotto primaverile,* the love affair between Tuscans and the outdoors.

# RISOTTO ALLA CONTADINA
*Risotto Peasant-style*

1 pound savoy cabbage, washed, dried, and separated into individual leaves
1 stalk celery, chopped
1 carrot, chopped
2 or 3 plum tomatoes, peeled and chopped
12 ounces string beans (haricots, if possible)
4 ounces pancetta (unsmoked bacon), diced
1 quart chicken broth (homemade or canned)
1 link sausage, removed from the casing and crumbled
3 tablespoons unsalted butter
3 cups Arborio rice
½ cup dry red wine
Salt and pepper
Parmigiano Reggiano, grated

1. Place the cabbage leaves, celery, carrot, tomatoes, beans, half the pancetta, and the broth in a pot; cover and cook over low heat for 1½ hours.

2. In a large skillet, brown the remaining pancetta and the sausage in the butter; add the rice and cook until the grains are lightly toasted.

3. Add the wine to the skillet and allow to evaporate.

4. When the vegetables are done, strain them through a colander, reserving the liquid. Add them to the skillet along with the salt and pepper.

5. Add the reserved liquid to the skillet, a little at a time, and continue to cook over medium heat, stirring frequently, until the rice has absorbed the liquid and the consistency is creamy.

6. Serve hot topped with Parmigiano Reggiano.

*Serves 4*

# RISOTTO AL COGNAC
*Risotto with Cognac*

4 tablespoons butter
4 tablespoons extra-virgin olive oil
1 onion, diced
4 ounces prosciutto, diced
½ cup dry white wine
3 cups Arborio rice
Salt and pepper to taste
2 quarts chicken broth (homemade or canned), heated
1 cup cognac

1. Melt the butter and oil in a large skillet; sauté the onion and prosciutto in the oil and butter until both are soft.

2. Add the wine and allow to evaporate.

3. Add the rice, salt, and pepper; stir with a wooden spoon until all the grains are coated with the wine mixture.

4. Add three or four ladles of hot chicken broth just to cover the rice; continue to stir over medium heat until all the broth is dissolved. Add another ladle or two and cook over low heat until absorbed, about 5 minutes; do not boil.

5. Heat the cognac in a small saucepan; light it with a match and, while aflame, pour it onto the rice; serve hot and, if possible, with the flame still burning.

*Serves 4*

# RISOTTO CON SPINACI
*Risotto with Spinach*

12 ounces fresh spinach, washed and dried
½ cup salted water
3 tablespoons unsalted butter
1 onion, diced
2 cups Arborio rice
Salt and pepper to taste
5-6 cups chicken broth (homemade or canned), heated
Parmigiano Reggiano, grated

1. Cook the spinach in ½ cup salted water; remove from pot and reserve the liquid.

2. Melt the butter in a large skillet. Add the onion and sauté until lightly browned.

3. Add the rice and toss until the grains are lightly toasted.

4. Slowly add the liquid from the spinach and a ladleful or two of the broth, and stir over medium heat until all the liquid has been absorbed; continue adding the spinach broth until all the liquid has been absorbed.

5. Add the spinach, another ladleful of the broth, and the salt and pepper. Stir until well blended, and continue cooking, over medium heat, until all the liquid is gone. Add the broth, one ladleful at a time, stirring frequently, until each ladleful has been absorbed. The rice is done when it is of a somewhat creamy consistency.

6. Just before removing from heat, add 7 or 8 tablespoons of the cheese and stir to blend. Remove from heat and let sit for 1 to 2 minutes or enough time to melt the cheese; serve hot.

*Serves 4*

# RISOTTO CON LA ZUCCA
*Risotto with Butternut Squash*

12 ounces butternut squash
½ cup salted water
8 tablespoons unsalted butter
1 small onion, diced
2 cups Arborio rice
1 quart chicken broth (homemade or canned), heated
4 ounces Parmigiano Reggiano, grated
Salt and pepper to taste

1. Peel the squash, seed it, and cut into small cubes; place the cubes in a saucepan with ½ cup salted water and 2 tablespoons of the butter. Boil until soft. Drain and reserve the liquid. Mash the squash with a fork to pastelike consistency. Add the salt and pepper.

2. Melt all but one tablespoon of the remaining butter in a large skillet; sauté the onion until soft. Add the rice and toss with a wooden spoon until the grains are toasted.

3. Add the cooking liquid from the squash and a ladleful of broth. Cook over medium heat until the liquid has been absorbed. Continue to add broth, a ladleful or two at a time, until the rice is cooked and the consistency creamy.

4. Just before removing from the heat, add the remaining tablespoon of butter and the cheese; remove from heat, stir to blend all ingredients, and let sit for a few minutes to allow the cheese to melt. Serve hot.

*Serves 4*

# RISOTTO PRIMAVERILE
*Springtime Risotto*

*For this risotto, use as many different kinds of fresh spring vegetables as possible—each in very small quantity.*

1 small onion, diced
3 tablespoons extra-virgin olive oil
4 tablespoons unsalted butter
1 medium stalk celery, diced
1 small carrot, diced
3 ounces fresh peas
1 small zucchini, diced
4 ounces fresh new green beans, sliced in half (best are haricots)
2 cups Arborio rice
1 quart chicken broth (homemade or canned), heated
4 ounces fresh spinach, washed, dried, and chopped
4 ounces Parmigiano Reggiano, grated
Salt and pepper to taste

1. Sauté the onion in a blend of olive oil and 2 tablespoons butter; add the remaining vegetables except the spinach and the salt and pepper and cook over low heat for 10 minutes.

2. Add the rice and stir until all grains are coated with the vegetable juices.

3. Add the broth, a few ladlesful at a time, and cook over medium heat until the liquid is completely absorbed; continue adding broth and stirring until the rice is creamy. If more liquid is needed, add boiling water, one ladleful at a time.

4. About 10 minutes before the rice is done, add the spinach and the remaining butter; cook, stirring constantly.

5. Remove from heat; add the cheese, toss, and serve hot.

*Serves 4*

# RISOTTO CON FRUTTI DI MARE
## *Rice with Shellfish*

*For dinner with the Signora and Amelia, the three of us prepared a risotto with squid and shellfish of every denomination. In preparing the broth, Amelia expressed her desire to use Orvieto, a wine that she classified as drier and more suited to the subtle textures of the fish. But the Signora insisted on Pinot Grigio. "Am I not right?" she asked at one point. Here is the final version of that exquisite dish.*

The risotto:
>  2 tablespoons unsalted butter
>  1 medium onion, minced
>  2 cups Arborio rice
>  2 cups dry white wine
>  2½ cups chicken broth (homemade or canned)
>  1 cup boiling water, or as needed
>  3 tablespoons finely chopped fresh parsley

The fish:
>  5 tablespoons extra-virgin olive oil
>  8 ounces small squid, cleaned, dried, and cut in thin slices
>  ½ cup dry white wine
>  1 pound mussels, scrubbed thoroughly under running water
>  1 pound small clams, scrubbed well
>  8 ounces medium shrimp, peeled and deveined
>    (shells reserved)
>  ½ cup water
>  12 ounces small scallops (ocean or bay)
>  Salt and pepper to taste

1. For the risotto melt the butter in a large skillet. Sauté the onion over medium heat until lightly browned.

2. Place the rice in the skillet and stir with a wooden spoon until each kernel is coated with butter.

3. Pour 1 cup of the wine and ½ cup of the stock into the skillet. Simmer over low heat until the rice has taken up all the liquid. Stir frequently throughout the process.

4. Pour ½ cup of the wine and ¼ cup of the stock into the skillet, and again, simmer until all the liquid has been absorbed.

5. Pour the remaining ½ cup wine and 1¾ cups stock into the skillet, and simmer until all the liquid is gone. If the rice is not al dente and creamy, pour in ½ cup of the boiling water and wait until the liquid is gone. Use the remaining water as needed to produce a slightly drier risotto than is called for by most risotto recipes. The traditional "soupiness" will come by adding the liquid from the fish.

6. While the risotto is cooking, prepare the fish. Place 2 tablespoons of the oil in a skillet large enough to hold all the fish; when the oil is hot, add the squid and cook over medium heat, stirring constantly for 3 or 4 minutes or until the color of the squid changes to pink.

7. Add the wine and allow to evaporate; reduce the heat to a simmer and cook for 20 minutes.

8. While the squid is cooking, put the remaining 3 tablespoons of oil in a large soup pot; when hot, add the mussels and clams, cover, and cook over high heat for 10 minutes or until the shells are all open. Turn off the heat and let cool until the fish can be handled.

9. Remove the clams and mussels from their shells; let the juices drip back into the pot in which they were cooked. Reserve the liquid but discard the shells; add the clams and mussels to the skillets with the squid.

10. Put only the shells of the shrimp into the pot with the juices from the mussels and clams; add ½ cup water and simmer for 15 minutes. Strain this broth through a sieve into the skillet with the squid.

11. Add the shrimp, scallops, salt, and pepper and simmer all ingredients for 5 minutes.

12. Blend the fish with its liquid into the risotto, add the chopped parsley, and stir with a wooden spoon until all the liquid is absorbed.

13. Serve hot with plenty of good white wine.

*Serves 6*

# BOMBA DI RISO PONTREMOLESE
## Rice Mold Pontremole-style

*In 1980, Angelo Paracucchi, the great Tuscan cooking instructor whose school in Ameglia de Sarzana draws chefs from all over the world, gathered his recipes from the Lunigiana region of Tuscany into a book published by Mario Spagnol of Lerici. This recipe was included in the book and subsequently became a menu staple in his Parisian restaurant, Carpaccio. The Signora had read it in the book and tried it to great satisfaction, and at her suggestion, I have reprinted it here with the gracious permission of the author.*

2 cups Arborio rice

1 small onion, diced

3 tablespoons extra-virgin olive oil

4 tablespoons unsalted butter plus butter for greasing the pan

4 ounces of veal, cubed

4 ounces of beef, cubed

1 link pork sausage, removed from its casing and crumbled

1 small carrot, chopped

1 medium celery stalk, chopped

Salt and pepper to taste

16 ounces canned Italian tomatoes, drained and chopped

½ cup chicken broth (homemade or canned), heated

Pinch of cinnamon

Juice of one lemon

2 whole eggs, lightly beaten

8 tablespoons Parmigiano Reggiano, grated

8 capers, minced

4 tablespoons dry, unflavored breadcrumbs

1. Boil 3 quarts of water in a large saucepan; add salt and the rice, and cook for 8 to 10 minutes or until it is half done; drain and cool.

2. In a large skillet over medium heat, sauté the onion in the oil and 2 tablespoons of the butter until lightly browned; add the meats—the veal, beef, and sausage—and the carrot and celery, and cook until all ingredients are lightly browned. Add salt and pepper and blend well.

3. Add the tomatoes, broth, cinnamon, and a dusting of pepper, and cook for 40 minutes, covered, over low heat.

4. Meanwhile, place the cooled rice in a large bowl with the lemon, eggs, half the cheese, capers, and a ladle filled with the sauce from the skillet; blend well with a wooden spoon.

5. Butter an aluminum mold that is approximately 9 to 10 inches in diameter; sprinkle with half the breadcrumbs, and fill with ⅘ of the rice mixture.

6. Dig a 3-inch hole in the center of the mold; fill with the meat mixture. Cover with the remaining rice, sprinkle with the remaining cheese and the remaining breadcrumbs, dot with the remaining butter, and bake in a preheated 350 degree oven for 30 minutes.

7. Remove from the oven, turn onto a serving platter, and serve hot.

*Serves 4 to 5*

*A street in Lucca.*

*Signora Giuseppina Lorenzoni*

*Chapter Five*

# CONTROLLING THE ELEMENTS

## VEGETABLES, EGGS, AND CHEESE

| | |
|---|---|
| *Quando i torbati vanno verso il mare,* | *When the storms go towards the sea,* |
| *Prendi la vanga e va a vangare.* | *Pick up a hoe and start hoeing* |
| *E quando i torbati vanno in su,* | *But when the storms go north,* |
| *Pigli la vanga e siedici su.* | *Take your hoe and sit on it.* |

*T*o spend more than a few hours in Tuscany is to realize that there are as many aphorisms pertaining to this blessed land as there are bureaucratic forms to be filled out. To eat more than one Tuscan meal is to understand that the love affair between Tuscans and fresh vegetables has to do with more than just gastronomy. To travel more than fifty kilometers through Tuscany is to comprehend that the land of Dante and Giotto and Brunelleschi and Carducci is also a land where *everyone* is a peasant.

To be a peasant here, however, means more than just knowing when to plant and when to water, when to prune, and when to leave things alone. It means, above all, a certain state of mind—as common to those who have never in their lives touched a clod of dirt as it is to the sun-baked olive growers who pass their days fertilizing the trees and hauling olives to the press. What it means is having control over something, over a piece of land, a process, a yield—*something!*

Make no mistake about it. Very little in life is more important to Tuscans than being in control. Just gaze for a moment at those ordered little villages, the perfectly terraced grape vineyards, the little black berets worn by the men, the tailored skirts favored by the women. Being Tuscan means rising at a certain time, having one's coffee precisely as one desires, having just enough sunshine, just enough rain, eating perfect purple figs, and washing them down with tiny glasses of properly aged *vin santo.*

And yet, if one is to give any credence to the words of Signora Giuseppina Lorenzoni, there is much about Tuscan life that is out of control. The winds, for example: the *libeccio,* which blows in suddenly from the turgid seas—from Spain—from the dark, mysterious alleys of Marseilles; the *scirocco* writhing in from the Casbah—from the hot heart of the dark continent bringing gray skies and wet, dirty clouds; the *grecale,* which comes up from the south, churning the heavy odor of sheep and horses and pecorino cheese; the *tramontana,* from the north—from Emiglia Romagna, with its chilly gusts that send everyone rushing for thick woolen jackets and hot bowls of hearty soup.

But, the Signora concedes, *those* things have always been and will always be. "It is more than that now," she says. "A sense that the dirt beneath our feet is being washed away with the tides. Tuscans have always had to deal with uncertainties. But, we always knew that in the end, however, we would manage the same way we have always managed—by the seat of our pants. But now our jails are filled with those who, only last year, sat in the Congress of Deputies, and the government is suggesting that the answer lies in making our old people work until the age of sixty-five. 'With our old people, we will build a bridge to the future,' they say. *Che shemi.* The only bridge to be built with old people is one that will fall apart as soon as the first person steps on it."

She takes my arm and lowers her voice to a whisper. "I'd like to thread those politicians on a skewer and grill them over an open fire," she says. But in the next second, her mood has changed. "Beh," she says. "Who needs politicians anyway? They do not control anything."

"Have you read Malaparte?" she says, changing the subject. I nod my head yes. "*Ecco un uomo che capisce* [there's a man who understands]," she says, and pulls out a well-worn text:

" 'In no place is the sky so near the earth as in Tuscany,' she begins to read. 'You find it in the leaves of the trees, in the herbs and grasses, in the eyes of oxen and babies, and above all, in the smooth foreheads of young girls.'

" 'The Tuscan sky is a mirror,' " she continues. " 'And always so close that your breath can mist it over. Hills and knolls are clouds; between them, the shadowy valleys, the green pastures, the fields with straight-plowed furrows. On clear days you can see, as if reflected in limpid water, the images of houses, haystacks, roads, gullies, and churches. At the fall of every hoe, air mixes with earth, and up from the clods spring furries of green and azure herbs. Larks and the larvae of crickets are born without warning. One need only touch it to feel that the earth is filled with little bubbles of air. On certain days, it yeasts and rises as if it might at any moment bring forth loaves of bread.' "

She puts the book aside and begins to talk in the same poetic voice as the author. "Malaparte is right," she says. "Travel throughout all of the Tuscan countryside, and wherever you chance to rest your eye, you will see green land blanketed with the tubular bodies of sheep—the white-faced Razza Sarda sheep that were brought a thousand years ago on large open ships from Sardinia—their faces spotted with a hundred small black dots, put there by the dirty fingers of a God attempting to wipe away the dried nodules of sleep."

Razza Sarda sheep, she explains, are the sweet-smelling variety prized for the creamy white milk used to make pecorino cheese. "Not the Pecorino Romano packaged into cartons with perforated shaker tops and sold around the world as an authentic Tuscan condiment," she asserts. "Not that pecorino. *Our* pecorino is Pecorino Toscano—marzolino, mucchino, brancolino, cacciotta—all smaller and creamier than Romano, more disposed to leaving on the blade of the knife that cuts it a soft, dewy residue."

During the next few days, I notice that each morning, before the bells of Vagli's Duomo have rung for the nine o'clock meeting of the Sacro Cuore volunteers, Signora Lorenzoni is dressed and already at work in her garden. The Signora lives in Vagli di Sopra (Valley of the Above), which is where she moved when her original home in Vagli di Sotto (Valley of the Below) was flooded by Enel, the government power entity, in 1940, to create a hydroelectric plant. Since then, the valley has been drained every ten years for repairs to the plant, and the resurrected village of Vagli di Sotto becomes, during those brief interludes, one of Tuscan's foremost tourist attractions. With its dozen or so homes surrounding a tiny Romanesque church, Vagli di Sotto rises from the waters like a phantasm evoking a time when similar self-sufficient villages dotted the Tuscan countryside.

On this particular morning, Signora Lorenzoni is dressed as always: knee to chin in the most somber of blacks—skirt, blouse, sweater, and stockings; on her feet she wears "zoccoli," the medium-heeled wooden slippers once worn by women all over Italy. She claws at the dirt with her hand-held rake. One thing is different however. In my honor, she has added a lace collar to her sweater and has donned a shiny string of pearls.

"The soil forgets you during the night," she says. "In the slanted light of the early morning, it often mistakes itself for being free, for not having on its finger the wedding band of duty. It presumes itself available for growing whatever seeps between its granules, selling itself equally to both weeds—the fine spores of clover and the thin underground hairs of the creeping limolia—and the valued seeds of your prized red radicchio. Not for it the fidelity that comes from having wed itself to only what was planted there by your own hand.

"What is necessary, therefore, is to remind it of the contract signed with the salt of your sweat. In order to make this soil productive, you must singe it with the heat of your fingers, strip it of the wide-leaved plantains and matted violets so that it may save its energy for the basils and flat beans and tomatoes that are its most heroic possibility."

Tending the soil is different today than it was decades ago, the Signora explains. "Back then, people owned great tracts of land and hired workers who stayed with them for a lifetime, living on the land in houses provided by the owner. The arrangement was usually half the yield for the owner, half for the worker. Of course, the half that went to the owner was always the best half—the first pressing of oil, the newest wine, the fruits without marks.

"But then came the sharecropper laws of 1960, and suddenly the workers had rights to land of their own and an increased yield, and it became impossible for many landowners to continue to maintain their estates. So they sold the land to the workers and, in many cases, moved to town. And just like *that*—an entire way of life was lost forever."

The Signora's memories are good ones even though her family owned no land of their own. In fact, her family worked for a large estate until just before the war, when many of her brothers and sisters emigrated to Chicago. She, however, could not bear to leave, so she stayed with her husband in Vagli, the two of them eking out a living as producers and vendors of pecorino cheese. The wartime years were hard ones, she remembers. Families banded together to conserve food supplies—one soup for twenty stretched a larder further than four soups cooked for five people—and there were always a great many people at any one dinner table.

"A popular meal during that time was called *Polenta e Stoccofisso,* stoccofisso being a type of salt cod fished from the Tyrrhenian. Everyone would receive one slice of polenta, and in the center of the table—just over everybody's head—would be hung a long, thin piece of stoccofisso. We would all take turns, each person placing the slice of polenta flat in the palm of his hand. Then we would slap it up against the *stoccofisso,* hold it there for a few seconds, slide it down the length of the fish, and plop it back onto the plate. In this way, we were able to get a small flavoring of fish and imagine we were eating a feast, rather than a plain plate of cornmeal."

Another specialty she remembers was called *Ragu con Tinca Fugita.* "Tinca [tench] is a freshwater fish that was once found in great numbers in our Serchio River. During the war, however, it was not wise to risk oneself standing at the side of the river for any part of an hour. So people made *ragu,* which is a kind of tomato stew, and called it *con tinca fugita,* which means " 'with escaped fish.' "

Turning from her wartime memories, the Signora snaps back to the present. "You see those artichokes," she says pointing to an overgrown clump. "Last year they got the better of me. I hesitated when I should have been firm and they took advantage. Certo, I saw them growing beyond their allotted space, but I let them go, because my relatives were visiting from America. *Que sbaglio*—what a mistake. It is as I have told you. Control is everything. You must never let go of the reins. Never!"

# TORTA D'ERBI DI VAGLI
*Vegetable Pie Vagli-style*

*Signora Lorenzoni prefers vegetables to either meat or poultry. Among Tuscans, this is not unusual. Traditionally a poor people, they have only recently become accustomed to serving meat more than once a week. In Vagli, the Signora says there are many wonderful dishes made solely from vegetables, with or without cheese. One of her favorites is a kind of vegetable pie that each neighborhood, each street, each family, makes according to its own specific taste.*

> *The filling:*
> 8 tablespoons extra-virgin olive oil
> 6 large leeks, cleaned and sliced (white part only)
> 6 large potatoes, peeled, boiled, and cut into tiny chunks
> 4 eggs, lightly beaten
> 3 ounces fresh pecorino cheese, grated
> Salt and pepper to taste
> Pinch of nutmeg
> *The crust:*
> 2 cups unbleached white flour
> ½ cup water
> 2 tablespoons olive oil

1. For the filling, heat the oil in a skillet; sauté the leeks until soft. Remove from heat and place in a large bowl.

2. Add the potatoes and the remaining ingredients; blend well.

3. Now make the crust: Blend together all the ingredients until a thick dough is formed.

4. Using a rolling pin, roll out 2 circles, one approximately 10 inches in diameter, the other approximately 12 inches.

5. Place the larger circle in a 9-inch pan that has been greased with olive oil; the dough should slightly hang over the edge of the pan. Add the ingredients for the filling.

6. Cover with the smaller circle of dough; roll the edges of the larger circle into a wide border. Press firmly in place.

7. Bake in a preheated 350 degree oven for 1 hour.

8. Serve hot with a mixed salad.

*Serves 6 to 8*

*Vagli di Sopra.*

# PATATE DEI POVERI
*Poor People's Potatoes*

*In the Signora's mental file of favorite foods are many recipes left over from wartime, when, as she says, mouths were many and resources few. This is one of them, a wonderful potato dish as simple to prepare as it is delectable to consume.*

> 4 tablespoons extra-virgin olive oil
> 4 leaves fresh sage
> 3 cloves garlic, crushed
> 1 tablespoon tomato paste
> 2 pounds potatoes, peeled and cut into large chunks
> Salt and pepper to taste

1. Heat the oil in a large skillet; add the sage and garlic and cook over medium heat until the garlic is lightly roasted.

2. Add the tomato paste, dissolve thoroughly, cover, and cook for 3 to 4 minutes until well blended.

3. Run the potato chunks under cold water and place them in the skillet still dripping; toss well to coat the potatoes with the oil-and-sage mixture. Add the salt and pepper.

4. Lower the heat, cover, and cook for 15 to 20 minutes or until the potatoes are very soft. Remove the sage and discard.

5. Serve hot with a mixed salad and slices of thick, crusty bread to soak up the sauce.

*Serves 6*

Travelers to Italy who long for tranquility have recently begun turning to a program called Agriturismo, *which enables them to experience the downhome Italy by spending their vacations in ancient farmhouses converted to comfortable resorts.*

*The Italian government is promoting* Agriturismo *in hopes that it will stimulate ailing rural communities and provide additional income for struggling farmers. Grants, loans, and tax credits are given to any person willing to open their working farm to guests. Thus far, the range of options with respect to accommodations includes both Spartan rooms in renovated barns, and luxurious apartments in sixteenth-century castles. Some even have the feel of exclusive spas.*

*Prices are lower than those charged by hotels and resorts, beginning at about $25 a night, and rarely climbing above $100. Because* Agriturismo *is only a few years old, regulations are a bit sketchy. A few practices however, have already become standard, among them the fact that farmers who participate cannot build new structures, but must restore existing ones. Also, when meals are provided for guests, the food must come either from the farm itself, or from one nearby. This way, the money spent on a farm holiday goes directly into the local economy.*

*The 7,000 or so farms participating in* Agriturismo *belong to one of three major organizations: Terranostra (39 646 821), Turismo Verde (39 6320 8300), or Agriturist (39 668 521). Each of the three has between 1,000 and 3,000 members and publishes its own guidebook.*

*One of the most beautiful of all the* Agriturismo *sites is Tuscany's Fattoria di Camporomano. A lovely farmhouse situated in a peaceful hilly area just minutes away from the Versilian Coast, Fattoria di Camporomano sits on the northern end of Lake Massaciuccoli in Massarosa, and has at its back, the Apuan Alps. Surrounded by olive trees, vineyards, and pastures, the main living area dates back to the 17th century and is still occupied by its owners. The grounds include a full-size swimming pool, several formal gardens, and an endless number of pastures filled with either horses or slowly-meandering cows.*

*In addition to the general peace and tranquility, this particular* Agriturismo *site houses a working* frantoio—*an olive press—which draws guests interested in learning how olive oil is made. Naturally, it is also possible to buy the oil, as well as the wine, which is made on the premises.*

## SALVIA FRITTA
*Fried Sage*

*While most Americans tend to think of basil or oregano as the herbs most represen-tative of Italian cooking, in Tuscany it is, in fact, sage that is used most frequently, whether in flavoring meats, soups, or vegetables. This recipe elevates sage from its everyday role as an accomplice to center-stage position. Salvia Fritta can be used either as an appetizer or as a secondo, an entree. It can either be surrounded by potatoes and vegetables, or served as the contorno, side dish, accompanying a platter of roasted veal. Anyway it is served, it is a truly splendid creation.*

8 canned anchovy filets, drained and rinsed to remove the salt
16 large leaves fresh sage
½ cup white flour
3–4 tablespoons extra-virgin olive oil, plus olive oil for frying

1. Place each anchovy filet between 2 leaves of the sage.

2. Make a paste of the flour and oil; coat the sage "sandwiches" with the paste.

3. Fry in hot oil, using no more than ½ inch of oil at a time, turning once. Cook until leaves are crispy and brownish.

*Serves 4*

In October, when the Tuscan passion for mushrooms and chestnuts has somewhat cooled (not because anyone has had "enough"—one can *never* have enough porcini mushrooms—but because the autumn rains make walking in the forest impossible), artichokes become the main attraction. Whatever type you choose, three large ones per person is generally adequate for a main dish served with plenty of bread and good red wine.

*l'olio*

# CARCIOFI FRITI
*Artichokes Standing Up*

*The artichokes used for this recipe are sort of purplish on the outside, and called mazzeferate.*

> 12 large artichokes
> 3 tablespoons finely chopped fresh parsley
> 3 ounces lean, ground sirloin
> 2 cloves garlic, crushed
> ¼ teaspoon each of salt and pepper (or to taste)
> Extra-virgin olive oil
> ¼ cup water

1. Remove the outer leaves of the artichokes and cut off the points of the leaves that remain; cut off the stems so that the artichokes "stand up."

2. Mix together the parsley, meat, and garlic; add the salt and pepper.

3. Spread the leaves of the artichokes to create pockets of space; fill the pockets with small quantities of the meat mixture.

4. Arrange the artichokes in a skillet large and deep enough to hold all of them (the sides of the skillet should be as high as the tops of the artichokes). Drizzle the tops with olive oil and add ¼ cup water to the bottom of the skillet.

5. Cook over medium heat, covered, for 20 to 30 minutes or until the artichokes are tender throughout (the exact cooking time will depend on their quality and size). Move the artichokes once or twice with a spatula to prevent sticking; add more water and oil if necessary.

6. Serve hot with thick slices of good bread.

*Serves 4*

# CROCCHETTE AL CUORE DI CARCIOFO
*Croquettes from Artichoke Hearts*

*Since Signora Lorenzoni lives, poised above a rushing river and surrounded by mountains of green, her table varies according to the seasons even more than that of other Tuscans. So when the autumn tramontana comes blowing through the valley and the artichokes begin to sprout from between those silvery frilled leaves, she sits herself down to a hearty dinner consisting of crispy artichoke croquettes served with pureed potatoes and a mixed salad. "Oh," she says, "and most important is a bottle of young red wine."*

8 medium artichokes, outer leaves removed
3 leeks, cleaned and minced (white part only)
1 potato, peeled, boiled, and mashed
4 ounces fresh pecorino cheese, grated (or Parmigiano Reggiano)
6 tablespoons extra-virgin olive oil
Salt and pepper to taste
2 eggs, lightly beaten
4 tablespoons milk
1 cup unflavored dry bread crumbs
½ cup white flour
Olive oil for frying (or vegetable oil)

1. Remove the stems from the artichokes, cut in half, and remove the choke; cut the remaining hearts into very small pieces.

2. Add the leeks, potatoes, cheese, oil, salt, pepper, and eggs, and blend thoroughly; add just enough milk to create a thick dough.

3. Form the dough into small, round croquettes, approximately 2½ inches in diameter; roll each croquette in the breadcrumbs, place on a dish, and refrigerate for 1 hour.

4. Place the flour in a small bowl; add just enough water to create a very liquid paste of a consistency to roll the croquettes and have them emerge coated with a thin layer of the flour-water mixture.

5. Heat the oil in a large skillet. Roll each croquette in the flour-water paste and fry in the oil, turning often until it has a golden crust on all sides.

6. Drain the croquettes on paper towels and serve hot with lemon wedges.

*Serves 4*

## CIPOLLE RIPIENE CON MANZO
*Onions Stuffed with Meat*

*There are few vegetable recipes more characteristic of the Lucchesía than onions stuffed with various combinations of ingredients. This recipe is based on one that was part of the Signora's household kitchen when she was growing up. It has more ingredients, however, and meat is used in place of bread. "We live in more prosperous times," the Signora explains, "and so I have embellished this dish with what I always imagined it needed."*

  4 large white onions, peeled
  3 tablespoons unsalted butter
  4 ounces lean ground sirloin
  2 links pork sausage, removed from casing and crumbled
  Pinch of nutmeg
  Pinch of cinnamon
  1 cup dry white wine
  1 egg, lightly beaten
  4 tablespoons fresh pecorino cheese, grated (or Parmigiano
    Reggiano)
  ½ cup Basic Meat Broth (page 95) or good quality canned

1. Cut one end of each onion so that it can stand by itself. Immerse the onions in boiling salted water and cook for 10 minutes.

2. Using a small knife, remove the inside layers of the onions so that only a thin shell remains; dice the removed parts.

3. Sauté the diced onions in the butter; add the ground beef, sausage, nutmeg and cinnamon. Cook until the meat is light pink; add the wine and cook until evaporated. Remove from flame and let cool.

4. Blend together the egg and cheese; add the cooled meat.

5. Stuff the onions with the meat and cheese; place in an oiled baking pan (the sides of the pan should reach no higher than to the halfway point of the onions). Bake in a preheated 350 degree oven for 25 minutes. Drizzle the broth, a few tablespoons at a time, over the tops if the onions seem too dry during cooking.

*Serves 4*

# FRIGO
## *Vegetable Medley*

*Frigó is a Tuscan term liberally applied to any mixture of vegetables tossed with olive oil and baked until crisp. The only constants are onions and potatoes. Important, however, is to use fresh vegetables in season, and to add them at appropriate times so that no vegetable is either raw or cooked too long.*

> 4 medium potatoes, peeled and cut into medium-size chunks
> 4 medium onions, peeled and cut in half
> 6 large carrots, sliced in half lengthwise
> 2 medium green peppers, seeded and cut in quarters
> 6 cloves garlic, peeled and thinly sliced
> ¼ cup extra-virgin olive oil
> 4 leaves fresh sage, chopped
> 2 tablespoons finely chopped fresh rosemary
> 4 tablespoons fresh thyme, chopped (or 1 teaspoon dried)
> Salt to taste
> 4 small zucchini, cut in half lengthwise
> 1 cup fresh champignon (white) mushrooms, cleaned and sliced in
>   half

1. Cook the potatoes in salted water for 10 minutes; drain.

2. Place all ingredients except the zucchini and mushrooms in a large baking pan (the sides no higher than 3 inches); toss well to blend.

3. Bake in a preheated 450 degree oven for 60 minutes turning often with a wooden spoon.

4. Add the zucchini and mushrooms; toss to coat well with the oil.

5. Cook 30 minutes longer or until the potatoes are crispy.

6. Serve hot as is, or cold with lemon wedges.

*Serves 4*

Throughout Tuscany, eggplants have been known as *petonciane* since the early 1600s when they were first brought from India. In the Middle Ages, it was believed that eating eggplant would lead to madness, a theory that eventually wound its way into the teachings of Mastro Taddeo, a noted Tuscan physician who recorded the following episode in his diary: A student, wanting to test the validity of the theory, ate only eggplant for seven days. When he reported to Mastro Taddeo that he had done so and had not, in fact, gone mad, the Mastro declared the experiment to have succeeded in establishing absolutely the theory's validity. "Who," he wrote, "would eat only eggplant for seven days except someone who had completely lost his mind?"

## PETONCIANE IN AGRODOLCE
*Sweet and Sour Eggplant*

>    1 medium eggplant, peeled and cut into large chunks
>    Salt
>    ¼ cup olive oil
>    1 tablespoon tomato paste
>    1 small stalk celery, diced
>    1 tablespoon sugar
>    2½ tablespoons good-quality red wine vinegar
>    ¼ cup water

1. Salt the eggplant chunks heavily, toss, and place in a colander for 1 hour weighted down by a heavy plate; rinse and dry.

2. Fry the eggplant in hot oil until it is soft; drain on paper towels.

3. Clean the skillet of any remaining oil, and add the remaining ingredients including the fried eggplant.

4. Cook over medium heat for 5 minutes or until the sauce has thickened.

5. Serve at room temperature.

*Serves 4*

# PEPPERONATA RUSTICA
*Peppers and Tomatoes, Rustic-style*

*The night I first arrived at the Signora's house, she made for me a wonderful zuppa di fagioli (bean soup) followed by roast veal served with pepperonata rustica, a half-cooked/half-raw blend of variously colored peppers, onions, and tomatoes. She explained that it is a typical dish of this mountainous region, and can be used either hot as a side dish, or cold as a spread. What a wonderful welcome!*

    1 small onion, diced
    1 medium onion, sliced
    3 tablespoons extra-virgin olive oil
    2 medium red peppers, thickly sliced
    2 medium yellow peppers, thickly sliced
    1 medium green pepper, thickly sliced
    4 peeled plum tomatoes (not too ripe), seeded and cut into small
        chunks
    Salt and pepper to taste

1. Sauté the diced onion in the oil; add the peppers and sliced onion. Cover and cook over medium heat for 15 minutes or until the vegetables are soft; stop just short of browning.

2. Remove the cover and continue to cook until all the liquid has evaporated.

3. Add the tomatoes; cook for 10 minutes or until the tomatoes are semisoft. Add the salt and pepper.

4. Remove from heat and serve hot as a side dish, or cold as either a spread for bread or an appetizer drizzled with lemon.

*Serves 4*

# PATATE ARROSTITE
*Roasted Potatoes*

*In Tuscany, potatoes are a quintessential side dish for meat. Roasted, fried, stewed, pan-fried, boiled, or grilled—the preparations are endlessly diverse. Here is a recipe for those who prefer their potatoes crisp, but at the same time not greasy. This dish differs from one in which the potatoes are roasted with the meat, in that the texture of the potatoes comes from baking them for a long time rather than from frying them in the fat from the meat (a method of preparation that is also very good).*

> 3 pounds red potatoes
> ¼ cup extra-virgin olive oil
> 4 cloves garlic, crushed
> 7 leaves fresh sage

1. Boil the potatoes in their skins for 15 minutes or until the outer half is done (the centers should still be fairly hard).

2. Peel them, and cut into large chunks.

3. Heat half the oil in a large, ovenproof skillet; sauté the garlic until the edges are golden. (Do not brown!) Add the sage and remove skillet from heat.

4. Add the potatoes and toss so that all pieces are coated with oil.

5. Bake in a preheated 400 degree oven for 1 hour.

6. Drizzle the remaining oil over the potatoes and turn with a spatula; cook 30 minutes longer or until the potatoes are golden brown and crispy. Serve hot.

*Serves 4*

A very popular vegetable dish among Tuscans is called a *sformato,* which translated literally means "hardened into the shape of a mold." These wonderful creations are nothing more than purees of vegetables mixed with a thick *besciamella*—a mixture of butter, flour, and milk—and sprinkled with a layer of Parmigiano Reggiano before baking.

The result: a piping-hot mixture of vegetables and bubbling melted cheese that looks very much like a pie. It can be used either as an accompaniment to a roasted chicken, or as an entree eaten with a tossed green salad and crunchy bread.

# SFORMATO DI CAVOLOFIORE
*Cauliflower Pie*

*This sformato is made with cauliflower, but fennel, string beans, spinach, onions, and potatoes will also do.*

  1 head firm, white cauliflower, cleaned and separated into individual florets
  2 tablespoons extra-virgin olive oil
  1 medium onion, diced
  4 tablespoons unsalted butter
  3 tablespoons white flour
  2 cups milk
  Pinch of nutmeg
  Salt and pepper to taste
  6 tablespoons Parmigiano Reggiano, grated

1. Place the cauliflower florets into boiling salted water over medium heat. Cook for 10 minutes or until the florets can be easily pierced with a fork; drain.

2. Heat the oil in a skillet over medium heat; sauté the onion until lightly browned. Add the cauliflower and continue to sauté until the florets begin to stick slightly to the pan; remove the cauliflower to a large bowl. Mash the florets with a fork until they become a thick, chunky paste. (Do not use a food processor as this would create too much liquid.)

3. Melt 3 tablespoons of butter in the same skillet; using a spatula, scrape into the butter any remnants of the cauliflower. Add flour and stir until you have a pastelike consistency. Add the milk, stirring constantly with a whisk until the mixture is thick and soupy; add nutmeg and stir until all ingredients are blended.

4. Return the cauliflower to the skillet; add salt and pepper and blend thoroughly.

5. Preheat the oven to 350 degrees; grease a 8- or 9-inch pie pan with the remaining tablespoon of butter. Pour entire contents of skillet into the pan; coat the top with the cheese, and bake for 45 minutes or until the middle is firm to the touch.

6. Slice and serve hot.

*Serves 4*

# VERDURA BOLLITA
*Boiled Vegetables*

*Tuscany is the land of boiled vegetable dinners, which are nothing more than the simplest of preparations turned into extraordinary dishes merely by drizzling across the top some of the extra-virgin olive oil that is the region's most precious possession. This dish serves as a fine accompaniment to broiled fish or chicken, but make sure to have good crusty bread on hand to sop up the rest of the oil.*

  4 medium red potatoes
  4 medium carrots
  4 medium sized onions
  1 medium butternut squash, peeled, seeded, and cut into large
      chunks
  4 small zucchini
  8 tablespoons extra-virgin olive oil (the very best quality is
      essential)
  Salt and pepper to taste

1. Place the potatoes, carrots, and onions in a large pot filled with cold water; boil for 8 minutes.

2. Add the squash; boil for another 8 minutes.

3. Add the zucchini and continue to boil until all vegetables are thoroughly cooked (test for softness by inserting a fork into the centers); remove from heat.

4. Peel the potatoes and cut them into small chunks; do the same with the other vegetables.

5. Place all the vegetables in a large bowl; drizzle the oil across the top, tossing to make sure that all vegetables are coated. Salt and pepper to taste.

*Serves 4*

# PALLINE DI ZUCCHINE
## *Zucchini Fritters*

*Whenever the Signora makes roast veal, she always accompanies it with these frit-*
*ters made of eggs, herbs, and grated Parmesan. She concedes, however, that the*
*palline would be equally delicious as an accompaniment to fried fish, roast beef, or*
*fresh Pecorino cheese.*

1¼ pounds small zucchini
Salt and pepper to taste
5 tablespoons Parmigiano Reggiano, grated
4 eggs, lightly beaten
2 tablespoons finely chopped fresh parsley
3 leaves fresh basil, chopped
White flour for dusting
1 cup dry unflavored breadcrumbs
Olive oil for frying

1. Boil the zucchini in very little water until almost done (the centers
should still be somewhat firm when pierced with a fork); drain and set
aside to cool.

2. Chop the cooled zucchini into very tiny slivers; add the salt, pepper,
cheese, half of the egg mixture, parsley, and basil. Blend all ingredients
until of a thick, pastelike consistency.

3. With floured hands, form tiny balls the size of walnuts; dust with
flour, roll in the remaining egg mixture, coat the balls with breadcrumbs and fry in hot oil until all sides are browned.

4. Drain on paper towels; serve hot.

*Serves 4*

# PISELLI CON PROSCIUTTO
# AL POMODORO
*Peas with Prosciutto in Tomato Sauce*

*"If I had to make a list of five vegetable dishes that are used, in one form or an-other, throughout the province of Lucca, I would definitely include* Piselli con Prosciutto al Pomodoro,*" the Signora said when I asked her to make just such a list. "Some people—namely those from Liguria—eliminate the prosciutto, but to my way of thinking, you are then left with no flavor at all. Beh, each to his own taste."*

1 medium onion, diced
3 tablespoons extra-virgin olive oil
4 ounces prosciutto, cut into small slivers
2 leaves fresh basil, chopped
2 leaves fresh sage, chopped
1½ pounds fresh peas, shelled (or 1 pound frozen, if absolutely necessary)
½ cup canned drained and chopped Italian tomatoes

1. Sauté the onion in the oil until lightly browned; add the prosciutto, basil, and sage. Continue to sauté for several minutes, stirring often with a wooden spoon.

2. Add the peas and the tomatoes, cover, and cook for 5 minutes over medium heat.

3. Remove the cover and cook for 5 minutes longer or until the sauce is somewhat reduced and slightly thickened.

4. Serve hot with plenty of thick bread and young red wine.

*Serves 4*

# TERRINA DI FINOCCHI
*Terrine of Fennel*

*In the fall, the Signora's garden is a maze of feathery clumps, each sprouting from the firm white bulbs of fennel that then become standard fare on Tuscan tables— whether sliced or served raw as an appetizer, cut into tiny chunks for a salad, or mixed with eggs and butter and cooked into a delicious terrine such as this one.*

4 medium-size bulbs of fennel
2 eggs
4 tablespoons Parmigiano Reggiano, grated
Pinch of nutmeg
Salt and pepper to taste
6 tablespoons unsalted butter
6 thin slices whole wheat bread

1. Cut the tops from the fennel and discard; slice each bulb into quarters lengthwise, removing any outside leaves that are damaged or tough.

2. Boil the fennel in salted water for 20 minutes; drain and set aside.

3. Beat the eggs with the cheese, nutmeg, salt, and pepper.

4. Using 1 tablespoon of the butter, grease a baking dish large enough to hold all 6 slices of bread in one layer.

5. Place the bread in the dish with no overlap. Melt the remaining butter and pour evenly over the bread.

6. Arrange the fennel over the bread; cover with egg mixture. Bake in a preheated 350 degree oven for 20 minutes; serve hot.

*Serves 4*

# PORRI ALLA PARMIGIANA
*Leeks with Parmesan Cheese*

*Leeks are very popular with Tuscans, who use them in soups and sauces and as a vegetable side dish. In general, the green part is discarded; the white part is then boiled in salted water for approximately 15 minutes and prepared according to the individual recipe. Most important is to clean the leeks thoroughly—sand tends to lodge between the layers around the root.*

4 pounds leeks
6 tablespoons unsalted butter
4 ounces Parmigiano Reggiano, grated
Salt to taste

1. Cut away and discard the green part of the leeks, cut into halves lengthwise, and wash the white parts thoroughly. Boil in salted water for 15 minutes; drain.

2. Arrange in a circular pattern on a heated serving platter so that the leeks resemble the rays of the sun, the root parts forming the nucleus.

3. Melt the butter in a small saucepan; drizzle evenly over the leeks.

4. Sprinkle liberally with the cheese, salt, and serve hot.

*Serves 4*

# INVOLTINI DI CAVOLO
## *Stuffed Cabbage Rolls*

*While most people tend to think of stuffed cabbage rolls as solely a northern European dish, it is also popular in Tuscany—albeit cooked in what the Signora refers to as "a much more delicious style."*

4 slices stale bread
½ cup milk
8 ounces lean, ground sirloin
1 egg, lightly beaten
Salt to taste
3 tablespoons finely chopped fresh parsley
1 head of savoy cabbage
2 ounces pancetta (unsmoked bacon), diced
3 tablespoons extra-virgin olive oil
8 ounces canned Italian tomatoes, drained and chopped

1. Soak the bread in the milk; using your hands, squeeze it "dry" and place in a large bowl.

2. Add the ground sirloin, egg, salt, and parsley; mix by hand until a thick dough is formed.

3. Remove 12 or so of the largest outer leaves of the cabbage (save the rest for another use), immerse the leaves in boiling water for several minutes until they are somewhat softened. Remove and drain.

4. Place a few tablespoons of meat filling in each of the leaves and fold into a tight package, first joining the two horizontal sides, then the vertical ones; fasten with a toothpick.

5. Sauté the pancetta in the oil for 3 minutes; add the cabbage rolls in one layer and cook for 8 minutes.

6. Add the tomatoes, cover, and cook over low heat for 1 hour; serve hot.

*Serves 4*

*Frittate*—omelettes—are very popular throughout the Lucchesía, both as appetizers and as first courses. To cook a perfect omelette, you need a heavy skillet, preferably made of iron; ideally, it should never be washed but merely wiped. The eggs should be very lightly beaten, dusted with salt and pepper, and then poured into the skillet with oil that has been heated to the point of smoking. Once the omelette has cooked for a minute or two, it should be turned. This is done by covering the omelette with a dish, and then—one hand on the dish—flipping the skillet so that the omelette is now, cooked side up, resting on the dish. It is then slid back into the pan and cooked for 3 to 5 minutes on the reverse side.

Following are three *frittata* recipes, each from a different town within the Lucchesía. The first, *Frittata con la Salvia* (Omelette with Sage), originated in Versilia, in the town of Pietrasanta just north of Viareggio; the second, *Frittata di Patate* (Potato Omelette) comes from Cardoso in Garfagnana; and the third, *Frittata di Aglio e Prezzemolo* (Omelette with Garlic and Parsley), hails from the area surrounding Bagni di Lucca, a spa town somewhat north of Lucca. All are delicious with mixed salads, crusty bread, and dry white wine.

# FRITTATA CON LA SALVIA
*Omelette with Sage*

2 slices bread, crusts removed
½ cup milk
6 eggs, lightly beaten
¼ cup unflavored breadcrumbs
6 leaves fresh sage, chopped
Salt
5 tablespoons Parmigiano Reggiano, grated
2 tablespoons extra-virgin olive oil

1. Soak the bread slices in the milk; wring dry and crumble into tiny pieces.

2. Place the lightly beaten eggs in a bowl; add the breadcrumbs, chopped sage, salt, cheese, and crumbled bread; blend well.

3. Heat the oil in a heavy skillet; when the oil smokes, pour the egg mixture into the skillet, beating constantly with a fork.

4. When the edges have set turn the omelette according to the directions on page 173; cook for 3 to 5 minutes or until the center is set. Cool to room temperature before serving.

*Serves 4*

# FRITTATA DI PATATE
*Potato Omelette*

3 tablespoons extra-virgin olive oil
1 clove garlic, crushed
2 tablespoons finely chopped fresh parsley
Salt and pepper
2 medium red potatoes, peeled and diced
6 eggs, lightly beaten

1.  Heat 2 tablespoons of the oil in a heavy skillet; sauté the garlic, parsley, salt, and pepper.

2.  Add the diced potatoes and 2 tablespoons water; cook, stirring often, until the potatoes are tender.

3.  Add the remaining tablespoon of oil, and pour the eggs over the potatoes; continue cooking.

4.  When the edges have set turn the omelette, according to the directions on page 173; cook for 3 to 5 minutes or until the center is completely done. Serve hot.

*Serves 4*

# FRITATTA DI AGLIO E PREZZEMOLO
*Omelette with Garlic and Parsley*

6 eggs, lightly beaten
3 cloves garlic, crushed
4 tablespoons finely chopped fresh parsley
Salt and pepper
2 ounces pecorino cheese, grated
2 tablespoons dry unflavored breadcrumbs
2 tablespoons extra-virgin olive oil

1. Place the eggs in a bowl; add the garlic, parsley, salt, pepper, cheese, and breadcrumbs. Mix until all ingredients are blended (do not overmix or the eggs will become too liquid).

2. Heat the oil in a heavy skillet until it smokes; add the egg mixture.

3. When the edges have set, turn the omelette, according to the directions on page 173; cook for 3 to 5 minutes or until the center is completely set. Serve hot.

*Serves 4*

# All About Eggs

*Eggs are a wonderful culinary resource: easy to make, adaptable to a variety of preparations, and appropriate for serving at any time of the day or night. Nutritionally speaking, they are a very good source of both protein and minerals, including iron, calcium, and phosphorus.*

*One egg weighs approximately 2 ounces, only 1.8 of which are edible. Of these 1.8 ounces, 15% is protein, 11% fat. An egg contains approximately 80 calories.*

*Fresh eggs are heavier than spoiled ones. To check for freshness, place the eggs in a deep bowl of water. The freshest will sink immediately to the bottom. Those that are five days old or less will remain near the bottom in a vertical position. Eggs that float in a horizontal position are at least fifteen days old and should not be used.*

*Eggs should always be refrigerated, but they should be brought to room temperature before using.*

*Vagli di Sotto.*

# UOVA IN CAMICIA AL VINO
*Eggs in Shirts with Wine*

*This is an ancient recipe from the Garfagnana region of Tuscany. A wonderful combination of poached eggs in a wine and mushroom sauce, it is generally served over slices of bread sautéed in olive oil. "In shirts" refers to the fact that the eggs are turned once during cooking so that only the white part (the shirts) are visible. The Signora remembers her grandmother making this dish on blustery winter nights when the whole family would gather around the table wearing mufflers and gloves.*

2 cups dry white wine
3 small onions, sliced
2 cloves garlic, crushed
¼ teaspoon dried thyme
½ bay leaf
Pinch of nutmeg
Salt and pepper
4 eggs
4 ounces fresh mushrooms (champignons), diced
3 tablespoons unsalted butter
1 tablespoon white flour
2 tablespoons extra-virgin olive oil
4 slices thick, crusty bread

1. Pour the wine into a heavy skillet; add the onions, garlic, thyme, bay leaf, nutmeg, salt, and pepper. Boil for 15 minutes over medium heat.

2. Lower the heat until the sauce goes from boil to simmer. Add the eggs, breaking them directly into the skillet with yolk intact; cook 1 minute.

3. Turn the eggs carefully with a spatula; the yolk should remain intact and be covered by a layer of white.

4. Cook for 2 minutes longer (at this point the yolks should be very soft but not runny); remove with a slotted spoon to a heated platter. Keep warm.

5. Remove the garlic and herbs from the wine sauce; leave in the onions. Place the sauce in a food processor and blend until the onions are thoroughly pureed.

6. Return the sauce to the skillet; add the mushrooms and cook for 10 minutes over medium heat.

7. Add the butter and flour and cook over low heat, stirring, until the sauce is somewhat thickened.

8. Heat the oil in a separate skillet; add the bread slices and toast on both sides.

9. Serve the eggs on the bread, covered with the sauce.

*Serves 4*

## POLPETTONE D'UOVA
*Meatloaf of Eggs*

*When the Signora invites her vegetarian friend, Fulvia, to dinner, she always makes this loaf because, she says, it fools the other guests, many of whom are fervent meateaters, into thinking they have eaten what they might have made for themselves at home. This hearty and flavorful dish is perfect for serving as an appetizer, a first course, or as the entree at a Sunday morning brunch.*

    8 eggs
    Salt to taste
    3–3½ cups white flour
    1 cup milk
    2 tablespoons finely chopped fresh parsley
    1 piece white cheese cloth, approximately 1 foot square
    1 tablespoon butter
    1 cup tomato sauce (homemade or canned)

1. Beat the eggs lightly with the salt; add the flour in a steady stream while continuing to beat.

2. Add the milk and the parsley and work into a somewhat thick paste. Use more flour if necessary.

3. Grease the cheesecloth with butter; place the egg mixture on the gauze and wrap into the shape of a meatloaf. Tie the ends with thread.

4. Place the loaf in a large pot filled with boiling salted water; boil for 10 minutes or until it has completely set. Remove from water and let cool.

5. Heat the tomato sauce.

6. Remove the loaf from the gauze, cut into slices, and serve topped with the sauce.

*Serves 4*

# MOZZARELLA IN CARROZZA
*Mozzarella in a Carriage*

*This dish gets its name from its appearance: a creamy white layer of mozzarella encapsulated between two slices of bread that have been fried to a lustrously golden color. Appropriate as an appetizer or for a brunch. The Signora recalls that she made this once for the American nephew of a close friend, and as he watched the preparation he said, "Oh, that's just the Italian version of a grilled cheese sandwich." Don't believe it. The two are as far apart as ketchup and a finely prepared sugo al pomodoro.*

> 4 thick slices of buffalo mozzarella, the same length and width as the bread; (approximately 1 pound)
> 8 slices stale bread, (any kind will do, from packaged white bread to rustic whole wheat—use what you like) crusts removed
> 2 eggs, lightly beaten
> 1½ cups milk
> Salt
> ½ cup white flour
> 2 tablespoons unsalted butter
> 4 tablespoons extra-virgin olive oil

1. Arrange the mozzarella between the slices of bread to form 4 well-packed sandwiches. If cheese slices are not as large as the bread, use a few smaller pieces side by side.

2. Place the eggs and the milk in a bowl; add the salt and blend all ingredients thoroughly.

3. Dust the sandwiches with flour and dip both sides in the egg mixture.

4. Heat the butter and oil in a large heavy skillet until the butter is lightly browned and the oil smoking. Place the sandwiches in the skillet two at a time until the mozzarella is creamy and the bread golden brown on both sides.

5. Drain on paper towels; serve hot.

*Serves 4*

# SPIEDINI DI MOZZARELLA ALL'ACCIUGA
*Mozzarella Skewers and Anchovy Sauce*

*When the Signora's husband was alive, the two of them ate this dish every Sunday night after the children had gone to bed. They would work together in the kitchen, talking over the week's events and threading their skewers with the mozzarella and bread. Her husband would always make the anchovy sauce, the Signora says, "because he claimed to have a special connection with fish." This dish works very well as an appetizer or as an entire meal served with a mixed salad and a good red wine.*

> 4 slices stale bread, cut in large chunks
> ¼ cup milk plus 1 tablespoon milk
> Skewers
> 1 buffalo mozzarella (approximately 1 pound), cut in thick chunks
> 6 tablespoons unsalted butter
> 4 anchovy fillets, canned in oil, rinsed to remove the salt and
>     mashed with a fork

1. Baste the bread with the ¼ cup milk.

2. Thread the skewers, alternating mozzarella with bread.

3. Melt the butter in a small skillet; brush the mozzarella and bread with half the butter.

4. Place in a baking pan so that both ends of the skewers rest on the sides of the pan and the mozzarella and bread do not touch the pan. Grill in a 500 degree oven until the bread is toasted and the mozzarella soft; turn once or twice so that all sides are cooked.

5. Meanwhile, sauté the anchovies in the remaining butter; add 1 tablespoon of milk and cook for 2 to 3 minutes or until the sauce is well blended.

6. Place the skewers on a serving platter; pour the sauce over them evenly. Serve hot.

*Serves 4*

# TORTA DI RICOTTA
*Ricotta Tart*

*Tuscan breakfasts are fairly undefined events, consisting as they do of a wide variety of catch-as-catch-can components. One mainstay however, is Torta di Ricotta which is served widely in homes as well as in bars (where Italians eat breakfast when they are out). A rich and delightful combination of ricotta and white wine, this particular recipe is for a torta salata—a salty tart, as opposed to a torta dolce—a sweet tart—which can also be made from ricotta, and is, as well, a breakfast mainstay for those with somewhat sweeter dispositions.*

1 cup white flour
6 tablespoons unsalted butter
Salt to taste
12 ounces fresh ricotta (from sheep's milk, if possible)
1 small onion, minced
2 tablespoons finely chopped fresh parsley
½ glass dry white wine
4 tablespoons Parmigiano Reggiano, grated

1. Place the flour and 4 tablespoons of the butter, softened, in a bowl; add salt and turn into a semithick dough, adding water by the tablespoonful as needed.

2. Place the ricotta in a large bowl; add the onion, parsley, and wine. Blend all ingredients thoroughly.

3. On a floured surface, roll out the dough into a 12-inch circle (the dough should be as thin as possible).

4. Line a 9-inch cake pan, bottom and side, with the dough; add the ricotta mixture, sprinkle with the grated cheese, and dot with the remaining butter.

5. Use the overhanging dough to make a rolled-edge crust.

6. Bake in a preheated 350 degree oven for 20 to 25 minutes or until the crust is golden brown. Serve at room temperature.

*Serves 4 to 6*

*Signora Eliza Angeli*

# Chapter Six

# A PAINTING IN
# PRIMARY COLORS

## FISH

*Insomma.* A word. An expression. The answer to a great many questions: How are you? How's your invalid mother? How go your exams? What did you think of Pavarotti's latest *Tosca?* How are you doing with your campaign to lose weight . . . find a job . . . stop smoking?

In its very purest translation, the word hovers somewhere between "so-so," and "What can one expect?" But on a more general plane, it is used to convey any one of a number of things: resignation to a fate worse than death; or suffering of a sort that must remain unmentioned for fear of overly burdening the listener; or even the speaker's judgment on, say, Berlusconi's chances of once again heading up a government or your cousin Silvia's new husband.

Don't press me any further, it implies, when what is really meant is: "I am dying to tell you." In the curtness of its abbreviation, it suggests the speaker will say no more—cannot, in fact, under threat of being beaten about the legs with a thorned thistle be induced to utter one additional word.

Nothing could be farther from the truth. Spoken as it is with an accompanying shrug of the shoulders and a helpless (or, when passing judgment, an *all-knowing*) look on one's face, it is the first step in a complicated social custom that requires—if etiquette is to be observed (and Tuscans are nothing if not masters of dramatic displays of etiquette)—a request for further information.

*Mi dici!* (You don't say!), this spoken with a shaking of the head and a darkening of the irises as if the two were now conspirators in a great plot against the heavens.

Drama. Peel away the skin of Tuscans, and what you will find is a brilliance of color, a bellowing of voice, a stridency of purpose in the consistent flailing of their arms towards the gods. *Dio Mio!* they cry at the slightest of provocations, their bodies bent in bewilderment over the tragedy of an ordinary occurrence. *Mamma!* they moan whenever they're in need, beseeching not the Creator, not their spouses, not their friends . . . *Mamma!*

Watch them as they engage in the quaint little ritual known as the *passegiatta,* which is literally translated as a simple little stroll around the piazza, but turns out to encompass a great deal more. Make no mistake about it, the *true* value of the *passegiatta* lies in the sheer number of people engaged, in the opportunities offered by such numbers for individual, highly explosive dramas.

"*Ciao* Fulvia, I saw your brother at the market last week. He looked quite well."

"*Insomma.*"

"I heard he was planning a trip to America."

"God forgive me, but would that He sees fit to crash the plane on route."

"Fulvia! What are you saying?"

"Oh Vincenzina, if you only knew what a cross I've had to bear these last few weeks with my brother and this business deal in San Francisco. Paolo wants to open a chain of stores there, which is all well and good. But what about his family? Can you imagine? He says he'll spend a few weeks here, a few weeks there. Such things are good for *young* men—*single* men. But my brother has a wife and two sons. And his partner! We won't even go into the problems his partner has already had with the payment of taxes. No, no, Vincenzina, my brother has lost his head. I can only thank the Lord that our sainted mother is not here to witness this turn of events."

This Tuscan penchant for drama was on full view during a visit to my friend Signora Eliza Angeli, who is, herself, a striking manifestation of theatricality. Together, we experienced a display of melodrama I will not soon forget.

Signora Angeli lives in Viareggio, a charming beach resort on the Versilian coast, which is the name given to the Italian Riviera from just below Viareggio, to—traveling north—the border between Tuscany and Liguria. Viareggio's attractions are many, not least among them the sight of the Apuan Alps in the background, and the two cool, shady pine forests at either end of the town. (*La Pineta Levante,* the pine forest to the east, and *La Pineta Ponente,* the one to the west).

But what I generally love best about Viareggio are its less natural beauties: the architectural splendor of the town's homes and its balconies which, from early March to late October, are awash with bougainvillea; the art deco bathhouses along the waterfront, many refurbished from the early 1920s, (the waterfront boulevard itself is named Viale Margharita in honor of Italy's Queen Margharita of Savoy); the winter *Carnevale,* which rivals that of Rio and New Orleans; and, of course, Viareggio's fascinating history, including the fact that it was just off this coast—and directly out to sea from the balcony of Signora Angeli's house—where Percy Bysshe Shelley drowned. (This event is commemorated with a slightly decomposing bust of young Percy erected in the nearby Piazza Shelley, where he was cremated and mourned by his fellow poet and bon vivant, Lord Byron).

On this one particular day in early autumn, I went to Viareggio because the Signora had promised to give me a lesson in the cooking of fish. The lesson was to begin with a bus trip to the market in Lucca where we would purchase a certain type of baccalà (salted codfish) sold only by a particular merchant. Little did I imagine what else I was to learn on this fateful trip.

We sat in the first seat, opposite the driver and behind the little folding chair on which the ticket taker traditionally sits. (He's the man who takes care of stamping and selling the tickets, as well as making sure that, if you already have a ticket, it's for the right day and not one you recycled from last week when he, on the spur of the moment, decided to take a little beach holiday.)

Ten minutes after boarding, the bus stopped at a railroad crossing. The barrier gates were down, and we were third in a long line that included two cars in front and a large number of cars behind. On the other side, also behind the gates, were a few cars as well as a long-distance type of bus, somewhat larger than ours. For a few seconds, we all sat patiently, waiting. Before long, however, the cars behind us began indiscriminately scooting around and through the gates, making a kind of "S" curve over the tracks. Whereupon some people from the back of our bus began agitating for our driver to do the same. In this they were supported by the ticket taker, who had glanced at his watch and realized he might not be home in time to pick up his car from the local garage.

"*Vai*," he urged the driver. Go. "You can see there is no train."

But our driver stayed put, and—to his credit—even remained calm, this despite the fact that a good one-third of the passengers had, by now, risen to their feet and assumed a position directly behind his right shoulder. At one point he turned around in his seat and tried pleading with them. "I *can't* just go around the gates," he implored in a number of different ways. "What if the train were to come? What if we were to get stuck on the tracks?"

As they say in Viareggio, he might as well have put away his sails.

By now, some of the cars on the other side of the tracks were also circumventing the gates. A sort of spontaneous courtesy had sprung up: If you were going to jump the barrier, you waved your arm out the car window so that the driver on the other side would understand your intentions and wait his turn. But then the long-distance bus went through the gates, and it was then that the hues and cries against our driver *really* began.

"*O toppino! Dove l'hai le palle?*" (Oh little mouse, where are your balls?) Some even flapped their arms and crowed like chickens.

Before too long, two-thirds of the passengers were crowded around this poor man, thrusting their watches in front of his face and pointing to briefcases filled with things that urgently needed attention. They yelled, threw up their arms, invoked God, His Mother, *their* mothers. In the middle of this mutiny, the ticket taker announced he could no longer wait for a resolution and demanded to be let off the bus. So the driver opened the doors—"*Beh, vai allora*" (So then, go)—and the little man took off, on foot, with his black shoulder bag, into the woods.

The drama proceeded in this manner for another five or so minutes with cars and buses streaming across the tracks in a steady flow. At one point, a car became stuck in the center of the railroad bed and had to be pushed by a number of volunteers amidst general shouting about how the right wingers were ruining public transportation with all their cost-cutting measures.

And then, at the height of the confusion, when it seemed as if Fellini's ghost might any minute round the corner with his videocam, the situation became even more surreal. An old man limped out of the woods, fished a key from the pocket of his bedraggled cardigan, and opened the door to a little shack sitting by the side of the tracks. He pulled out a wooden mallet, strolled over to the barrier gates, and pushed the end of it into an odd, cylindrical container attached to one of the gates' arms.

And, miraculously, both arms lifted.

But it is what happened subsequently that, to this day, most remains embedded in my memory. Our driver simply and quietly closed the door to the bus, the passengers simply and quietly (well, not *totally* quietly—these *were*, after all Tuscans) resumed their seats, and we were once more on our way, everyone acting as if nothing had ever happened. And when we reached our destination, the driver and two of the most vociferous of the passengers ambled off together to the local cafe for an espresso.

"I'm surprised no one threw a bottle at his head," Signora Angeli said later in summation. "We Tuscans are a volatile people. Everything we do is with drama—processions, cleaning, serving coffee, waiting tables. Why do you think we have so many balconies, so many benches on the street, so many seats in cafes if not to feed our great desire to perform for a crowd?

"That's why it's so easy for us to lie," she continued. "Why speak the truth if the truth will not please your audience? If you know, for example, that it will take four weeks to deliver the new dishwasher, and the person in front of whom you're performing is obviously going to be upset with that news, why not simply say, 'Yes, you will have it on Tuesday next'? That way, you're happy, your audience is happy, and the strength of the performance is maintained. Your next encounter will be more dramatic, of course, but that is also part of how we in Viareggio live."

Back home with the baccalà, the Signora instructed me in its preparation. She first informed me that cod was the most stubborn of all fish, that it would try in every way possible to strip me of my dignity, to take over. I must not let it, she warned. I must fight back, showing I have what it takes to maintain the upper hand. Above all, I could not allow it to seduce me into its mood, or the resulting sauce would be far more bitter than even the very earliest of midwinter dandelions.

"The first thing you must do," she told me, "is to soak the baccalà in water for twenty-four hours. One reason is to rid it of its excess salt. More important, however, is to rid it of its stridency, to submerge its need to dominate so that it can blend harmoniously with all the other ingredients in your dish. Strong flavors are needed when cooking baccalà. Garlic. Parsley. Onions. Place it in a pan with the subtle leaves of fennel, and the result will be a fish that strangles you with the force of its nature."

The next day, after the fish had been soaked and rid of its salt, the Signora began the preparation for what would be a delicious dish of baccalà simmered in the oven with potatoes, onions, and parsley, and called simply *Baccalà al Prezzemolo* (Baked Cod with Parsley).

She whirled around the kitchen for hours, laughing, complaining, exhorting, damning—all directed towards the baccalà. *"Accidenti a te!"* (Damn you!) she admonished the fish on more than one occasion. At the end of this performance, we sat down to dinner, the two of us accompanied by eight other culinary friends, all contributing to the exalted sense of a victorious battle with life, circumstances, and of course, the baccalà.

*Statue commemorating the drowning of Percy Bysshe Shelley—Piazza Shelley.*

Baccalà—dried cod—is one of the most popular fish dishes in this part of Tuscany. At one time, it was peasant food and cost nothing to buy. Today, however, depending on the type, baccalà can go for upwards of 28,000 lire per kilo, which works out to roughly $8 a pound.

Baccalà can be prepared in any number of ways—fried, stewed, with polenta, with tomato sauce, with anchovies, with olives and capers. When preparing any dish, it is important to soak the fish at least twelve hours in fresh water. In Tuscany, where water is plentiful, many soak it in the sink and let the water run over it. What works just as well and is far more practical is to change the water several times.

# BACCALÀ AL PREZZEMOLO
*Baked Cod with Parsley*

*This preparation is simple but takes full advantage of baccalà's ability to blend harmoniously with onions and herbs.*

    ½ cup extra-virgin olive oil (approximately)
    1 pound potatoes (preferably red), sliced into pieces ½ inch thick
    2 large onions, sliced
    2 pounds dried baccalà, soaked in fresh water for 12 to 24 hours,
        rinsed, and then cut into 2 x 3 inches.
    15 tablespoons finely minced fresh Italian parsley
    Salt and pepper to taste

1. Spread some oil over the bottom of a large roasting pan (preferably with a cover). Layer the ingredients in the following order: potatoes first, then onions, baccalà, parsley, salt, pepper, and finally, a drizzle of oil.

2. Repeat. Continue until all ingredients are used.

3. Cover (or seal with foil) and bake in a preheated 350 degree oven for 1 hour, or until the potatoes and fish are tender.

*Serves 6*

# FRITTELLE DI BACCALÀ
*Baccalà Fritters*

*Here is another magnificent recipe using baccalà, this time in the form of fritters. For this preparation, it is wise to soak the baccalà for at least two days, since it is necessary to reduce it to a form that can be grated with a fork.*

1 pound baccalà
10 tablespoons flour (approximately)
Milk
3 tablespoons olive oil
½ cup dry white wine
1 egg
½ teaspoon baking soda
Vegetable oil for frying
Salt to taste

1. Soak the baccalà for 48 hours in fresh water (change the water at least 6 times during this period). Give it a thorough final rinsing and dry with paper towels.

2. Using a fork, "grate" the baccalà into flakes and place in a large bowl.

3. Add the flour and enough milk to create a creamy consistency that is not too dense.

4. Add the olive oil, wine, egg, and baking soda; blend all ingredients thoroughly, cover with a cloth, and let sit for at least 3 hours.

5. Add vegetable oil to a large skillet until approximately one inch deep; heat the oil and fry the baccalà by dropping it by the tablespoonful into the hot oil.

6. When each fritter is golden brown on one side, turn with a spatula and fry to the same color on the other side.

7. Drain on paper towels, sprinkle with salt, and serve hot.

*Serves 4*

Fish, whether from salt water or fresh, is a very nutritious food, rich in both calcium and phosphorus. For this reason, as well as for the fact that they are bordered on the west by the Tyrrhenian Sea, Tuscans eat fish several times a week. At one time they ate it every Friday because it was forbidden by religious dogma to eat meat.

When selecting fish, it is important to choose the very freshest variety. Fresh fish is denoted first of all by smell—the lighter the scent of the sea, the fresher the fish. Heavy "fishy" odors indicate that the fish is somewhat past its prime. The flesh should be firm, the eye of the fish alert—not glazed over—and the gills pink and wet (not gray and dried out). The scales should be firmly attached and quite difficult to remove.

If the fish is to be kept for any length of time greater than twenty-four hours, it should be salted and frozen in aluminum foil. The purpose of the salt is to draw the water to the surface of the fish, rather than allowing it to remain in its interior where it would tend to soften the flesh.

## Methods of Cooking Fish

**Poached in Bouillon:** *The term "bouillon" can mean merely water that has been salted and herbed. To prevent the fish from dissolving into a mass of flakes, never boil the bouillon, but merely simmer, creating a kind of fermenting action over the surface of the fish. Before placing the fish in the bouillon, cook the liquid with its ingredients for at least 45 minutes, and then chill. Cooking times for fish poached in bouillon should average approximately 10 minutes per pound from the time the liquid begins to simmer. If the fish is to be eaten cold, it should be chilled in the bouillon so that it will be both more flavorful and more tender.*

*For especially large or firm fish, figure approximately 3½ quarts of water in which are placed 1 medium-size, thinly sliced onion; 1 medium carrot, sliced; 1 celery stalk, sliced; ½ cup red wine vinegar; and ¼ teaspoon each of salt and pepper. Boil the mixture over medium heat for at least 45 minutes.*

For finer fish, such as sole, trout, or salmon, substitute white wine for the vinegar.

**Sautéed in Butter:** Dip the fish first in milk, and then in a light flour. The butter should be very hot but never browned. Salt the fish during cooking, and turn once. Fish cooked in butter tends to be more tender than when fried in oil.

**Fried in Oil:** Only small fish or small pieces of fish should be fried whole. Those weighing more than ¼ pound should be either cut into smaller pieces or cooked some other way. For an especially crispy crust, first dip the fish in lightly salted milk, then bread it in flour. Fish is fried in oil rather than butter because oil can reach higher temperatures without burning. Vegetable oil is preferred over olive oil because it creates a lighter end product. Only a small quantity of fish should be fried at a time to avoid cooling the oil. Salt fried fish after it is removed from the skillet to avoid compromising the crispiness of the outer crust.

**In Parchment:** Parchment is used to seal in the flavors. This method works equally well with larger fish, such as snapper, and small groupings of sardines. Parchment paper itself may be used, but aluminum foil works just as well and is less trouble to assemble. Once the fish has been washed and dried, place it in the parchment with all the other ingredients. An especially good mix for almost any fish consists of a few tablespoons of chopped rosemary, olive oil, and lemon that have been first whisked together, and minced parsley. Equally good are mushrooms and various types of marinated vegetables.

Fish cooked in parchment should be sealed just before placing in the oven, cooked in high heat (400 degrees) for approximately 15 minutes per pound, and served in its casing.

**Cooked in the Oven:** This method works well for large, solid fish. If smaller, more tender fish are used, they should first be covered with either a layer of lard or of fatty meat, such as prosciutto or mortadella, in order to avoid drying.

Oven-cooked fish are generally placed on a bed of vegetables, including a blend of chopped onions, carrots, and celery, as well as a few tablespoons of chopped thyme and a leaf or two of bay. Pour olive oil and water over the top (white wine can also be added), and spoon the liquids over the fish at least once every 10 minutes during cooking.

Oven temperature should be at 350 degrees, and the fish cooked for approximately 15 to 20 minutes per pound.

   *Grilled:* Fish for grilling should be abundantly brushed with olive oil in order to keep the flesh tender. Heat should be high, and the fish salted and oiled a few times during the grilling period.

# GAMBERI ALL'AGLIO E PREZZEMOLO
*Shrimp with Garlic and Parsley*

*The western part of the province of Lucca borders entirely on the Tyrrhenian Sea, a geographical reality that orients its cuisine very much towards fish—especially crustaceans. And there are few crustaceans more beloved by Tuscans than gamberi, shrimp. This recipe, sublime in its simplicity, exhibits yet again the artistry of Tuscan cooking with its reliance on a minimum of ingredients to create a maximum of flavor.*

   2 pounds of very fresh shrimp (size is irrelevant so long as freshness
      is evident)
   3 or 4 tablespoons extra-virgin olive oil
   4 or 5 cloves of garlic, finely minced
   1 large bunch Italian parsley, finely chopped
   1 cup dry white wine

1. Clean the shrimp, removing the shells and veins; dry thoroughly.

2. Place the oil in a large skillet and, over high heat, sauté the garlic and parsley; do not allow the garlic to turn brown.

3. Add the shrimp, tossing together all the ingredients with a wooden spoon until the shrimp turn pink.

4. Immediately add the wine; toss for another minute or so until all ingredients are well blended.

5. Remove from pan and serve hot.

*Serves 6*

Fish soups are very popular along the Versilian Coast, and none more so than a simple fish broth served over a crisply toasted *bruschetta*. To make a good broth, you need a good fish. Which fish, however, is of very little importance. Broths can be made with snapper, carp, pike, mullet, whitefish—lean fish are better than fatty. The important thing is that it be fresh and that you use the whole fish, since flesh alone produces a very skimpy broth.

# BRODO DI PESCE ALLA VIAREGGINA
*Fish Broth Viareggio-style*

*The difference between this and fish broths from other areas lies in the use of tomatoes and chili pepper.*

> *For the broth*:
> ¼ cup olive oil
> 3 cloves of garlic, finely minced
> 2 fresh chili peppers (or dried)
> 3 quarts water
> 1 whole fish, approximately 2 pounds or more, eviscerated and scaled
> 12 ounces canned Italian tomatoes with liquid
> 6 tablespoons extra-virgin olive oil
> Salt and pepper to taste
> *For the bruschetta*:
> 6 thick slices good-quality bread (the more rustic, the better)
> 2 cloves garlic, sliced in half

1. For the broth, place ¼ cup olive oil in a skillet over medium heat and fry the garlic and chili until the garlic just starts to turn brown around the edges; remove from heat.

2. Fill a large soup pot with 3 quarts of water; add the garlic and chili blend and the fish, cover, and bring to boil over high heat.

3. Add the tomatoes and cook, covered, for 1½ hours; stir once or twice during cooking.

4. Pour the soup through a fine-mesh sieve, pressing down on the fish so that the bones crackle and as much of the juice as possible gets through.

5. Pass the soup through yet another sieve to remove any trace of sol-ids. Add the salt and pepper.

6. Now make the bruschetta. Rub both sides of the bread with garlic, and toast both sides in the oven.

7. Place a slice of bread in each bowl, and pour the soup over it.

8. As a finishing touch, drizzle one tablespoon oil in each bowl, and serve hot.

*Serves 6*

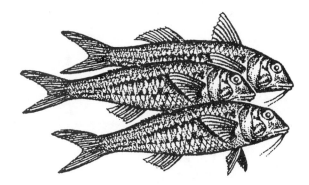

# FARRO

*Farro,* or spelt, is a cereal grain with a long and colorful history that has been traced back to the beginnings of civilization. It was originally cultivated by the shepherds and nomads of Syria and Egypt, and was later discovered in the tombs of the ancient pyramids. Homer paid tribute to *farro* in many of his odes, and the Romans used it almost to the exclusion of any other grain. Mixed with flour, it became the national dish of the Roman Republic, *pula,* and is referred to in many of the ancient Roman texts. When Rome entered its "Imperial" age, *farro* became important in religious ceremonies where it was used mainly as the basis for offerings to the gods on the first of the year.

Today *farro* is cultivated mainly in the forests of the Garfagnana in northern Tuscany. Highly resistant to disease, adaptable to almost any terrain, and extremely high in nutrients, this early food source has recently become very trendy among health-conscious culinarians; in the United States in fact, it is generally sold only in health-food stores where it is known as spelt. For those unable to find spelt, barley makes a very good substitute.

# FARRO CON IL PESCE
*Spelt with Seafood*

*This recipe combines the sturdiness of farro with the delicate texture of shrimp and tiny squids to produce a dish that is served in many of the best restaurants in Viareggio.*

12 ounces spelt
3 tablespoons extra-virgin olive oil
2 cloves garlic, minced
½ chili pepper, minced
8 ounces shrimp, peeled and deveined
12 ounces baby squid, cleaned and chopped into small pieces
Pinch of salt and pepper
1 cup dry white wine
3 leaves fresh basil
4 fresh plum tomatoes, diced
4 tablespoons finely chopped parsley
1 cup vegetable broth (bouillon cubes or canned)

1. Rinse the spelt well; soak in cold water for 6 to 8 hours or overnight.

2. Place the olive oil in a large, heavy skillet; sauté the garlic and chili over medium heat until the garlic takes on a golden color.

3. Add the shrimp squid, salt, and pepper.

4. Add the wine and continue cooking until all ingredients are done, approximately 3 minutes.

5. Add the basil and tomatoes, and cook for 5 minutes longer.

6. Drain the spelt; add to the fish and tomato mixture. Add the parsley and vegetable broth; cover and cook for 30 minutes or until the spelt is tender.

7. Preheat the oven to 350 degrees. Place the fish and spelt mixture in a buttered baking dish and bake in the oven uncovered, for 40 minutes or until the spelt is fully cooked and the top is gratinée.

8. Serve hot.

*Serves 4*

Of all the places to buy fish along the Versilian Coast (and there are many), *Pescheria La Sirena* is probably the most popular. Filled to the rafters with fish of every color and size, *La Sirena's* produce comes from as far away as Indonesia, and as close as 20 miles out on the Mediterranean. The owner, Aldo Barcaroli, is an extraordinary cook who is known throughout the province for his original fish recipes.

## RAVIOLI DI PESCE
*Fish Ravioli*

*The recipe for* Ravioli di Pesce *(Fish Ravioli) is one that Barcaroli says he uses "whenever I have a houseful of company and want to impress them with the exquisite flavors that, to us, are second nature."*

*The filling*:
　　1 pound fresh cod (or any other type of meaty white fish)
　　½ pound medium shrimp, cleaned and deveined
　　3 tablespoons extra-virgin olive oil
　　Pinch of grated nutmeg
　　Salt and pepper to taste
　　½ dry white wine
*The dough*:
　　4 cups unbleached white flour, sifted
　　4 eggs, lightly beaten
　　½ teaspoon salt
*The sauce*:
　　4 tablespoons unsalted butter
　　½ pound small shrimp, cleaned and deveined
　　1 pound filet of sole
　　2 fresh basil leaves
　　2 tablespoons cognac
　　½ cup heavy cream

1.  First make the filling: place the cod in a heavy skillet and cover with water; bring the water to a boil and boil the fish for 10 minutes; remove

the cod from the water and flake with a fork until you have a plateful of flaked cod; reserve the water.

2. Place the shrimp in the water from the cod; bring to a boil and cook for 5 minutes.

3. Heat the oil in a heavy skillet; add the fish along with the nutmeg, wine, and salt and pepper; cook for 5 minutes stirring constantly with a wooden spoon; cool to room temperature.

4. Now make the dough: place the flour in a large bowl; add the beaten eggs and stir with a fork until the ingredients are well blended.

5. With floured hands, work the dough for 5–7 minutes or until you have a ball (if the dough is too watery, add more flour a tablespoon at a time; if the dough is too dense, add a tablespoon or two of water); cover the ball of dough and let rest for 15 minutes.

6. Using a floured rolling pin, roll the dough into a thin sheet; cut the dough into individual ravioli rounds using the mouth of a water glass that is approximately 3 inches in diameter.

7. When all the dough has been cut into rounds, roll the remainder into a ball, spread with a floured rolling pin and resume cutting; continue until all the dough has been used.

8. Fill each round with a teaspoon of filling; to seal, fold the ravioli over itself so that you have a half-circle shape; seal the ends with the tynes of a fork.

9. To make the sauce: heat the butter in a heavy skillet; add the sole and cook for 5 minutes or until it can be flaked with a fork; add the shrimp and cook for another 2–3 minutes.

10. Add the basil and cognac and cook, stirring constantly, for five minutes or until the fish is well coated with the sauce; stir in the heavy cream and blend thoroughly with the rest of the ingredients (do not allow to boil).

11. Cook the ravioli in a large pot of salted boiling water for 15–20 minutes; drain and place in a large bowl; cover with the sauce and serve hot.

*Serves 6*

# TONNO BRIAO
## Drunken Tuna

*According to the Signora, fish recipes in this part of Tuscany are divided into two distinct categories: those that are more elegant, and those that are more rustic, like this one. In local slang,* briao *(bree-OW) means drunk. And indeed, Tonno Briao does a good job of inebriating the slices of fresh tuna by immersing them in* vino giovane—*the youngest of red wines, the first pressing that, taken indiscriminately, goes immediately to the head.*

> 4 tablespoons extra-virgin olive oil
> 4 tuna steaks (approximately ¼ pound each)
> Salt and pepper to taste
> 2 tablespoons white flour
> 1 clove garlic, minced
> 1 medium onion, minced
> 3 tablespoons finely chopped parsley
> 1 cup new red wine

1. Over a medium flame heat the oil in a heavy skillet large enough to accommodate the 4 steaks in one layer.

2. Salt and pepper both sides of the steaks; dredge them in the flour, shaking off the excess.

3. Sauté the garlic and onion until both are a golden color; add the parsley.

4. Place the steaks in the skillet side by side; cook over medium heat until browned on the outside (the insides should be "medium" at this point). Turn with a spatula and cook until browned on the other side.

5. Pour the red wine over the steaks, cover, and cook for 20 minutes or until the sauce is reduced by half.

6. Serve hot, spooning the sauce over the steaks.

*Serves 4*

# PESCE LESSO CON SALSA DI PREZZEMOLO
*Poached Fish with Parsley Sauce*

*Tuscans consume a large quantity of fish poached in vinegar. Traditionally, such fish is accompanied by a green sauce made primarily from parsley and olives, and served with boiled potatoes and, perhaps, a green vegetable such as zucchini sautéed with a pinch of thyme.*

*The fish:*
4 fish steaks (halibut, swordfish, red snapper, sea bass, or monk-fish)
1 medium carrot, sliced lengthwise
1 celery stalk, cut in 3-inch lengths
1 medium onion, quartered
2 tablespoons finely chopped fresh parsley
4 tablespoons good-quality red wine vinegar
Extra-virgin olive oil for brushing
3 quarts water for poaching

*The sauce:*
4 tablespoons finely minced fresh parsley
5 tablespoons extra-virgin olive oil
1 clove garlic, finely minced (optional for those who prefer the taste of the fish to remain unobscured)
½ teaspoon salt

1. Poach the fish in a bouillon consisting of the carrot, celery stalk, onion, chopped parsley, and vinegar (see directions for poaching, page 193).

2. Leave the fish in the bouillon until it has come to room temperature.

3. Meanwhile make the sauce by mixing the minced parsley with 4 tablespoons of the oil, the salt, and garlic until it forms a fine paste.

4. Remove the fish from the bouillon and place on serving platter; brush with the remaining tablespoon of oil.

5. Brush it with the sauce and serve at room temperature.

*Serves 4*

# CACCIUCCO ALLA VIAREGGINA
*Cacciucco, Viareggio-style*

*Cacciucco, the Italian version of bouillabaisse, holds all the flavor of the Medi-
terranean in one deep bowl. This type of* cacciucco *(there are as many preparations for this popular soup as there are fish in the local waters) is somewhat less
spicy than, for example, the one made in Livorno to the south. "Alla Viareggina"
refers not only to the style itself, but also to the fact that it is the most popular type
served both in the homes and restaurants of Viareggio. Important here is to assemble as wide a variety of fish as possible (at least a third should be crustaceans
and mollusks). A good distribution would be 1 pound large, solid fish; 1 pound
tender, white fish; and 1 pound clams, shrimp, and scallops.*

> 3 tablespoons extra-virgin olive oil
> 1 medium onion, minced
> 1 clove garlic, minced
> 1 small carrot, chopped fine
> 1 celery stalk, chopped
> 2 cups canned Italian tomatoes, chopped and with liquid
> ½ teaspoon black pepper
> ½ teaspoon salt
> ¼ teaspoon crushed red chili
> 1 cup dry white wine
> 1 pound large fish, cleaned and cut into medium-size chunks
> 1 pound tender white fish, cleaned and cut into medium-size
>   chunks
> 1 pound mixture of clams, shrimp, and scallops
> 4 slices thick, crusty bread
> 2 cloves garlic, sliced in half

1. Heat the olive oil in a medium-size skillet; add the onion, garlic,
carrot, and celery and sauté until golden brown.

2. Add the tomatoes, black pepper, salt, and chili; continue cooking.
Mix with a wooden spoon until all ingredients are well blended and the
tomatoes have come to a boil.

3. Add white wine, cover, and cook over medium heat for 10 minutes.

4. Transfer the wine and tomato mixture to a large soup pot or dutch
oven; add the chunks of large, solid fish. Cover and cook for 10 minutes.

5. Add the white, tender fish; cook for 10 minutes more, adding water if necessary to maintain the souplike consistency of the liquid.

6. Meanwhile, clean the clams by scrubbing them under running water. Steam open the clams by placing them in boiling water until the shells separate.

7. Clean and devein the shrimp; wash the scallops.

8. Add the clams (including the shells), shrimp, and scallops to the soup; cook for 5 minutes, stirring frequently to blend all ingredients.

9. Rub the bread slices with the garlic; toast the bread on both sides.

10. Place one slice of bread in each bowl; top with soup, making sure that each plate receives a portion of each kind of fish.

11. Serve hot with plenty of red wine.

*Serves 4*

*A fishing boat returning to Viareggio.*

# MUSCOLI ALLA MARINARA
*Mussels in Tomato Sauce*

*Viargeggio is known for its blue mussels, which are smaller in size than those in the United States and slightly more tender if fished from the waters between September and April. In the absence of this particular type, however, any mussel will do as long as it is very fresh.*

    3 pounds mussels, cleaned and scrubbed
    1 cup dry white wine
    1 small carrot, chopped
    1 medium onion, minced
    3 tablespoons finely chopped fresh parsley
    1 bay leaf
    1 clove garlic
    Salt and pepper
    2 tablespoons salted butter
    4 slices thick, crusty bread (peasant bread works well)

1. Put the mussels in a large skillet with the remaining ingredients except the bread; cover and let cook over medium heat until all the mussels open. Remove pan from heat.

2. Toast the bread slices on both sides; place each slice in an individual dish.

3. Remove half the mussels from their shells; divide them into four portions and place one portion in each of the four dishes on top of the slices of bread.

4. Divide the mussels still in shells also into four portions; place these on each of the dishes around the bread.

5. Strain the sauce through a sieve and spoon over all the mussels and bread.

6. Serve hot with plenty of red wine.

*Serves 4*

# COZZE ALLA PANNA
*Clams in Heavy Cream*

*When purchasing clams, according to Signora Angeli, you should always look for the dirtiest; the clean ones may have already lost the water from inside the shells in the cleaning process, and, therefore, have no "sauce" to offer. They must be washed well many times, but never left immersed in water, or the clam will exchange its water for your water. To open clams, place them in a pot over medium heat with a minimum of liquid—they can even be placed in a pan with no liquid; as soon as they open, they're cooked. This recipe makes use of heavy cream, which is a very popular ingredient along the Versilian Coast.*

> 3 pounds clams (any kind)
> 1 large onion, chopped
> 3 tablespoons finely chopped fresh parsley
> Salt and pepper to taste
> 1 cup dry white wine
> 2 eggs, lightly beaten
> ½ cup heavy cream

1. Wash the clams in several changes of water; do not submerge them.

2. In a large skillet, place the onion, parsley, salt, pepper, and wine; add the clams on top of this layer.

3. Place over high heat for 10 seconds or so, then lower the heat to medium and continue cooking until the clams open.

4. Remove the clams from the shells and set aside; keep warm.

5. Pass the cooked vegetables through a sieve into a bowl; add the eggs and heavy cream and blend thoroughly.

6. Heat the cream and vegetable mixture to just before boiling; do not allow it to boil.

7. Pour the mixture over the clams and place on a serving platter.

8. Decorate the platter with an empty clam shell or two, and serve hot.

*Serves 4*

# PESCE SPADA IN UMIDO AL VINO
*Swordfish Stewed in Wine*

*Swordfish is a delicacy in Versilia, if only because of its size, which means it can only be found in much deeper waters than the local fishermen generally navigate. However, the Signora says, when you go to the market and see those large pieces of firm flesh, only a fesso (a fool) would pass them up. This recipe relies on that indispensable aspect of Tuscan cooking—the soffrito (see page 16) to give this meatlike fish its succulent flavor.*

3 tablespoons extra-virgin olive oil
4 swordfish steaks, cleaned and dried
1 small minced onion
1 clove minced garlic
3 tablespoons chopped parsley
Salt and pepper to taste
½ cup dry red wine
12 ounces fresh green peas, shelled (or frozen)
¼ cup canned Italian tomatoes, chopped, with liquid

1. Heat the oil in a skillet large enough to hold the fish in one layer; sauté the onion, garlic, and parsley over medium heat until the edges of the onion are just turning brown.

2. Add the fish and brown on both sides; add the salt and pepper.

3. Pour the wine over the fish and allow to evaporate.

4. Add the tomatoes and liquid, and an additional tablespoon or two of water.

5. Add the peas, stirring into the tomato sauce; cook for several minutes or until the peas are tender.

6. Cover and cook over low heat for another 10 minutes.

7. Serve hot.

*Serves 4*

# SALMONE ALL'OLIO E LIMONE
*Salmon with Oil and Lemon*

*Like swordfish, salmon is also a very large fish sold in the form of steaks. It has a more refined flavor than many of its large-fish comrades, however, and a beautiful red color that only becomes more brilliant as it cooks. Generally, salmon tastes best when poached or grilled.*

> 4 salmon steaks, cleaned and dried
> 3 quarts water for poaching (see page 193)
> 3 tablespoons extra-virgin olive oil
> Juice of 2 lemons
> 3 tablespoons finely chopped fresh parsley
> Salt to taste

1. Poach the salmon in the bouillon (make sure to substitute white wine for the vinegar) for 20 minutes.

2. Cool the salmon in the poaching liquid, drain and place on a serving platter.

3. Whisk together the oil and lemon; pour over the cooled fish.

4. Just before serving, sprinkle the parsley over the fish and add salt.

*Serves 4*

# SOGLIOLE FRITTE
*Fried Fillets of Sole*

*Fish can be prepared in many ways, but the preparation Signora Angeli prefers above all others is fried in oil—a choice apparently shared by many people in Viareggio, where restaurant menus feature fried fish in dozens of varieties. This recipe works best with small fillets of sole; larger ones, the Signora says, are better made in* umido, *which means stewed in a sauce.*

    4 small fillets of sole
    Milk for soaking
    Flour for breading
    Vegetable oil for frying
    Salt to taste
    2 tablespoons chopped fresh parsley
    2 lemons, sliced in half

1.  Clean the sole and remove the dark outer skin.

2.  Soak the fillets in milk for approximately 10 minutes. Drain.

3.  Coat the fillets with flour, shaking off any excess.

4.  Heat the oil over medium-high heat; fry the fillets, 2 at a time, until both sides are lightly browned.

5.  Drain on paper towels; sprinkle both sides with salt. Place on a platter sprinkled with the parsley and accompanied by the wedges of lemon.

6.  Serve immediately while still hot.

*Serves 4*

Castruccio Castracani degli Antelminelli was Lucca's most prominent military leader during the thirteenth and fourteenth centuries. At one time, his empire consisted of Pistoia, Pisa, Altopascio, and the environs of Florence. He died in fact, while attempting to add Florence to his empire. The cause of death was malaria which, the Signora says, he undoubtedly contracted in the swamps of the Maremma. In the centuries since his death, his fame has been surpassed only by that of his biographer: Niccoló Machiavelli.

The following recipe for a delicious dish of smoked herring served cold is an ancient one, adopted in modern times by both home-based cooks and restauranteurs throughout the Lucchesía. Originated in the Buca di Sant'Antonio, which is the oldest restaurant in Lucca (founded in 1782), it was dedicated to Castracani by the restaurant's original owner.

# ARINGHE AFFUMICATE
# ALLA CASTRUCCIO
*Smoked Herring, Castruccio-style*

6 smoked herrings
5 cups of milk
½ cup heavy cream
Juice of 2 lemons
3 hard-cooked eggs
8 ounces beets, boiled in salted water until tender and chopped
　　into tiny chunks

1. Starting at least 6 hours prior to serving, soak the herrings in the milk (in order to remove the salt).

2. Wash the herrings under running water, dry them well, and place them side by side in a serving dish.

3. Whisk the cream with the lemon juice until both ingredients have blended together into a creamy consistency.

4. Spread the cream mixture over the herrings.

5. Separate the yolks of the eggs from the white; slice the yolks into thin strips. Do the same with the whites.

6. Place the beets, egg yolks, and egg whites over the herring so that they form three different color stripes across the surface of the serving dish.

7. Refrigerate for at least one hour before serving.

8. Serve cold with either dry white wine or cold vodka.

*Serves 6*

# MERLUZZO ALLE ACCIUGHE
*Fresh Codfish with Anchovies*

*In addition to the infinite number of preparations for the ubiquitous* baccalà, *or dried codfish, of which Tuscans are so fond, there is also great variety in recipes utilizing* merluzzo, *fresh codfish. Some of these recipes call for steaks, which are generally cut from codfish larger than 7 or 8 pounds; others indicate fillets. This recipe combines fresh codfish steaks with fresh anchovies to create a dish that is both delicate and flavorful, and very popular along the Versilian coast.*

 8 tablespoons extra-virgin olive oil
 4 fresh codfish steaks
 Salt and pepper to taste
 1 cup dry unflavored breadcrumbs
 2 ounces fresh anchovies, cleaned, boned, and cut into very small
     pieces (or canned, although the resulting flavor will be some-
     what different)
 Juice of 1 lemon

1. Using 2 tablespoons of the oil, brush both sides of the codfish steaks, salt and pepper them, and coat with breadcrumbs; reserve 3 tablespoons of the breadcrumbs.

2. Place the steaks in an ovenproof dish greased with 2 tablespoons of the oil.

3. Sauté the anchovies in 2 tablespoons of the oil over medium heat for 3 to 5 minutes or until they form a saucelike consistency; remove from pan and let sit until cool.

4. Spread the cooled anchovy sauce over the codfish and sprinkle with the reserved breadcrumbs.

5. Place the baking dish in a preheated 350 degree oven for 20 minutes or until a golden crust forms over the steaks.

6. Drizzle the remaining 2 tablespoons of oil over the steaks and cook for 5 minutes longer.

7. Just before serving, pour the lemon juice over the steaks, making sure to distribute it evenly. Serve hot.

*Serves 4*

# SARDINE ALL'ACETO
*Pickled Sardines*

*In Tuscany, sardines are both well loved and cost-effective, their popularity a result of the ease with which they lend themselves to a great number of preparations. In planning a sardine recipe, calculate approximately 6 per person. To clean them, merely slice them open lengthwise and lift out the spine.*

> 5 tablespoons extra-virgin olive oil
> 3 tablespoons chopped parsley
> 1 clove minced garlic
> 2¼ pound of sardines (approximately 24), cleaned and deboned
> Salt and pepper to taste
> 1 tablespoon good-quality red wine vinegar

1. Heat the oil in a pan large enough to hold all the sardines; mix together the parsley and garlic and sauté in the oil for one minute;

2. Add the sardines, salt, and pepper; cook for 4 minutes on each side.

3. Splash with the vinegar and a tablespoon or two of water.

4. Cook for 8 minutes more.

5. Serve hot as a main course, or cold as an appetizer.

*Serves 4*

# TROTELLE AL BURRO E SALVIA
*Small Trouts in Butter and Sage*

*One morning as I stopped by Signora Angeli's house for some basil, which she grows in a pot on her terrace, she was cleaning several small trout she had just bought in the large market claiming Viareggio's center. In Tuscany today, small trout are almost all farm-bred; the particular vendor who sold them to Signora Angeli claims to sell hundreds of these delicacies every day. "Stay for lunch," the Signora commanded. Which I did with great pleasure as she prepared this trout quickly and simply with just a little butter and a few leaves of the sage that grows alongside the basil.*

    4 small trout, cleaned and dried
    2 cups milk
    Flour
    4 tablespoons unsalted butter
    4 leaves fresh sage (or dried whole leaves)
    Salt and pepper to taste

1. Soak the trouts in the milk for 30 minutes.

2. Dredge them in the flour.

3. Heat the butter in a skillet large enough to hold the trout in one layer; add the sage.

4. Sauté the trout in the butter over medium heat for 5 minutes per side.

5. Place them on a serving platter; add salt and pepper. Serve hot.

*Serves 4*

*Signora Minnie Gragnani*

# Chapter Seven

# A LUST FOR THE WILD

## GAME, PORK, AND POULTRY

*T*he next time you find yourself in Torre del Lago Puccini or any other town in northern Tuscany, try this exercise: Look over your head, at the pinkish yellow sky and the wavering tops of trees. Stand there for a few minutes, locking your eyes on the natural beauty all around you. Let yourself be pulled by the sense of having come from far away and suddenly being home. Allow yourself to notice that, in your absence, something has vanished, that there's something missing—a movement, maybe, that has been stilled; a vision, perhaps, that's been erased, a sound, hushed. What is it?

Ask this of yourself as you search the air around your head: "What have I always counted as an integral part of my existence that is no longer here?" Close your eyes and wait for the answer, and suddenly, it will come. Flight . . . song . . . birds . . . birds! Birds. The sky is clear and wide and uninterruptedly blue, and nowhere can you see the infinite number of wings that once flew across the heavens.

Suddenly—and it *is* sudden, just as sudden as the proliferation of satellite dishes across the valleys—there is no song, no trills and quivers and *cu-cu-cu-ruuus* tossed across the winds, no flight, no nests left behind in the crooks of branches, no rustling among the leaves.

There are no *petetti rossi* (robin red breasts), no *porporati* (cardinals), no *rondini* (swallows), no *perpolli* (finches). All that's left is an endless series of charts, posted in hunting offices all over Italy and showing in full color and brilliant design, the pictures of birds that have been brought to near or total extinction by Italy's lust for hunting.

*"Sono quelli,"* the head of Torre del Lago Puccini's *Officio di Caccia*—Hunting Office—told me with a gracious smile. That's them over there. What I see when I glance in the direction of his pointing finger are a wall full of posters depicting endangered birds.

Signora Gragnani walks with me through the tree-lined streets of Torre del Lago Puccini, one of the loveliest towns in all of Versilia. Built along the western shore of Lago di Massaciuccoli, the town is named after its most famous resident, Giacomo Antonio Domenico Michele Secondo Maria Puccini, who—in 1894—married Elvira Gemignani and moved to a pink stucco villa on its lakefront. There he composed two of his most famous operas: *La Fanciulla del West,* and the unfinished *Turandot.* There too, he died—in November 1924, after being unsuccessfully treated in a Brussels clinic for throat cancer. In 1930, after the death of his wife, the villa was turned into a museum. His remains are interred on the grounds.

Today, one has only to look at the street signs to understand how thoroughly the Great Maestro's aura still pervades Torre del Lago Puccini: there's Via Butterfly, Via Tosca, Via Boheme, Via Manon. In summers, the town hosts an opera season, conducted in a huge open-air theater on the lakefront opposite the Villa Puccini. Music lovers come from all over the world and for weeks, the only music to be heard anywhere—restaurant, dry cleaners, or fruit store—is that written by the Great Maestro.

Torre del Lago's most ingenious tourist attraction however, continues to be its residents, most of whom either remember *"Sor Giacomo"* themselves, or have parents who do. Signora Minnie Gragnani belongs to both groups. Her name in fact—Minnie—was given to her by Puccini himself just after he'd completed *La Fanciulla del West,* whose main character is a cowgirl named Minnie. *"E nata Minnie,"* the great Maestro telegraphed the newborn's father, Arnoldo, who, at the time, was serving in the military. Minnie is born.

Arnoldo Gragnani was one of Puccini's closest friends; the two were united by both their passion for hunting, and their love of great music. Since Puccini's house was directly across the street from Gragnani's, the men spent much of their leisure time together. The Signora recalls one particular occasion, when Puccini and her father were out walking in the fields behind their two homes ("at one time, these were *all* fields," the Signora says, gesturing around her head in a 360-degree arc).

"It was a beautifully moonlit night, she remembers, "and the two of them had already been out there quite some time, singing parts of songs and throwing around poetic phrases the way they sometimes did.

"At one point my father pointed to the sky and uttered a particularly lyrical line, using the flowery dialect of that period. *'E lucean le stelle,"* he orated, *'E stridea l'uscio dell'orto.'* The stars are shining, and the doorway to the garden creaks.

"Whereupon Puccini grabbed Pappa's arm and propelled him into the study of his house. 'For Tosca!' he said, 'I will use that line in Tosca!' And so he did—right at the end, during the big death scene."

Many of the Signora's anecdotes pre-date her birth and, as such, have been entrusted to her care by other members of her family. One of these ensued during The Great War, when her father was called up for the military. "Pappa, naturally, did not want to go to the front," she says, "but it was more than that: he really wanted to be in the band. So he wrote a letter to his friend Puccini, who, by then, was already quite well known, and Puccini wrote a letter to the minister of War. Three weeks later, my father's orders were changed and he was assigned to the military band."

The Signora is a frail little woman who chain smokes with the fury of a female Toscanini. She recounts these stories while bustling around her living room in search of a cigarette, which she is ultimately unable to find. "Let's go to the *bar,"* she says nervously. "I cannot exist knowing I am completely out."

So we walk through the Signora's garden and make our way next door, to the *Bar Maria,* whose walls are covered with photos of Puccini hung alongside newspaper clippings trumpeting a recent lotto winner who bought her ticket here. In Puccini's time, the bar was a private home; today, it is a gathering spot for the town's residents, who come here for morning coffee and the latest word on the political intrigue of the day. Signora Gragnani introduces me to the proprietor, Signora Anna Muzzetti, who promptly begins telling me her *own* Puccini stories.

Signora Muzzetti's stories come by way of another Puccini intimate. "My mother-in-law, Carmelinda, told me how he would always come bursting through the door precisely at mealtimes, and go directly into the kitchen—that room over there." She points to a room off to the side. "And Carmelinda would stand there as he lifted all the covers off the pots. *'Si,'* he would say if all was good, or *'No, un puo piu sale'* [a little more salt]."

The discussion winds its way toward the topic of Puccini, the hunter. "It was his third greatest passion," says Signora Gragnani. "First, of course, came Music, although that often slipped to number two or, sometimes, even three, behind Women, and Hunting. The Maestro was a superb hunter. He and my father would go out once, sometimes twice a week. They'd go after ducks, geese, squirrels—whatever was in season. Then they'd bring them back and my mother would cook them up.

"Sometimes however, they'd catch nothing." The Signora shows me a photograph of Puccini given to her father with the following dedication—*"Al mi collego padillare."* *Padillare,* she says, is taken from the noun *"padella"*—skillet—and means when a hunter goes out and brings nothing back to put in the pan. "Of course, those were the days when hunters killed for food," she says. "It was *also* a sport, but you *ate* your kill then. Not like they do now—pa-pa-pa-pa-pah—and then the hunters walk away.

"Hunting today has gotten out of hand," she says. "A good example is the fact that hunters are supposed to stay 300 ft away from people's houses. But sometimes, especially if you live nearer the woods, you hear a *cannonata* [a repetitive volley] and you rush out behind your house only to find a group of men with their rifles pointed at the sky directly above your head. And it's not only the danger. In Italy, we have almost no animals left."

She gestures outside, in the direction of the large forested areas that surround the lake on its northern and southern fronts. *"Accidenti loro, tutti quanti!"* she says, slapping the air with the back of her hand. Damn them, all of them!

Her outburst reaches a man and a woman sitting at a table in the front of the bar having coffee. They shake their heads in agreement. At one time, hunting was an activity integral to survival. No longer.

The anti-hunting lobby is now as large as the one in support of the activity. Made up of three different organizations—LAC (Lega Anti Caccia [hunting]), WWF (World Wildlife Fund), and LIPU (*Lega Italiana Protezione Uccelli* [birds]), the movement, now a potent political force, is referred to throughout Italy as simply *Il Verdi*—the Greens. For many, however, its power comes too late.

"As recently as ten years ago," the Signora says, "you could open your window in the morning, and your ears would be filled with a symphony of birds, all in competition as if auditioning for The Great Maestro himself. Now there is nothing, unless you count old Ugo who sings the arias of *Tosca* as he sweeps away the refuse."

*La Caccia* (hunting season) traditionally starts on a Sunday, usually in September. One and a half million men take part. Of all the nations in the world, Italy has the second highest density of hunters—approximately five for every square kilometer. Only Malta has more. From the cleaning of the rifle, to the decision over which game to track, to the arranging with mothers and wives for a late-morning delivery of undressed catch, there is little to match the fervor with which hunters treat the sixteen or so weeks allowed by law.

Of paramount importance is having the proper license, which, in many cases, is very difficult, and costly, to obtain. The average rate is $1000, although it can drop to as little as $100 for the disabled. Italian law requires hunters both to prove their shooting expertise and to identify the various species populating local forests. Even with all of that, there is often a stiff wait. Nevertheless, the Signora says, when it comes to the opening day of *la caccia,* the forests are thick with "the heavy breath of men wearing leather bandoliers slung over their fat torsos."

"Last year, a friend of mine spent millions of lire to fence in his property. His fear was of men with short sights mistaking his dogs for *faggiani* [pheasants]. But do you think that stopped them? *Madre di Dio,* they trampled the fence until it resembled the flat dough one used in making *focaccia.* If it wasn't for my friend's wife who heard the hunters coming and called back the dogs, they most likely would have surfaced on a hunter's dinner table, dressed with berries in their skins the way you do with wild boar."

The Signora saves her wrath for the hunters of birds and pheasants. Wild boar is quite another story. "Nobody is upset when a hunter shoots a boar. One need only stand in a garden at sunset to feel the fear of those monstrous wild pigs with their long tusks and bristly snouts. Not only do they rob us of those wonderful truffles that grow at the base of our trees, but they have no manners. They charge into villages and trample our vegetables whenever a whiff of something becomes lodged in their nostrils; something aromatic enough to throw them completely off the course of their forest paths and into your tomatoes."

No sooner has she uttered the last word of her sentence than I catch a whiff of something emanating from the Signora's kitchen. "Lunch is ready," she says, noticing my look of hungry appreciation. And in we go, to a delicious meal of *Pappardelle al Cinghiale,* a wonderful combination of homemade noodles and wild boar cooked in young red wine.

## CINGHIALE

A boar is a wild pig—or piglet, if it is younger than six months. In northern Tuscany, wild boar is a delicacy, one, however, that is sold in most large markets and specialty butcher shops, where it hangs alongside rabbit and pheasant and deer with its coarse black hair and menacing tusks. Young boar meat is tender and pink, although a bit bland. Mature boars are less tender but succulent in both color and taste. Preparations vary; boar meat can be stewed *(in umido)*, roasted *(arrosto)*, grilled *(a la griglia)*, or pan fried in a ragout *(salmi)*.

# CINGHIALE AL SUGO
## Wild Boar with Tomato Sauce

*This preparation calls for pan frying the boar in a complex blend of marsala and tomatoes to crate a thick, zesty sauce.*

2 pounds lean wild boar loin (or pork loin★)
2 cups water
1 cup red wine vinegar
Salt and pepper to taste
1 bay leaf
3 tablespoons finely chopped fresh parsley
1 cup extra-virgin olive oil
2-ounce slab of pancetta (or bacon), diced
1 medium onion, diced
1 cup marsala
1 tablespoon tomato paste
½ cup meat broth

1. Soak the boar for no less than 8 and no more than 24 hours in a marinade made of 1 cup of water, the vinegar, salt, pepper, bay leaf, and parsley.

2. Heat the olive oil in a large skillet; add the pancetta and onion and sauté until the onion is lightly browned.

3. Remove the boar from the marinade and add to the skillet; brown on all sides.

4. Add the marsala and cook over high heat until the liquid has evaporated.

5. Dilute the tomato paste in 1 cup water; add to the meat, lower the heat, and cook, covered, for 1½ hours or until the center of the meat is slightly pink. Add the meat broth if necessary to maintain a thick, saucelike consistency.

6. Serve hot.

*Serves 4*

*★If using pork, marinate for no more than 6 to 8 hours.*

# CINGHIALE IN UMIDO
## *Boar Stewed in Wine and Herbs*

*One of Signora Gragnani's favorite recipes for cooking wild boar involves marinating the meat for 24 to 48 hours in a blend of red wine and juniper berries before placing it in the oven to roast to a moist, tender succulence. In lieu of boar, she says, one can also use pork, in which case you reduce the marinating time to 8 to 12 hours, but no longer.*

*The marinade:*
>2 cups dry red wine or enough to cover the meat
>10 juniper berries, crushed
>1 bay leaf
>2 cloves garlic, minced
>2 tablespoons finely chopped fresh parsley
>2 tablespoons finely chopped fresh rosemary

*The boar:*
>2 pounds boar loin (or pork loin)
>6 tablespoons extra-virgin olive oil
>2 small onions, minced
>1 tablespoon finely chopped fresh rosemary
>1 bay leaf
>1 red chili, minced (or ½ teaspoon crushed red chili)
>8 ounces canned Italian tomatoes with liquid

1. Combine all the ingredients for the marinade. Pour over meat and let sit for 24 to 48 hours, turning four or five times to make sure that the flavor will be absorbed.

2. Remove the meat from the marinade; discard all but 5 tablespoons of the liquid.

3. Heat 3 tablespoons oil in a large ovenproof pot over high heat; brown the meat on all sides.

4. Place the remaining oil in a separate skillet; sauté the onions until lightly browned.

5. Add the onions to the meat; add the remaining ingredients, including the reserved marinade. Blend well.

6. Cover or seal with foil; bake in a preheated 350 degree oven for 1½ to 2 hours or until the meat is pinkish-white in the center.

*Serves 6*

*Puccini memorabilia in the Signora's sitting room.*

# PAPPARDELLE AL CINGHIALE
*Pappardelle with Boar Sauce*

Pappardelle *are wide strips of pasta generally made by hand and served fresh. Sauces are, by necessity, of the heavier, more flavorful variety since the size of the pasta requires a topping that can "sit" on it rather than be absorbed by it. Here this wonderful cut of pasta is combined with a sauce made of boar and red wine. Pork may be substituted for the boar.*

*The pasta:*
- 3 cups white flour
- 3 eggs, lightly beaten
- 1 tablespoon extra-virgin olive oil
- ½ cup water
- ⅛ teaspoon salt

*The sauce:*
- 1 clove garlic
- 1 tablespoon fresh rosemary, chopped (or ¼ teaspoon dried)
- 1 dried chili pepper
- 2 whole cloves
- 6 tablespoons extra-virgin olive oil
- 2 ounces boar loin (or pork loin), chopped finely
- Salt and pepper to taste
- ½ cup dry red wine
- 4 tablespoons tomato paste
- 2 cups water

1. For the pappardelle, mix all ingredients together to form a ball of dough that is light enough to be kneaded easily.

2. Flour a large surface; roll out the dough with a rolling pin to ⅛ inch in thickness.

3. Cut into rectangles, approximately 3 x 1½ inches.

4. To make the sauce, sauté the garlic, rosemary, chili, and cloves in hot oil; add the boar, salt, and pepper.

5. Just as the garlic is about to brown, add the wine and allow to evaporate.

6. Add the tomato paste and 1 cup water; cook over low heat, covered, for approximately 2 hours or until the boar is tender and the flavors are thoroughly blended.

7. Cook the pappardelle in boiling water for 4 minutes; drain.

8. Remove the garlic clove from the sauce, pour it over the pappardelle, and serve hot.

*Serves 4*

*Giacomo Antonio Domenico Michele Secondo Maria Puccini.*

# ARISTA DI MAIALE CON FINOCCHIO AL OLIO E PATATE AL'ORO

*Roasted Pork Loin with Braised Fennel and Potatoes with Bay Leaves*

*This is a classic Sunday or holiday recipe used throughout the province of Lucca. A wonderful blend of roasted pork cooked with anise, and crispy potatoes cooked with bay leaves, the dish will instantly transport you to the festive dining room of a typical Tuscan home.*

*The roast:*
   4 cloves garlic
   1 tablespoon finely chopped fresh rosemary
   3 tablespoons fennel seeds
   Salt and pepper to taste
   2 pounds pork loin, bones split
   3 onions, halved
   4 tablespoons extra-virgin olive oil
   ½ cup dry white wine

*The fennel:*
   3 large bulbs fennel (tops removed and discarded), each cut into
      vertical slices ½ inch thick
   ⅓ cup extra-virgin olive oil
   Salt to taste

*The potatoes:*
   12 fresh bay leaves
   12 small potatoes, sliced in half, lengthwise
   Salt and pepper to taste
   4 tablespoons extra-virgin olive oil

1. Chop the garlic and rosemary together until they form a thick paste; add the fennel seeds, salt, and pepper, and blend thoroughly.

2. Stuff the herb mixture into the cuts in the pork where the bones were split.

3. Place the pork and the onions in a roasting pan; drizzle 4 table-spoons oil over the top. Roast at 350 degrees for 1½ hours or until the center of the pork is a pale pink.

4. In the meantime place the fennel in a covered saucepan with ⅓ cup oil, salt, and enough water to cover.

5. Boil for 25 to 40 minutes, or until fennel is soft and creamy.

6. Place a bay leaf between each set of potato halves; salt and pepper.

7. Heat 4 tablespoons oil in a roasting pan on top of stove. Place assembled potatoes in pan.

8. Roast the potatoes in the oven for the last hour of the pork's cooking time.

9. Remove roast from pan; pour off fat. Place pan drippings and the softened onions into a saucepan with the wine; cook for 3 minutes, stirring constantly with a wooden spoon. Keep warm in a sauceboat.

10. Cut the roasted pork into thick slices.

11. Assemble the dish by placing the pork slices on top of the fennel on a large serving platter; arrange the potatoes around the outside of the platter. Serve hot with onions in sauceboat.

*Serves 4*

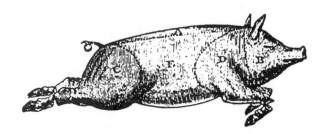

# ARROSTO DI MAIALE, MORTO
*Roast Loin of Pork, Dead*

*The Signora advances this recipe for roast pork, which she received from a longtime friend in Lucca. "It's a very old recipe, handed down through ten generations or so, and yet no one has ever been able to discover why the word* dead *is used to describe the preparation." It is a roast whose juices must remain, more or less, on the liquid side—like a sauce, she says. In obtaining this consistency, you might need to add, just before serving, a piece of butter and a little flour. This dish goes very well with roast potatoes, which cook in the juices of the meat. To do so, peel and cut 4 medium potatoes into small cubes; add to the roasting pan, turning a few times during cooking. (If adding potatoes, broth will definitely be needed to create a sauce.)*

> 2 pounds loin of pork, bone out
> 2 sprigs fresh rosemary
> Salt and pepper to taste
> 2 tablespoons olive oil
> 2 tablespoons unsalted butter, plus additional 2 tablespoons, if necessary
> 2 cloves garlic
> 3 leaves fresh sage (or 3 whole dried leaves)
> ¼ cup meat broth
> 2 tablespoons flour

1. Make a series of small slits in the roast; place a leaf or two of rosemary in each slit, and dust the pork with salt and pepper.

2. In an ovenproof dish, place the oil, butter, garlic, sage, and finally, the roast.

3. Roast in a 350 degree oven for 45 minutes to 1 hour, basting every now and then with the juices from the pan (if, at any time, the pan seems too dry, add some of the broth).

4. Remove the roast from the pan; stir the juices into a semithick sauce. If the sauce is too thin, add the 2 tablespoons butter and the flour, 1 tablespoon at a time; if the sauce is too thick, thin with a little of the broth.

5. Cut the roast into thin slices and top each slice with a teaspoon of the sauce; serve hot.

*Serves 4*

# ARROSTO DI MAIALE CON LATTE
## Pork Roast in Milk

*One of Puccini's favorite foods, according to his memoirs, was this dish of roast pork cooked in milk. The milk not only gives flavor to the pork but tenderizes it as well.*

8 ounces unsalted butter
1 medium celery stalk, diced
1 leek, diced
2 cloves garlic, minced
2 plum tomatoes, seeded and chopped
2½ pounds boneless loin of pork
2 tablespoons fresh thyme
Salt and pepper to taste
Flour
6 cups milk, heated to boiling

1. Melt the butter in a large ovenproof dish over low heat; add the celery, leek, garlic, and tomatoes. Cook slowly until the onion and garlic are lightly brown.

2. Make a series of 10 to 15 tiny slits along the surface of the meat; insert a few leaves of thyme in each. Dust meat with salt and pepper, and tie it into a tight roll using kitchen string.

3. Roll the meat in flour; shake off any excess.

4. Add the meat to the garlic and onion mixture and brown on all sides.

5. Pour the hot milk over the meat; cover (or seal with aluminum foil) and place in an oven preheated to 350 degrees.

6. Cook for 2 hours.

7. Remove the meat from the baking dish; blend the sauce together using a fork. Cut the roast into thick slices and serve, topped with the milk sauce.

*Serves 4*

"New Year's eve is, for us, a time for gathering around the table with family and friends," says Signora Gragnani. "In that, it is not very different from what we do on any other holiday except that the foods are specific to this particular night. One traditional dish I especially love is served around 10 p.m. as an appetizer and is called *Zampone con Lenticchie*. I'm not sure if you have *zampone* in America, but I hope for your sake that you do."

The Signora need not have worried. *Zampone,* while not yet available in the local A & P, can be found in most Italian specialty stores. Essentially an oversized sausage (average weight is 2½ pounds), its main ingredient is pork, which is diced and the mixed with various herbs and spices. *Zampone* must always be soaked overnight before cooking.

# ZAMPONE CON LENTICCHIE
*Zampone with Lentils*

1 zampone, soaked overnight in fresh water
½ pound lentils, picked through for stones, and rinsed 2 or 3 times
1 medium onion
1 celery stalk, cut in 3 pieces
Salt and pepper to taste
1 small carrot, diced
1 celery stalk, diced
2 tablespoons extra-virgin olive oil

1. Pierce the skin of the zampone in 4 or 5 places; cover with cold water in a large soup pot. Boil over low heat for 2 hours.

2. Cover the lentils with cold water; add the onion and the pieces of the celery, salt, and pepper. Boil over low heat for 20 minutes; drain well.

3. Sauté the diced carrot and celery in 2 tablespoons of the oil over medium heat; add the drained lentils.

4. Skim the fat from the water in which the zampone was cooked; add ¼ cup of the liquid to the lentil mixture. Let sit for 15 minutes or until the liquid has been absorbed.

5. Cut the zampone into thick slices; place on a serving platter surrounded by the lentils. Drizzle olive oil on top and serve hot.

*Serves 4*

*Coniglio* (rabbit) has always been a quintessential part of the Tuscan diet, prized for its white, lean meat, and slight hint of gaminess. While small-town inhabitants often raise their own rabbits, those that are purchased are always farm raised, which distinguishes them from *lepre* or wild rabbits. At one time they were considered economical; today they cost much more than poultry. There is a big difference in the taste between young rabbits and old; one way to tell a rabbit's age is to look at it: the younger the rabbit, the smaller its "knees" and the more flexible its hindquarters.

Rabbit can be bought whole or in sections; best are the loins near the back, and the hindquarters. If the rabbit is not young, it is best to marinate it overnight in white wine, sliced carrots, diced onions, and a leaf of bay. If it *is* young, it is still best to soak it in water for at least ½ hour before cooking. Rabbits must always be dried well, however, since they tend to give off much liquid of their own during cooking.

# CONIGLIO STUFATO AL FORNO

*Oven-roasted Stuffed Rabbit*

1 tablespoon salt
Pepper to taste
1 whole young rabbit, skinned, cleaned, and with head and fore-
   legs removed by butcher
6 cloves garlic, minced
1 large link of sweet sausage
1 bunch fresh fennel stalks (the tops), chopped
6 or 7 very thin slices of pancetta (or bacon)
Extra-virgin olive oil

1. Rub salt and pepper into both the outside flesh of the rabbit and its inside cavity.

2. Place the garlic inside the cavity, spreading it evenly throughout.

3. Prick the sausage in 4 or 5 places; add sausage and fennel to the cavity.

4. Using needle and thread, sew up the cavity so that the filling is firmly enclosed.

5. Cover the outside of the rabbit with the pancetta (or bacon), and drizzle olive oil over its entire surface.

6. Place the rabbit in an ovenproof dish, and roast in a 350 degree oven for 1 hour or until the juices run clear when you prick the rabbit.

7. Remove the sausage and fennel from the cavity. Cut the rabbit into serving pieces; slice the sausage. Place the rabbit on a serving platter surrounded by sliced sausage layered with cooked fennel.

*Serves 4*

# CONIGLIO ALLA CACCIATORA CON POLENTA
*Rabbit over Polenta Hunter-style*

*In all of northern Tuscany, the most popular way to cook rabbit is the "HUNT-ERS" way: in a tomato sauce flavored with wine and herbs and dried mush-rooms, served over polenta. The Signora, in fact, remembers many nights when her mother would make extra polenta "knowing that in some mystical way, the odor would filter across the street through Puccini's window, and before long, he'd stroll through the front door and sit himself down at the big table in the kitchen along with the rest of us. And there we would sit for hours, eating plateful after plateful, soaking up the sauce with thick slices of bread, and washing it all down with liters of strong red wine." (See more about polenta, page 127.)*

*The rabbit:*
  3 ounces dried porcini mushrooms
  2 tablespoons unsalted butter
  1 medium onion, diced
  2 ounces prosciutto, minced
  1 whole skinned rabbit, cleaned, dried, and cut into small pieces
  1 glass dry red wine
  ¼ teaspoon dried thyme
  Salt and pepper to taste
  1 35-ounce can Italian tomatoes with liquid
*The polenta:*
  4 cups coarse-grain polenta
  3 quarts water
  ½ teaspoon salt

1. Soak the mushrooms in warm water for ½ hour; squeeze them "dry," discarding all but 2 tablespoons of the liquid.

2. Heat the butter in a skillet over medium heat; sauté the onion, pro-sciutto, and mushrooms until the onion is lightly browned.

3. Add the rabbit, and brown on all sides.

4. Add the wine, thyme, salt, and pepper; cook, covered, over medium heat for 15 minutes.

5. Dice the tomatoes and add them to the rabbit; lower the heat and cook, uncovered, for another 30 minutes or until the sauce has thickened somewhat.

6. In the meantime, make the polenta: Fill a large, thick pot with 3 quarts of salted water; add the polenta in a steady stream and cook over medium heat, stirring with a wooden spoon, until the spoon stands by itself in the center and the polenta pulls away from the sides of the pot.

7. Serve the polenta in large bowls topped with the rabbit.

*Serves 6*

*All the streets in Torre del Lago are named with the maestro in mind.*

# CONIGLIO ALL'ARANCIA
*Rabbit in Orange Sauce*

*The cooking of Tuscany is best known for its simple, peasant style—fresh ingredients and joyous consummation. Occasionally, however, Tuscans choose to bring to their kitchens a touch of the elegance for which they are well known in the worlds of international fashion and design. The following is an "elegant" recipe, one that elevates rabbit to the world of nouvelle cuisine.*

      2 rabbit fillets, cut from the saddle
      2 tablespoons extra-virgin olive oil
      ½ cup chicken broth
      Salt and pepper to taste
      2 large bulbs of fennel, tops removed
      Juice of 1 medium navel orange

1. Remove any fat from the rabbit fillets; rinse under cold water and dry thoroughly.

2. Place in an ovenproof dish with the oil, broth, salt, and pepper; cover, and cook in a 350 degree oven for 15 minutes.

3. In the meantime remove and discard the outer leaves of the fennel bulbs. Cut into fourths and then cut each quarter into small pieces.

4. Boil the fennel in salted water until it is cooked well, at least 10 minutes. Remove from water and place in a food processor with salt and pepper and pulse until reduced to a creamy consistency, or press through a food mill.

5. Remove the rabbit from the oven. Add the orange juice to the liquid in the pan; blend well with a fork.

6. Cut the saddles in half.

7. Divide the fennel cream into four equal portions. Place each portion on an individual plate; the cream should cover the center of the plate and form a nice, neat round.

8. Place one saddle half on each dish, topped with the juices from the bottom of the pan; serve hot.

*Serves 4*

# CONIGLIO ALLA BRACE
## Grilled Rabbit

*One of the very best ways to prepare rabbit is to grill it over hot coals, whether whole or in individual sections. A typical Tuscan picnic often consists of just such a rabbit served with, maybe, a cold salad of white beans, plenty of crusty bread, cheese, and good red wine.*

> 1 whole rabbit, or 2 pounds sections
> 5 tablespoons chopped fresh parsley
> 2 cloves garlic, minced
> 4 leaves fresh sage, minced
> Extra-virgin olive oil
> Salt and pepper to taste

1. Soak the rabbit in a solution of 4 parts water to 1 part vinegar for ½ hour before cooking.

2. Rinse under cold water; dry thoroughly.

3. Make a paste of the parsley, garlic, sage, oil, salt, and pepper.

4. Place the rabbit over the grill and baste with the parsley and garlic mixture; turn once and baste the other side.

5. Total cooking time should be no more than 25 minutes; the rabbit is done when its juices run clear when pricked with a fork.

*Serves 4*

Wild rabbit, or hare, is indeed, a culinary delight—difficult to prepare, but as the Signora says, "those who seek Paradise should be prepared to earn it."

A wild rabbit is best when caught (or sold, as the case may be) between September and December; its meat, unlike that of its domestic counterpart, is dark. One should never buy an old hare; the most flavorful are from six months to one year old. Before cooking, it is always first necessary to soak the hare in a wine or a vinegar-based marinade for at least 12 to 24 hours—the longer the better.

In the province of Lucca, the most popular method for preparing hare is the following recipe for *Lepre in Salmí* Ragout of Hare. The flavor of the dish depends on adding, at the last minute, the blood of the hare, which gives the sauce its body. When purchasing the hare, ask the butcher to cut the meat into chunks and to package it with both the liver and several tablespoons of the blood.

## LEPRE IN SALMI
*Ragout of Hare*

*The marinade:*
- 1 quart dry red wine
- 2 cloves garlic, crushed
- 1 medium onion, studded with 4 or 5 whole cloves
- 1 medium celery stalk, cut into 3 pieces
- 1 small carrot, cut into 3 pieces
- 5 whole peppercorns
- ¼ teaspoon dried thyme
- 1 bay leaf, crushed

*The ragout:*
- 1 hare, approximately 3 pounds, cut into chunks
- 1 small onion, diced
- 1 small carrot, diced
- 3 tablespoons extra-virgin olive oil
- Salt and pepper to taste
- 2 tablespoons flour

2 or 3 tablespoons blood from the hare

1 hare's liver, minced finely

1. Place all the marinade ingredients in a large bowl; soak the chunks of hare, making sure they are completely covered. Cover and let sit at room temperature for 12 to 24 hours.

2. Drain the hare and dry with paper towels; reserve the marinade.

3. In a large skillet, brown the onion, carrot, and the chunks of hare in the oil over high heat.

4. Add the salt, pepper, and flour, blend together with the hare and continue to brown for a few more minutes.

5. Add the marinade with all the ingredients; bring to boiling and then lower the heat and cook, covered, for 2¾ hours.

6. Just before serving, add the blood and the liver and cook for 5 minutes, blending all ingredients thoroughly.

7. Remove the hare to a heated platter; pass the sauce through a food mill.

8. Serve the hare covered with the sauce.

*Serves 8*

# ANATRA LESSATA
### *Poached Duck*

*The following recipe comes from the Gastronomic Almanac of 1912, and is credited to Maestro Giacomo Puccini. According to the Almanac, it was, for a long time, a specialty served only in Torre del Lago Puccini.*

> 1 whole young duck, 3–5 pounds including heart and kidney,
>   rinsed under cold water and dried thoroughly
> 3 small onions, diced
> 2 tablespoons unsalted butter
> Salt and pepper to taste
> 1 lemon, thinly sliced
> 1 lemon, cut into wedges

1. Chop the heart and kidney of the duck into small pieces; add the onion, butter, salt, and pepper. Using a fork, blend into a pastelike consistency.

2. Stuff the mixture into the cavity of the duck; sew up the cavity using a needle and threat.

3. Wrap the duck with heavy thread, as if it were a roast (in order to prevent its falling apart during cooking).

4. Submerge the duck completely in salted boiling water.

5. Cook for 90 minutes.

6. Remove the duck from the water, unwrap the thread, skin, and cut into serving pieces. Discard the skin.

7. Serve on a heated platter surrounded by the lemon slices; spoon the filling over the duck and drizzle with lemon.

*Serves 4*

# ANATRA ALLA GRAPPA
*Duck with Grappa Sauce*

*Puccini was a great duck hunter. Many are the times he would sneak into the kitchen of Signora Gragnani's house and leave a duck on the table without saying a word to anyone. Then he would come back at dinnertime, knowing, of course, the exact contents of that evening's menu.*

*This dish combines the pungent flavor of duck with the equally pungent flavor of grappa, which is a brandy made from the residue of wine grapes. The duck is first boiled in water to remove most of the fat.*

1 3-pound duck
3 medium onions, whole
Salt and pepper to taste
3 tablespoons extra-virgin olive oil
1 medium onion, sliced
2 tablespoons unsalted butter
3 leaves fresh sage
2 tablespoons chopped fresh rosemary
1 cup grappa (use *grappa*—not marc brandy)

1. Place the duck in a soup pot filled with water; add the 3 onions and some salt and pepper. Boil over high heat for 30 minutes.

2. Drain the duck and dry with paper towels.

3. Place the duck in an ovenproof dish; add the oil, the sliced onion, butter, sage, rosemary, salt, and pepper.

4. Cook for 30 minutes in a 350 degree oven, turning every 15 minutes; baste often.

5. Douse with the grappa and cook for 10 minutes longer.

6. Place the duck on a heated serving platter; pour the grappa sauce over the top and serve hot.

*Serves 4*

Like rabbit, geese for eating are, today, almost completely farm-bred. Their flesh tends to be quite fatty, although succulent. The younger the goose, however, the less the amount of fat. To achieve a good balance between fat and flavor, geese should be no larger than 3 or 4 pounds, and those caught between September and February are best in terms of taste. When buying sections, the anterior quarter of a goose tends to be the most tender.

In preparing a whole goose *(OCA),* roasted or stuffed is best, since cooking it in any kind of sauce would compromise the wonderful crackliness of the cooked skin. Also, because of its high fat content, there's no danger of its drying out, but it is important to use a roasting rack to prevent the goose from "sitting" in its own fat during cooking. Many recipes allow for boiling the goose first in order to eliminate much of the fat. In general, cooking times tend to be approximately 1 hour for the first two pounds and 15 minutes or so for each additional pound.

# OCA RIPIENA DI MELE
## *Goose Stuffed with Apples*

> 2 pounds slightly sweet medium-sized red apples (MacIntosh or
>    Rome would work well)
> 2 tablespoons sugar
> ⅛ teaspoon cinnamon
> Juice of 1 lemon
> 1 young goose, 2 to 3 pounds
> 2 tablespoons unsalted butter
> Salt and pepper to taste
> 1½ cups cognac

1. Two hours before cooking, peel the apples, remove the core, and cut into thin slice; sprinkle with the sugar and cinnamon, drizzle with lemon, and let sit to blend the flavors.

2. Wash the goose inside and out; dry thoroughly with paper towels. Stuff the cavity with the apples. Sew closed.

3. Melt the butter in a large skillet over medium-high heat; add the goose and brown on all sides, basting frequently with the fat from the bottom of the pan.

4. When the goose is completely browned, dust it with salt and pepper; cook, uncovered, for 1½ hours, turning it every 10 minutes or so.

5. When it is almost cooked, drizzle the cognac over the meat, turning constantly so that all sides absorb the flavor; cook, uncovered, for 20 minutes longer.

6. Remove the goose from the skillet and place on a cutting board; spoon the apples from the cavity and sauté them for 3 minutes in the skillet with the drippings.

7. Cut the goose into serving pieces, place on a heated platter, and serve with the sauce spooned over the top.

*Serves 6*

When buying a chicken, choose only those with skin that is uniform in color; spotting or discoloration indicates that the chicken is not as fresh as it should be. In northern Tuscany, there are many ways to cook chicken; among the most popular:

**Arrosto (Roasted):** More than any other preparation, roasted chicken requires a bird of very high quality. Before cooking, it should be salted inside only, and for best results, the breast should be coated with prosciutto or pancetta to retain moisture and insure a crispy outer crust.

**Al Forno (Baked):** Oven temperatures should be low to medium for the duration of the cooking time. Baking works especially well with older or larger chickens whose meat would otherwise be too dry for roasting or even grilling.

**Lessoata (Boiled):** To insure that the meat remains white during boiling, sprinkle it first with lemon and let it sit for 10 to 15 minutes. Chicken should always be boiled with carrots, celery, and onions, both to give flavor to the meat and to create a flavorful broth. Free-range or natural chickens create better broths than the typical mass-market varieties.

**In Umido (Stewed):** Ideal for chicken that has already been cut into sections. In Italy, sauce variations include tomato, curry, mushroom, beer, marsala, wine, oil and lemon, and cream. Chicken in umido should be cooked over medium heat and slowly enough to allow the flavors to infiltrate the meat.

**Alla Griglia (Grilled):** Can be barbecued over charcoal, or grilled in an oven broiler. Chickens cooked in this way are split down the middle, flattened somewhat, and then cooked under a stone to ensure even grilling.

**Fritto (Fried):** Tuscan fried chicken is far superior to its American counterpart in that the pieces are first marinated in milk, salt, and pepper for 15 minutes in order to render them more tender. The pieces are then battered in flour and fried in olive oil.

# POLLO AFFOGATO
## Smothered Chicken

*The following recipe is a staple throughout the Lucchesía, both for the succulent flavor of the chicken and for the sauce, which is then spooned either onto crostini—small wedges of toast—or onto pieces of polenta fried in oil.*

2 pounds chicken pieces, skinned
4 tablespoons unsalted butter
1 pound small white onions, peeled
1 bottle dry red wine (for those in the mood for splurging, Barolo wine is best)
3 ounces dried porcini mushrooms, soaked for 20 minutes in warm water, drained, and chopped
Salt and pepper to taste
¼ teaspoon dried thyme
1 tablespoon flour

1. Wash and dry the chicken. Heat the butter in a large skillet over medium heat; place the chicken in the butter, a few pieces at a time, until all sides are browned. Drain on paper towels.

2. Place the onions in a saucepan filled with boiling water and cook for 3 minutes; drain.

3. Place all ingredients except the flour in a large skillet; cook, uncovered, over medium heat for 1 hour, turning the chicken often.

4. When everything is cooked, add the flour, and stir until the sauce is somewhat thickened.

5. Serve with slices of fried polenta or with crostini.

*Serves 6*

## A CHICKEN STORY

A friend of the Signora tells the story of how she was once finagled out of her two plumpest chickens. "When I was young," she says, "we had many animals, among them a large number of chickens. One day, I came out and saw the two finest ones—the ones we were saving for my father's birthday dinner—dead. I asked the workers what had happened but no one knew anything. So I asked the young man who took care of the chickens to take them away and burn them. After all, I thought, if they're diseased, I don't want the disease to spread.

"Many years later, after we had sold the farm and all the workers were employed elsewhere, I found out that the young man in charge of the chickens—who had always been well fed but obviously not enough to his liking had put a needle through the heads of the chickens, a procedure that had killed them instantly and without any trace of conspiracy. I found this out from my grandson whose schoolmate just happened to be the grandson of the young man. The boy had been told the story by his grandfather and had now recounted it in an essay written on the topic of *'Quei Bel Tempi'* [Those Wonderful Days of Yore]."

The following recipe was probably the one employed by the young man in cooking the chickens since it has always been extremely popular throughout northern Tuscany.

# POLLASTRINO AL MATTONE
*Small Chicken Cooked with a Stone*

*A wonderful variation on this recipe involves marinating the chicken in all the rest of the ingredients plus 2 tablespoons of red wine vinegar for 1 hour per side, and then grilling the chicken in the broiler pan for 20 minutes per side, basting often with the marinade. Try this recipe first however.*

1 smallish chicken—2-2½ pounds (*pollastrino* means "small chicken")
Juice of 1 lemon
1 clove garlic, crushed
2 tablespoons finely chopped fresh rosemary
4 tablespoons extra-virgin olive oil
2 teaspoons coarse salt
½ teaspoon coarsely ground pepper

1. Wash and dry the chicken; split it down the middle and flatten it with a cooking stone or large heatproof weight until you hear most of the bones break.

2. Make a paste of the remaining ingredients, and rub the paste onto both sides of the chicken.

3. Place the chicken in a skillet over medium heat; flatten with the stone or an ovenproof dish weighted down with a water-filled jar.

4. Cook the chicken under the weight for 20 minutes on each side; when done, the skin should be quite crispy.

5. Serve hot with roasted potatoes and a green salad.

*Serves 4*

# POLLO IN SALSA BIANCA E PREZZEMOLO
*Chicken in White Sauce with Parsley*

*One of Puccini's favorite preparations for chicken (or fish, or meat of any kind) was* in bianco, *which means in a white sauce. This recipe blends the dryness of white wine with the luxuriousness of heavy cream to create a truly elegant dish.*

> 1 3-pound chicken
> 1 cup water
> 1 cup dry white wine
> Salt and pepper to taste
> 4 tablespoons unsalted butter
> 2 tablespoons flour
> 1 cup milk
> 1 quart chicken broth (homemade or good quality canned)
> ½ cup heavy cream
> 4 tablespoons freshly chopped parsley

1. Clean and dry the chicken; place in a casserole with 1 cup water, the wine, salt, and pepper. Bring to boiling over medium heat.

2. Skim the top, cover, and place in a preheated 350 degree oven for 2½ hours.

3. Meanwhile, prepare the sauce. Melt the butter in a skillet over low heat; remove the skillet from the burner and add the flour, stirring with a fork until of a thick, creamy consistency.

4. Add the milk to the flour and butter, and gradually add the broth, stirring constantly; bring to a boil, add the cream, and whisk into a thick, creamy sauce.

5. Remove the chicken from the casserole (save the wine broth for another use); cut into pieces and place on a serving platter.

6. Pour the sauce over the chicken, sprinkle with parsley, and serve hot.

*Serves 6*

# POLLO AL SALE
*Chicken Encrusted in Salt*

*This is an ancient recipe, culled from a book belonging to one of Torre del Lago's most famous home cooks of the 1940s: Signora Silvia Montigioso. In her notes, the Signora claims to have made this for Puccini on the day he finished* Madame Butterfly. *"He told me of his need for a culinary celebration," she wrote, "and I made this wonderful chicken encrusted in salt, which he ate as if tomorrow would never come." The recipe creates a salt crust that encapsulates the chicken during cooking to create a tender, succulent bird with a crackling outer "coat."*

    1 large chicken (3–5 pounds)
    Pepper to taste
    3 pounds coarse salt

1. Clean and dry the chicken; dust inside and out with pepper.

2. In an ovenproof casserole place a sheet of aluminum foil large enough to line the bottom of the casserole and fold over the chicken.

3. Pour the salt on the aluminum foil; place the chicken on the salt and spread it so that the chicken is completely covered. Add salt if necessary.

4. Bring the edges of the foil together and seal.

5. Cook in a preheated 400 degree oven for 1½ hours.

6. Remove from oven and open the foil package; the chicken will be encrusted with a hard layer of salt. Transfer the chicken to a chopping block and break the salt layer with a kitchen mallet; under the layer the chicken will have formed a golden crust.

7. Cut the chicken into serving pieces and arrange on a platter; serve hot.

*Serves 6*

*Signora Adriana Forasieppi*

# Chapter Eight

# THE IMPORTANCE OF LA BELLA FIGURA

## BEEF, VEAL, AND LAMB

What do these answers have in common?

A person, especially a woman, over the age of eighteen wearing shorts on Sunday for any occasion other than exercising (and even then, the activity should be restricted to a *palestra,* a gym);

Using the informal *tu* instead of the more formal *lei* when addressing people who are not strictly family;

Asking to take home the uneaten portions of a restaurant meal;

Attempting to get to the point without an initial inquiry on the state of one's health and family;

Skimping on anything when in company—a meal prepared for guests, the choice of food or wine when inviting someone to a restaurant, the style of clothing worn in public.

The above are all examples of a dire social breach the Italians refer to as *brutta figura.* The words require no translation, spoken as they are with eyes raised towards the heavens and a subsequent shaking of one's head. *Brutta figura.*

I am sitting on the terrace of *Il Antico Ristorante Forasieppi* overlooking the vineyards and olive groves surrounding Montecarlo; a lovely 14th century hill town near the eastern edge of the Lucchesía. With me is Signora Adriana Forasieppi of the famous family who founded this restaurant over 300 years ago.

Where we are sitting is not the original restaurant site; that location is elsewhere—in the Piazza Garibaldi, opposite the walled castle built in

1554 by Cosimo I dei Medici after the end of the Sienese wars. The original restaurant is now in ruins—an unfortunate by-product of the Tuscan landmark laws which make it prohibitively expensive to restructure buildings in an advanced state of decay. This new site had been, for hundreds of years, a *frantoio*—an olive press; when construction began, eight ancient gold coins were found in one of the outside walls.

One of Tuscany's most famous restaurants, *Il Antico Ristorante Forasieppe* seats over 200 people and is generally filled to overflow, especially in the first two weeks of October, during the Wine Festival. Then, as in summer, the terrace teems with hungry visitors who come to sample the many house specialties, among them, *Arrosto di maialino* (Roast Suckling Pig), *Tagliatelle alla Salsiccia* (Homemade Pasta with Sausage), and *Risotto ai funghi porcini* (Risotto with Porcini Mushrooms). One of the restaurant's most illustrious gastronomes, Giacomo Puccini, was a great friend of the Signora's father-in-law, Giovanni Forasieppi, who owned the restaurant until he died.

*Il Antico Ristorante* notwithstanding, there are a great many additional reasons to come to Montecarlo—among them: the quaint 200-seat Rococo-style theater built in 1750, whose modern-day repertoire ranges from Rossini to Donizetti to Verdi to—of course—Puccini; the aforementioned walled castle with its formally-designed interior gardens; and the beautifully-maintained Church of Sant'Andrea Apostolo, with its 14th century frescoes (among them a huge depiction of the Madonna and Child painted by Angelo Puccinelli of the Lucchese school in 1387). Montecarlo's main attraction however, is its wine—especially the whites, which in 1969 were awarded the prized D.O.C. (Denominazione ad Origine Controllata).

The Signora and I are having a cup of afternoon tea. The water for the tea was steamed in a copper pot which, she says, should have gone to the wartime effort, but "I forgot it under my bed when the army came to collect all our metals. Otherwise, it too, would have been melted down for armaments."

She talks to me of a young female visitor, an Australian, who stayed with her a few weeks earlier. "She came to the restaurant late on the night of *ferragusto* (August 15th, which is the beginning of Italy's official summer holiday season), and, of course, there were no empty rooms anywhere in town. So I told her she could use Giovanni's study (Giovanni is but one of the names by which the Signora refers to her late husband. His alternate aliases, Dino, Felice, Iacopo, and Giove, resulted from an indecision on the part of his parents as to what, exactly, they would call their firstborn son).

"*Poverina,*" the Signora says shaking her head. "What could I do? The girl had such a pathetic look about her, after all those days of traveling. And thin? She was so thin that, before doing anything else, I immediately brought her some bread and prosciutto, which she consumed with the appetite of ten men.

"Beh, when she was done, I showed her to the room and told her she was welcome to stay for the next two nights, after which the painters would be arriving to begin their work. She threw her arms around my neck and kissed me on both cheeks. '*Grazie,*' she kept saying in her close-mouthed way. '*Grazie!*' But as I turned to go, I saw her throw her dirty bag on my husband's upholstered chair."

The Signora rolls her eyes in a counterclockwise fashion. "I should have known then that a disaster would occur the first time she stepped foot outside. *Que brutta figura che a fatto.*" What a bad showing she made.

The Australian, it seems, had spent the entire morning photographing the local cemetery. And as if it wasn't bad enough her treating the cemetery like a tourist attraction, she had been dressed in shorts and a T-shirt, and had a backpack slung around her shoulder. Her hair was uncombed, and she was wearing sneakers. "Imagine," says the Signora, "the embarrassment of finding all this out from Signora Vellini, the seamstress across the street, who called me to say that the whole town was talking. I tried to present a good face, to excuse the girl by virtue of Australia's geography. So removed is it from any formal center of civilization. But imagine . . ."

The Signora sips her tea, obviously distressed at the shame of having been phoned not only by Signora Vellini but also by the magistrate's wife, who had gone to the cemetery to visit with her newly departed father.

"What happened when the girl got back?" I asked, wondering at the nature of the conversation that must have followed this scene.

"Oh, I mentioned none of this to her," she says quickly. She leans across the table to refill her cup with more of the tea. "What could I have said?"

Indeed. What *could* she have said? For that matter, what would the girl have said had she been approached by either Signora Vellini or the magistrate's wife while the scene was still in progress.

She probably would have apologized profusely, explaining her amazement at the beautiful marble tombs that sit above the earth, as high

as one's thighs, side by side and attached to each other like newly baked biscuits.

She might have begged their forgiveness, mentioning in her defense the surprise that she'd experienced from seeing both the photographs of the deceased—the framed images set prominently on the tops of the tombs beside electrified marble lamps—and the flowers, the dazzling display of roses and lilies and faintly scented orchids set in granite vases beside the photographs, and changed daily by Montecarlo's widows.

She might have pleaded ignorance, acknowledged rudeness, exculpated herself by slinking from the cemetery in a supplicating posture.

But the Signora is right. What could she have said?

We finish our tea, and she points me towards the *drogheria,* the drugstore, where she has said I can purchase a new tube of toothpaste. *"Aspetta,"* she says as I'm almost out the door. "I will go with you. You will not know how to ask if you go by yourself."

On the way, we pass the pizzeria from which a local youth has just exited, carrying a large slice of pizza on the customary scrap of white paper. He walks down the road, eating his pizza as he swings his body to the rhythm of whatever music is being piped into his ears.

*"Guarda como siamo ridotti"*—look at what we have been reduced to—the Signora says, closing her eyes in a weary sort of desperation. I assume she refers to his long ponytailed hair and the headphones encircling his head like a surgical clamp. But I am wrong.

*"Come che non ci fosse un tavolo per mangiare in casa sua"*—as if in his house there were no dining table on which he could eat. After all, she points out *sotto voce,* he *is* the son of the doctor. End of conversation.

Back at the house, I go to my room to ponder the importance given to bad showings and good showings in this country, where all behavior is codified according to the way in which it adheres to the rules. I ponder also the difference between these immutable codifications and the laconic adherence to rules in general.

In Tuscany, the most serious threat one person can make to another is *ti sistemo io*—I'll systemize you. *Sistemare,* the verb, means to arrange, to put in order, to settle, to find a job for, to find a husband for, to fix. *Ti sistemo io,* a mother might say to a son who has brought home bad grades on his report card. *Ti sistemo io,* a wife might say to a husband who spends too much time playing cards at the local cafe. All are variations on the theme of organizing according to the rules.

How does it happen, then, that this is also a country known for *not* living by the rules—the same country where, for instance, telephone bills present merely the total owed with never any itemizing of calls? Where, when the government first passed a law mandating seat belts, the hottest selling item immediately became a T-shirt emblazoned across the front with an airbrushed seat belt?

"The only reason we may have been assigned this reputation," says the Signora when I broach the subject, "is because others do not understand our system. There is nothing here that does not run in the way we want it to run. If our trains are not on time, it is because we live in a culture that allows for meeting someone on the street and remaining for an extra minute's chat. If it takes three months for the plumber to come to fix the drain, it is because he was living the same life we are living—a life that takes into account what is important and what is not. *Certo* we could—how do Americans say it—run a tighter ship. We could work harder, produce more, streamline our systems, but what would we have to give up? No, no, no. We will stay with what we have and wait for the rest of the world to catch up to us."


That night, the Signora sends her nephew to call me down to dinner. She has prepared a wonderful meal of *Manzo Bollito,* Boiled Beef, with a spicy sauce made of garlic, chili, and Parmigiano cheese. The aroma fills the room—the sweet smell of beef broth weaving through the delicate lacework of the Signora's hand-crocheted window panels—before it floats outside, there to blend with the delicious odors of Montecarlo's wine-saturated air.

From the look on Signora Forasieppi's face, I can tell she is pleased, that she thinks I will be pleased, that she has honored both herself and her town, that she can rest easily for the remainder of the evening knowing she has truly made a *bella figura.*

# BISTECCHE DI MANZO ALLA GRIGLIA
*Grilled Steak*

*In Tuscany, the act of preparing a fine, grilled steak is an achievement akin to any of the great works of Michelangelo. A Tuscan steak is at least 1 inch thick, cut from the rib of a young steer, and well aged. Ideally, the Signora says, one would have available an outdoor grill and some finely scented wood—cypress or olive. If not that, a charcoal grill, and if not that, a stovetop grill, the kind made of iron with virtually no sides and a corrugated cooking surface. Keep the meat about 3 inches from the heat and cook for about 7–8 minutes on each side. Tuscan steaks are generally "medium" in doneness.*

> 4 steaks, porterhouse or sirloin, each at least 1 inch thick
> Pepper and salt
> 4 tablespoons extra-virgin olive oil
> 4 lemon wedges

1. Dust the steaks with pepper; do not salt until after the meat is done to prevent toughness.

2. Place the steaks on a very hot grill for 7 or 8 minutes per side.

3. Remove from grill; brush immediately with olive oil and salt.

4. Serve accompanied by lemon wedges.

*Serves 4*

# POLPETTONE SERAVEZZINO
## *Meatloaf, Seravezza-style*

*Seravezza is near Pietrasanta, once the headquarters of the marble industry and the home of thousands of marble miners who toiled from early morning till late at night in the surrounding hills to extract pure white marble for the likes of Michelangelo Buonarroti. Today, however, the image of the lowly, overworked miner has been replaced by that of marble artists who populate the bars and cafes of Pietrasanta in their black turtlenecks and Timberland deck shores. But this recipe retains perfectly the flavor of "peasant" heartiness and the no-holds-barred joy that comes from sitting down to a wonderful meal at the end of a long, hard day.*

8 ounces lean ground beef
1 link pork sausage, removed from casing
4 ounces prosciutto, diced
2 cloves garlic, crushed
4 tablespoons unsalted butter
4 tablespoons Parmigiano Reggiano, grated
1 egg, lightly beaten
1 2-pound veal breast (with a pocket cut into it for stuffing)
½ cup Basic Meat Broth (page 95)

1. Mix together the beef, sausage, prosciutto, and garlic until all ingredients are well blended.

2. Add 2 tablespoons of the butter, the cheese, and egg; blend thoroughly.

3. Lay the veal on a flat surface, interior side up. Spread the meat mixture evenly over the surface. Roll up jellyroll fashion starting at the thickest part of the breast. Tie securely with kitchen string.

4. Heat the remaining butter in a skillet; add the meat, browning on all sides. Cook over low heat for 1½ hours. Sprinkle every now and then with the broth to prevent drying.

5. Remove the string; cut into slices and serve hot.

*Serves 4–6*

# BRACIOLINE IN UMIDO CON INSALATA
*Bracioline in Tomato Sauce with Escarole*

Bracioline *are thin strips of beef (or veal) that are generally either rolled around a filling and stewed in a sauce, or cooked like scallopine which means lightly battered and quickly fried. This unusual and delightful dish, originally from Versilia, combines both methods: First the meat is battered and panfried, and then it is cooked very briefly in a delicious sauce made from tomatoes and escarole.*

1¼ pounds very thin beef fillets
1 egg, lightly beaten
½ cup unflavored breadcrumbs
6 tablespoons extra-virgin olive oil
1 onion, diced
3 tablespoons unsalted butter
12 ounces canned Italian tomatoes, with liquid
1 cup Basic Meat Broth (page 95)
2 pounds escarole, washed, dried and cut into strips
Salt and pepper to taste

1. First prepare the sauce. Sauté the onion in the remaining oil and the butter; add the tomatoes and the broth and cook for 5 minutes until all ingredients are well blended.

2. Place the escarole in the sauce; add salt and pepper, cook, covered, over low heat for 40 minutes.

3. Now prepare the meat by drying it first with paper towels, dipping each fillet into the beaten egg batter, and then coating them with breadcrumbs. Pan fry each fillet in 4 tablespoons of the hot oil until both sides are lightly browned.

4. Place the fillets in the sauce in one layer and cook for 2 to 3 minutes or until the meat is heated throughout.

5. Serve with thick, crusty bread, and plenty of red wine.

*Serves 4*

# FILETTO ELISA ALLE ERBE
*Beef Tenderloins with Herbs "Elisa"*

*When Elisa Bonaparte, Napoleon's sister, married Felice Baciocchi, she came to live in his hometown of Lucca. The piazza immediately visible upon entering Lucca through the western walls bears a commemorative statue erected in her honor. A true Renaissance woman, Elisa was once described by Metternich as the Semiramide del Serchio—The Semiramis of the Serchio River Valley—for her love of beauty, elegance, and especially, good food. This dish, a wonderful blend of herbs, beef fillets, and brandy, was appropriately named in her honor.*

6 steaks cut from the beef tenderloin, each 1½–2 inches thick
White flour
2 tablespoons extra-virgin olive oil
¾ cup brandy
1 tablespoon Dijon mustard
1 cup heavy cream
1 tablespoon finely chopped fresh mint
1 tablespoon finely chopped fresh marjoram (or ¼ teaspoon dried)
5 green peppercorns, in brine, drained and crushed
1 tablespoon finely chopped fresh coriander
½ cup Basic Meat Broth (page 95)
Salt and pepper to taste

1. Dust the fillets with the flour and shake off any excess.

2. Heat the oil in a skillet large enough to hold all the fillets in one layer; brown the fillets on both sides.

3. Add the brandy and allow to evaporate. Add the remaining ingredients, and cook for approximately 15 minutes or until the flavors have completely blended.

4. Serve hot accompanied by either *Crostini al Funghi* (see page 12) or pureed potatoes.

*Serves 6*

In Tuscany, boiled meat dinners were once exclusively the fare of poor people. Today, however, they enjoy a new prominence evoking, as they do, memories of a simpler, more accessible Tuscany. Their return to popularity also rests on the complex blend of flavors—the succulent meats, the spicy sauces—and the fact that boiled meats are far less fatty than their roasted or panfried counterparts.

*Carne bollite*—boiled meats—require very specific preparations and an understanding of the difference between *lessare,* which means immersing the meat in cold water and then cooking it, the result being a very fine broth but tasteless meat—and *bollire,* which means immersing the meat in boiling water so that the heat seals in the flavor.

Following are two recipes for Tuscan boiled meat dinners: one, a simple dish of boiled beef served with a wonderfully spicy pepper sauce, the other, a cold dish of boiled veal with a classic sauce made of tuna and capers.

## MANZO BOLLITO CON SALSA PEARA
*Boiled Beef with Pepper Sauce*

*The beef:*
  2 pounds beef rump roast
  1 carrot
  1 stalk celery
  1 onion
  Salt to taste
*The sauce:*
  3 tablespoons unsalted butter
  4 ounces beef marrow, chopped
  1 clove garlic, crushed
  1½ cups dry unflavored breadcrumbs
  ½ cup broth from the boiled beef
  5 tablespoons Parmigiano Reggiano, grated
  1 dried chili pepper, crushed
  Salt to taste

1. Fill a large soup pot with salted water; heat until boiling. Add the meat and cook for five minutes.

2. Add the vegetables and cook, covered, over medium heat for 2 hours, skimming the liquid every 15 minutes or so to clear the broth.

3. Meanwhile make the sauce. In a small saucepan, sauté the marrow in the butter, add the garlic and breadcrumbs and cook until the breadcrumbs are toasted.

4. Add ½ cup broth from the soup pot to the saucepan and stir with a wooden spoon until the breadcrumbs have absorbed the broth; cook for 1 hour over low heat, adding more broth if necessary to maintain a saucelike consistency.

5. Add the cheese, chili pepper, and salt; blend all ingredients thoroughly.

6. Remove the meat from the broth; slice, salt, and place on a large serving platter. Sprinkle with a tablespoon or two of the broth.

7. Serve hot accompanied by the pepper sauce.

*Serves 4 or 5*

*The Signora in the cemetery.*

# VITELLO TONNATO
*Boiled Veal with Tuna and Capers*

*The veal:*
> 2 pounds veal loin, trimmed of all fat and tied
> ½ onion
> 1 small carrot
> 1 celery stalk
> 1 bay leaf
> 1 teaspoon salt

*The sauce:*
> 8 ounces tuna packed in olive oil, drained and crumbled
> Juice of 1 lemon
> 3 anchovies, drained
> 2 hard-cooked eggs
> 10 capers plus a few extra capers for the garnish
> ¼ cup extra-virgin olive oil
> Salt
> 1 lemon, sliced
> 1 carrot, julienned

1. Fill a large soup pot with cold water; bring to boiling. Add the veal, skimming the top after a few minutes to clear the broth; add the vegetables, bay leaf, and salt.

2. Boil, covered, for 1 hour over low heat; let cool in the broth.

3. When completely cooled, remove the meat from the broth, wrap in foil, and refrigerate. Save the broth and the vegetables for another use.

4. Meanwhile, make the sauce: Place the tuna and lemon juice in a bowl; mix well and let marinate for 1 hour.

5. Pass the marinated tuna, anchovies, eggs, and capers through a food mill, or in a food processor, reduce to pastelike consistency.

6. Dilute the sauce with the oil and salt to taste.

7. Remove the veal from the refrigerator; cut into thin slices. Serve on a platter covered with the sauce, surrounded by thin slices of lemon, julienned carrot, and a few capers, if desired.

*Serves 4–6*

# BRACIOLINE DI VITELLO CON L'AGNELLO
*Veal Rolls Stuffed with Lamb*

*Nothing pleases a Tuscan more than the* bella figura *achieved by serving a good meal, in this case, thin* bracioline *of veal stuffed with a creamy mixture of finely ground lamb and spices.*

> 6 ounces ground lamb
> 1 small onion, diced
> 2 tablespoons finely chopped fresh parsley
> 5 tablespoons extra-virgin olive oil
> Salt and pepper to taste
> 1½ pounds veal scallopini (pounded very thin)
> Toothpicks (the strong, round type)
> ⅔ cup dry white wine
> ⅔ cup canned Italian tomatoes, drained and pureed

1. Mix the lamb with the onion, parsley, and 2 tablespoons of the oil.

2. Add a pinch of salt and pepper and blend thoroughly.

3. Lay the scallopini flat on a counter and, over each spread equal portions of the lamb mixture.

4. Roll up loosely and fasten with a toothpick inserted through the roll like a stitch (do not insert horizontally or the rolls will be hard to turn during the cooking).

5. Heat the remaining oil in a skillet large enough to hold all the bracioline in one layer; place the meat in the pan and brown on all sides. Transfer to a heated platter and keep warm.

6. Add the wine and the tomatoes to the skillet; simmer, stirring from time to time, for 15 minutes.

7. Return the bracioline to the pan, lower the heat, and cook for 1 minute—just enough to heat through; serve immediately.

*Serves 4*

# FETTINE DI VITELLO ALLA SALVIA
*Veal Scallopini with Sage*

*One recipe that has been a staple on the menu of Ristorante Forasieppi for years is this blend of thin slices of veal, prosciutto, and sage. It is, the Signora claims, not only a veritable crowd pleaser but also a delight to cook because of the fragrant odor of sage wafting from the pan.*

8 thin scallopini of veal
8 thin slices prosciutto
8 leaves fresh sage
4 tablespoons unsalted butter
½ cup dry white wine
Salt and pepper to taste

1. Pound the scallopini with a kitchen mallet until they are as thin as can be without creating holes; lay a slice of prosciutto and a leaf of sage on each. Cover with another scallopini.

2. Heat the butter in a skillet large enough to hold all the scallopini in one layer. Brown the scallopini in the butter, drizzle with the wine, turn carefully, brown on the other side and—at the last minute—dust with salt and pepper. Total cooking time should not exceed 8 minutes.

3. Serve hot from the skillet accompanied by a mixed salad.

*Serves 4*

# GRIGLIATA MISTA
*Mixed Grill*

*There are few* secondi *(entrees) in Tuscany that are more characteristic than a mixed grill—Grigliata Mista—of meats. As with other recipes in this section that call for grilling, cooking over an outdoor grill with scented wood is optimal. Equally good, however, is cooking in an iron skillet, the kind with almost no sides and a corrugated bottom. The pleasure with this particular recipe is the ability it offers to sample small quantities of many different kinds of meats, each prepared in its own delicious way.*

4 lamb chops
1 sirloin steak, approximately ¾ pound, cut into four pieces
2 pork cutlets, cut in half
4 small pork sausages
½ cup extra-virgin olive oil
Juice of 1 lemon
Salt and pepper to taste
2 tablespoons finely chopped fresh parsley
2 tablespoons unsalted butter
2 ounces Gruyère cheese, cut in thin slices

1.  Place all the meats in a large bowl. Mix together the oil, lemon, salt, and pepper, and pour over the meat; toss to blend well, and let sit for approximately one hour.

2.  Heat the grill until it sizzles. Place the meats on the grill, a few at a time; cook for 3 to 4 minutes per side. Arrange the cooked meats on a heated serving platter.

3.  Blend the chopped parsley with the butter; spread over the steak.

4.  Place each slice of the Gruyère over one of the sausage links.

5.  Serve hot with a mixed salad and an assortment of pickled vegetables.

*Serves 4*

# AGNELLO CON LE OLIVE
## *Lamb with Olives*

*Tuscans are not known for their love of leftovers. Blessed with the ability to shop locally and cook twice a day using fresh ingredients, they are rarely seen eating something that has been reheated. According to the Signora, however, this recipe—while excellent on the first day—is even better the second, third, or fourth. Whenever it is made at the restaurant, therefore, it is always made in greater quantity than needed to accommodate the Signora's desire for* rimasti—*leftovers.*

> 2 pounds leg of lamb, cut into cubes
> 2 tablespoons extra-virgin olive oil
> 3 or 4 cloves garlic, crushed
> 1 tablespoon finely chopped fresh rosemary
> 1 cup dry white wine
> Salt and pepper to taste
> 1 35-ounce can Italian tomatoes, drained and chopped
> 8 ounces oil-cured olives, pitted
> ¼ cup Basic Meat Broth (page 95)

1. Place the lamb in a hot skillet and brown over medium heat. Remove the lamb and its juices to a heated dish.

2. Heat the oil in the same skillet and sauté the garlic and rosemary; add the lamb with its juices, wine, salt, and pepper. Cook over medium heat for 3 minutes, stirring often. Remove the lamb once again and keep warm on a heated platter.

3. Add the tomatoes and olives to the skillet; cook over medium heat for 10 minutes.

4. Add the lamb and the broth; cook for 10 minutes.

5. Serve hot with a mixed salad.

*Serves 4*

*Signora Velia Fontanini*

# Chapter Nine

# THE DEMANDING LIFE
# OF THE SAINTS

## DESSERTS

"*T*uscans have a habit of never greeting anybody first, not even in Paradise. Upon encountering a Tuscan floating along a heavenly cloud, it is God who extends the first *Buon giorno*."

Velia Fontanini talks about religion and the people of Gioviano, a mountain hamlet built along the left bank of the Serchio River, just above Borgo a Mozzano. She sits with me in the kitchen of her home, built in 1635 (the date is inscribed on the peak of the gothic arch framing the front door). From her back terrace, there is a magnificent view of the Serchio River Valley; in the distance are the forests of the Garfagnana.

If you lean far enough over the southern wall of the terrace, your view is of Borgo a Mozzano's most famous tourist attraction, the Ponte della Maddalena—Maddalena Bridge—which is also called the Devil's Bridge *(il Ponte del Diavolo)* due to an ancient legend regarding how it came to be built: Supposedly the architect, short of funds, asked the devil for help, and the devil agreed on one condition, that the first person to cross the bridge would be his to claim. When the bridge was finally completed, however, the architect proved wiser than the devil in that the first to cross the bridge was his cat.

Gioviano is home to exactly 158 people. Not included in this count are a Texan couple who spend the greater part of every summer in a house near the Signora's, which they bought thirteen years ago and have since restored. Although the Signora is great friends with the two, she is never sure whether or not to lump them into the population total even though, as she says, "they have taken great pains to learn our language."

As we sit in the light of the afternoon sun streaming through *le Persiane,* the shutters, Signora Fontanini waxes at length about Tuscan saints and especially the saints of the Lucchesía. "We are very close to our saints here," she says. "But not because we hold them up as exalted personages, hovering above us on pedestals. *Our* saints are everyday people, people who understand what is expected of them, and perform accordingly, people who know better than to characterize their miracles as anything out of the ordinary—as anything that would set them apart from others.

"Flamboyant miracles would simply not be tolerated by the people of Gioviano," she says solemnly. "When one of *our* saints performs a miracle, it is never one of those fantastic feats executed merely for the spectacle. It's an everyday affair, like San Davino who restricts himself to curing headaches. But then, how else could it be in a land where the extraordinary is the substance of everyday life? The extraordinary is what we have all around us—look at our mountains, our coast, the sky sparkling with sunshine. What could the saints possibly do that would be better than that?"

She sets about making a cup of espresso. "And then there is the question of what they would have to do to distinguish themselves even if we *did* allow them that privilege." She places the pot on the stove. "Tuscany, after all, is the home of Michelangelo, of Giotto, of Leonardo da Vinci. What could a saint possibly do to top the Pietá? No, no, no," she says firmly, "our saints can do nothing other than limit themselves to necessary kinds of miracles—nothing conspicuous—nothing loud or flagrant. And even then, there are still times when, no matter what they do, they are just not in our favor and are denounced in the same way as everybody else."

She launches into the story of her niece, Daniela, who works in the maternity wing of Borgo a Mozzano's central hospital. "Santa Anna, you know, is the patron saint of pregnant women," she says by way of background. "But the insults hurled against that poor saint when it comes time for women to give birth—well, according to Daniela, they will turn your ears red. One woman supposedly carried on for eight hours. *'Accidente a te, Santa Anna, a chi t'a fatto!'* [Damn you, Saint Anna, and He who made you], she screamed."

The coffee is ready. The Signora pours it into dainty porcelain cups and sits herself down across from me. "But it is more than the question of what we expect from our saints here in Tuscany, or how they carry out their mandate. It is also a question of their personal characteristics, which, like Tuscans at large, are different from those of other people. We Tuscans are proud people. We are not often found kneeling in Church asking for large homes or extravagant vacations. Consequently, when we *do* ask for something, we do not expect the donor to grant our wish in a way that would require a great profusion of thanks. After all, we could probably have gotten along without the favor in the first place."

Of course, the Signora says, what this creates is a way of giving that can only be characterized as somewhat recalcitrant. " 'Take it,' our saints say when they *do* decide to bestow a favor. 'Take it and be off with you.' "

By way of example, she points to Lucca's *Volto Santo*—Holy Face— which is a huge, ebony figure of the crucified Christ that hangs in the Church of San Martino. "According to legend," she explains, "a wealthy aristocrat once employed a violinist of limited means to play for his daughter's wedding. But when the wedding was over and the violinist had performed to everyone's gratification, the aristocrat refused to pay. So the violinist went to pray before the *Volto Santo*. 'O Dio,' he beseeched the luminous statue. 'My wife is lame and my children sick. I have no money and no food. Please help me.'

"And the *Volto Santo,* whose feet are adorned with slippers made of solid gold, kicked one off, and flicked it in the face of the violinist. When the poor man recovered from his initial shock, he took the gift and scampered off, eager to sell it and buy some food for his family. But as he exited from the church, he was spotted by a *carabiniero* [a police officer] who accused him of having stolen the slipper.

" 'No,' said the violinist. 'It was given to me by the *Volto Santo.*'

"The police officer laughed. 'As a present for your birthday, or simply on account of your good looks?' he asked, confiscating the golden treasure. And then he had a thought. 'Before I haul you off to jail,' he said, 'I'm going to give you a chance to stand before the Lord and beg Him for forgiveness.'

"So they walked back into the church. But when they reached the altar and the officer leaned forward to put the slipper back in place, the *Volto Santo* once again flicked it in the direction of the violinist. The officer tried again, and again, and each time the same thing happened. And so," the Signora says, "to this day, the *Volto Santo* stands above the altar in the Church of San Martino in Lucca, one slipper on, the other held up by a silver chalice.

"But do you see what I mean?" she asks. "If it had been another

Christ figure—the one in Naples, for example, or the one in that cathedral in Bari—the slipper would have floated delicately into the violinst's hands or, at least, hovered above him with some gentility. But not in Tuscany. Here, if you *do* receive a favor, it is thrown at you. 'Take this and don't ask me again!' "

The reason for this, she says, is that Tuscans do not like to have things done for them in the first place. For one thing, they do not want to be in anyone's debt. But more important is that, throughout history, they have become accustomed to fending for themselves *alla garibaldina,* in a make-shift way. (The term is attributed to Garibaldi, one of nineteenth-century Italy's great leaders, even though his efforts were, for the most part, hap-hazard and temporary.) So ingrained is this tendency among Tuscans that there's even a word for it—*arrangiarsi*—which means "to make do with your own resources."

"Wherever you go, a thousand times a day, you'll hear someone hurling the word at someone else, usually in instances where a piece of advice has been offered and refused: *allora arrangiarti* [so then, handle it yourself], to which the inevitable comeback is always: *E, naturalmente!* [naturally]."

Not all Tuscans are so *sfacciati*—brazen—however. The Signora points to the patron saint of the province of Lucca, Santa Zita, as an example of the gentle and beatific side of the Tuscan character, a side that, even the Signora admits, is more exception than rule. "Santa Zita was a simple soul," she says. "A model of humility not often found among the people of Tuscany, whose rate of hip injuries is higher than that of any other province."

"Why is that?" I ask, surprised by this apparent non sequitur.

"Because our noses are always in the air instead of pointed towards the ground, watching where we're going, that's why!"

"Beh," she says returning to the story, "poor Zita worked as a servant for one of Lucca's most aristocratic families, and every day, when she would go to the local market to buy food, she would be accosted by the poor and lame of the city, who would beg for even the smallest crumb. So she began filling her apron with slices of bread and distributing them to those who crossed her path. One day, however, as she was preparing to leave the house, Zita was spotted by one of the higher servants and reported to the master, who raced downstairs and accosted her as she was exiting the front gate. 'What do you have in your apron?' the brute demanded.

"'Roses and flowers,' St. Zita responded in her sweetest voice. And sure enough, when she opened her apron, the cloth was covered with magnificent buds of every color and fragrance.

"Of course," the Signora says, "poor Zita was martyred anyway. Which, as my husband would say, is what she gets for not having told the master to mind his own business."

The Signora explains to me about *piatti settimanali*—food for special occasions. "Tuscans eat well every day," she says. "But on holidays such as Easter, or the feast day of a certain saint, we prepare certain foods that are above and beyond our normal fare. Usually, these are sweets, made in great quantity and with a great number of ingredients."

A typical menu for such an occasion might include: an *antipasto;* a *minestra* and perhaps another type of *primo;* two or three *secondi* complete with *contorni;* fruit; cheese; an initial dessert such as *panna cotta* with espresso and a variety of liqueurs; and—as the crowning glory of this holiday meal—a special *dolce,* such as one of the ones on the pages that follow.

*The Ponte della Maddalena (Il Ponte del Diavolo).*

# BUCELLATO DI LUCCA
*Sweet Loaf of Lucca*

*This simple bread, perfumed with anise and stuffed with raisins, is the traditional dessert of Lucca. Generally made at home, it can also be bought in stores throughout the province of Lucca. The most favored and authentic can be found in Lucca itself, at a two hundred-year-old shop called Taddeucci in the Piazza San Michele 34, right behind the Cathedral.*

    1 tablespoon yeast
    2 cups sugar plus 2 tablespoons dry granulated sugar
    Warm water
    2 pounds unbleached flour, sifted
    1½ ounces anise seeds
    8 ounces golden raisins
    1 tablespoon unsalted butter
    1 pint heavy cream
    1–2 tablespoons fruit liqueur

1. Dissolve the yeast and 1 tablespoon of the sugar in ⅓ cup warm water; place the cup in a pot of hot water that surrounds the cup almost to the top. Let sit for 20 minutes or until the yeast is foamy (if the yeast has not foamed, it is dead and should be discarded).

2. Place the flour in a large bowl; add the foamy yeast, the 2 cups of sugar, the anise, raisins, and ¾ cup warm water. Mix well by hand, adding additional water, one tablespoon at a time, until a soft dough is formed. Knead on a floured counter for 2 or 3 minutes and replace in the bowl; cover and let sit for 30 minutes.

3. Stretch the dough into a long rectangle no more than ¾ inch thick; place on a baking sheet greased with butter. Preheat the oven to 350 degrees.

4. Mix the remaining tablespoon of sugar with the egg white; add 1 tablespoon warm water and beat with a fork into a liquid paste. Brush the top of the bucellato with the egg paste.

5. Bake for 20 minutes or until the top is golden brown.

6. Serve with fresh cream whipped with a tablespoon or two of fruit liqueur.

*Serves 6*

# BACI GARFAGNINI
*Kisses, Garfagnana-style*

*These small white cookies, similar to meringues, are of ancient tradition in the Garfagnana region of Tuscany. Today they are served for Easter dinners, weddings, baptisms, and local festivals. The recipe for this simple and delectable dessert has been passed down from family to family since the 1700s. Baci must be cooked at very low heat so that they retain their characteristic whiteness; cooking at higher heat will render them yellow.*

> 5 egg whites
> 2 cups sugar

1. Beat the egg whites to foamy consistency (if necessary to achieve the desired lightness, add another egg white). Add the sugar and beat into soft peaks.

2. Drop the "dough," 1 teaspoon at a time, onto a cookie sheet.

3. Cook in a preheated 200 degree oven for 20 minutes until firm.

*Yields approximately 30 baci*

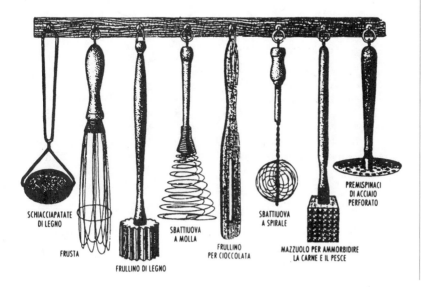

SCHIACCIAPATATE
DI LEGNO

FRUSTA

FRULLINO DI LEGNO

SBATTIUOVA
A MOLLA

FRULLINO
PER CIOCCOLATA

SBATTIUOVA
A SPIRALE

MAZZUOLO PER AMMORBIDIRE
LA CARNE E IL PESCE

PREMISPINACI
DI ACCIAIO
PERFORATO

The *Befana* is an old woman who is the Italian equivalent of Santa Claus: According to legend, all year long, this kindly old soul—dressed in rags and a head scarf and always pictured with a straw broom in hand—lives in her house in a remote section of the mountainous Garfagnana, preparing wonderful presents for good little girls and boys. Unlike Santa Claus, however, she delivers the presents on January 6th in commemoration of the day the Three Kings came to Jerusalem bearing gifts for the Christ Child.

The following recipes are traditionally prepared for January 6th, the feast of the Epiphany, which is also the day of the *Befana*. *Paste della Befana* is a type of "strudel" characteristic of many of the towns along the Versilian Coast. It is an ancient recipe, but one that is still in use.

*Befanani* are cookies usually brought first to the church for blessing, and then eaten with *vin santo,* whose literal translation is "holy wine" for reasons that have never been accurately determined.

## PASTE DELLA BEFANA
*Pastry for the Befana*

6 ounces toasted almonds
½ cup sugar
½ cup unbleached flour
1 egg plus 1 additional egg white
¾ teaspoon finely ground espresso
¾ teaspoon cocoa
1 tablespoon butter

1. Place the almonds and the sugar in a food processor and reduce to a paste; remove to a bowl.

2. Add the eggs, the additional egg white, the espresso and cocoa, stirring constantly with a fork.

3. Add the flour, pouring in a steady stream and continuing to beat with the fork until a thick, consistent paste is formed.

4. Roll out to ½-inch thickness; cut into diamond shapes and place on a buttered baking sheet.

5. Bake in a preheated 350 degree oven for 30 minutes or until crispy and cooked throughout.

*Makes approximately 20 diamonds*

# BEFANINI
*Epiphany Cookies*

>   4 cups unbleached flour, sifted
>   12 tablespoons butter
>   5 eggs, lightly beaten
>   ¼ teaspoon vanilla
>   ½ cup sugar
>   ½ teaspoon lemon juice
>   ¼ teaspoon mixed grated orange and lemon rinds

1. Place all ingredients in a large bowl; mix by hand into a thick dough.

2. On a floured surface, roll out the dough to ½-inch thickness; cut into shapes, such as circles, stars, and animals, or use cookie cutters.

3. Place on a baking sheet in a preheated 350 degree oven; bake for 15 minutes or until golden brown.

*Makes approximately 30 cookies*

# PASTA FROLLA
*Basic Pastry Dough*

*This is a simple but very good, useful dough to use for fruit tarts and tartlets, pies, shortcakes, and ricotta cakes. A porous dough, pasta frolla easily absorbs liquids from whatever is placed on top of it; it should, therefore, be consumed on the same day or within a day of baking. Pasta frolla can also be used for savory pies, in which case omit the sugar and add another pinch of salt.*

    2 cups unbleached flour, sifted
    ½ cup sugar, finely ground
    4 ounces unsalted butter, softened to room temperature
    1 egg yolk, lightly beaten
    ⅛ teaspoon grated orange rind
    Pinch of salt

1. In a large bowl, blend the sugar, flour, and salt.

2. Cut in the butter, then add the egg yolk and orange rinds. Mix with a wooden spoon until a thick but malleable dough is formed.

3. Roll into a ball, place in a clean bowl, cover, and refrigerate for at least 30 minutes.

4. When ready to use, place on a piece of waxed paper and flatten with a rolling pin; turn over the waxed paper on top of a baking pan or sheet, and peel away.

*Makes enough for 2 nine-inch pie crusts, 6 three-inch double-crusted tartlets, 2 nine-inch fruit tarts with crisscrosses on top, or 1 nine-inch shortcake*

# DOLCE ECONOMICO DI PATATE

*Economical Potato Dessert*

*Here, the Signora says, is a dessert that was enjoyed on many occasions when she was a child—not only for the reason implied by its name (although that was certainly a big part of it) but also for its complex blend of potatoes, rum, and caramelized sugar.*

3 eggs, separated
3 large potatoes, boiled, peeled, and cooled
½ cup sugar plus ⅓ cup for caramelizing
3 tablespoons light rum

1. Beat the egg whites until they form soft peaks. In a separate bowl, lightly beat the egg yolks.

2. Mash the potatoes; add the egg yolks, ½ cup sugar, and rum. Blend thoroughly by hand.

3. Fold the egg whites into the potato mixture, being careful not to liquify the consistency.

4. Place the ⅓ cup sugar in the bottom of a 9-inch cake pan; cook over very low heat until caramelized (until the sugar turns to a liquid brown). Be careful; this happens very suddenly.

5. Pour the potato mixture into the cake pan; place the cake into a larger pan filled with water that reaches halfway up the side of the cake pan. Bake in a preheated 350 degree oven for 20 minutes.

6. Serve at room temperature.

*Serves 6*

# TORTA DI RICOTTA CAMPAGNOLA
*Country-style Ricotta Cake*

*Despite its name, this elegant cake is used for weddings, baptisms, and confirmations. It is the best of the dozens of ricotta cakes made in either Versilia or Garfagnana, which all use the highly prized ricotta made in the mountainous regions of the Lucchesia.*

*The filling:*
> 1½ pounds fresh sheep's milk ricotta
> 1 ½ cups sugar
> 8 ounces assorted candied fruit, diced (or all one type, such as cherries)
> 6 ounces dark chocolate, melted
> ½ teaspoon vanilla
> ⅓ cup anisette, pastis, or sambuca
> 4 egg yolks, lightly beaten

*The shell:*
> ½ recipe Pasta Frolla (page 280), at room temperature
> 1 tablespoon unsalted butter for greasing the pan

*The meringue:*
> 3 egg whites
> 6 tablespoons sugar
> 2 ounces almond slivers

1. Pass the ricotta through a food mill or place it in a food processor and reduce to a pastelike consistency; add the sugar and stir with a wooden spoon to blend. Add the candied fruit, chocolate, vanilla, anisette, vanilla and egg yolks, one at a time, and stirring well between additions.

2. Place the pasta frolla on a piece of waxed paper; roll to ⅛-inch thickness and 12 inches in diameter.

3. Butter a 9-inch cake pan whose sides are at least 3 inches high; place the dough into the pan, shaping it so that the edge overlaps the pan somewhat.

4. Pour the ricotta mixture into the cake shell and shape the overlapped edge to create a rolled crust; bake in a preheated 350 degree oven for 40 minutes.

5. Meanwhile make the meringue: Beat the egg whites with the sugar to a thick, snowy consistency.

6. Remove the cake from the oven; spread the meringue over the top and sprinkle with the slivered almonds; replace in oven and bake for 10 minutes longer or until the meringue is well set.

7. Cool before serving.

*Serves 8*

*Gioviano.*

# TORTA COI BISCHERI
## *Cake with Scalloped Edges*

*Another extraordinary ricotta cake, this one completely different, has bischeri, or scalloped edges, signifying the towers of ancient medieval castles. A traditional dessert recipe originally from the Versilian Coast area, this particular preparation comes from Stazzema in northern Versilia, where it is generally made for Easter Sunday.*

1½ pounds fresh sheep's milk ricotta
6 eggs
5 cups milk
Rind of 1 lemon, grated
1 teaspoon vanilla
3 tablespoons light rum
1 cup dry unflavored breadcrumbs
½ recipe Pasta Frolla (page 280)
1 tablespoon unsalted butter

1. The day before, line a wire-mesh sieve with cheesecloth. Place the ricotta in it, set over a bowl, and allow to drain. Discard the liquid.

2. The next day, mix by hand the ricotta, eggs, milk, lemon, vanilla, and rum; add breadcrumbs as needed to create a semiliquid consistency.

3. Bring the pasta frolla to room temperature; place all but one handful on a piece of waxed paper and roll with a rolling pin to a diameter of 12 inches and a height of ⅛ inch. Reserve the handful for a topping.

4. Arrange the dough in a buttered 9-inch cake pan that is at least 3 inches in height; overlap the edges somewhat.

5. Pour the ricotta mixture into the pan; roll the edges and flatten between thumb and forefinger to form an evenly shaped edge standing at least 1 inch higher than the edge of the pan. Using a knife, cut the edge into a pattern resembling a series of towers. Bake in a preheated 350 degree oven for 30 minutes.

6. On waxed paper roll the reserved handful of dough into a rectangle; cut into strips approximately 1 inch in width. Arrange on top of the cake in a lattice pattern to resemble the barred windows of the castles;

if possible, do not remove the cake from the oven while arranging the latticework, but only slide it towards you on the oven shelf. Bake for 15 minutes more, or until a knife placed into the center of the cake comes out relatively dry. Remove from pan and cool on a rack.

7. Serve at room temperature.

*Serves at least 8*

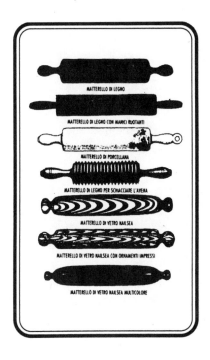

*Cenci* (rags) are fried pieces of sweet dough prepared for Carnival. Known throughout Italy by a host of different names—*chiacchiere* in Milan, *galani* in Venice, *crostoli* in Trent, *frappe* in Rome, and, in other places *stroppole, fiocchi, fiochetti, nastrini,* and *donzinelli*—the Tuscan *cenci* is, according to the Signora, the most appropriate name for this treat because of their appearance, which resembles that of irregularly shaped rags. "Of course," she says, "those Pratese (the people of Prato in the province of Florence are known for being the center of the textile industry and for housing thousands of 'ragpickers')—*they* think the name *cenci* belongs to them." She points an angry finger in my direction. "*You* try convincing them otherwise."

# CENCI
*Carnival Rags*

¼ teaspoon granulated yeast
2 tablespoons sugar plus ½ tablespoon for proofing the yeast
½ cup warm water
2 cups unbleached flour, sifted
1 egg, lightly beaten
2 tablespoons extra-virgin olive oil
½ cup vin santo or port
Rind of ½ lemon, grated
Olive oil for frying
Powdered sugar for dusting

1. Place the yeast and the ½ tablespoon of sugar in ½ cup warm water; place the cup in a pot filled with enough hot (not boiling) water to rise almost to the top of the cup. Let sit for 30 minutes or until very foamy.

2. Place the flour in a large bowl; add the egg, the 2 tablespoons of oil, 2 tablespoons sugar, vin santo, the yeast mixture, and the lemon rind. Mix by hand until a ball of dough is formed (do not knead); cover, refrigerate, and let rest for 30 minutes.

3. On a floured surface and using a rolling pin, roll out the dough to a large rectangle approximately ½ inch high; cut into shapes or circles, stars, squares, diamonds, etc.

4. Fry in a large skillet filled with very hot oil until both sides are golden brown; dust with the powdered sugar and serve hot.

*Makes about 50 cenci*

*Passimata* is a traditional dessert made throughout the mountainous Garfagnana region for Easter Sunday when it was brought to church, along with eggs decorated especially for the occasion, by young children to be blessed by the priest.

The following song was traditionally sung on Holy Saturday during the long and tedious preparations (among them, the making of the *passimata*) that would render a house suitable for celebrating Easter, which is to Italians the most important religious festival of the year. Note that this ancient ditty contains the complete menu for a traditional Easter dinner of old.

| | |
|---|---|
| *Sabato Santo* | Holy Saturday |
| *Perche sei stato tanto?* | Why did you take so long to end? |
| *Domenica mattina* | Sunday morning |
| *una grossa gallina* | a large chicken |
| *un quarto di capretto* | a quarter of a sheep |
| *un uovo benedetto* | a blessed egg |
| *una fetta di passimata* | a slice of *passimata* |
| *Oh! Che vita beata!* | Oh! What a wonderful life! |

# PASSIMATA
*Easter Cake*

1 teaspoon granulated yeast

2 cups sugar plus 1 tablespoon for proofing the yeast

½ cup warm water

8 cups unbleached flour, sifted

5 eggs, lightly beaten

8 ounces unsalted butter plus 1 tablespoon for greasing the pan

½ cup vin santo or port

8 ounces golden raisins, soaked for 1 hour in warm water, drained, and dried

1. Dissolve the yeast along with 1 tablespoon sugar in ½ cup warm water; place the cup in a saucepan filled with enough hot water (not boiling) to reach halfway up the side of the cup. Let sit for 30 minutes until the yeast is very foamy.

2. Place the flour in a bowl and cut in the 2 sticks of butter. Add the eggs, vin santo or port, ¾ pound sugar, and the yeast mixture. Work with your hands until a soft dough is formed; cover and let sit in a warm place for 1 hour or until risen to twice its size.

3. Add the raisins and knead with your hands until they are well blended; cover and let sit in a warm place for another hour or until doubled in size.

4. Butter a 9-inch cake pan whose sides are at least 3 inches high; place the dough in the pan, cover, and let sit for 30 minutes in a warm place.

5. Bake in a preheated 350 degree oven for 30 minutes or until a fork inserted into its center comes out dry.

6. Cool to room temperature before serving.

*Serves 8*

# PASTA REALE
## *Regal Cake*

*This is a popular type of cake served throughout the Versilian Coast area, especially on Easter Sunday and local feast days. In the northern Versilia town of Cardoso di Stazzema, it is commonly made for the feast of Saint Maria, patron saint of Cardoso. The Cardosans eat it as is, with a plentiful quantity of good red wine; in the mountainous areas, however, it is more commonly served sliced into two layers and filled with fresh whipped cream.*

    6 eggs, separated
    1 cup sugar
    2 cups unbleached flour, sifted
    ½ teaspoon vanilla
    Rind of 1 lemon, grated
    1 tablespoon butter for greasing the cake pan

1. Using a fork, beat the egg yolks with half the sugar.

2. In another bowl, beat the egg whites with the remaining sugar into stiff peaks.

3. Add the flour to the egg yolk mixture and blend thoroughly. Add the vanilla and grated lemon.

4. Fold the egg whites into the dough, blending delicately with a spatula until a soft dough is formed.

5. Place the dough in a greased 9-inch cake pan at least 3 inches in height. Bake in a preheated 200 degree oven for approximately 2 hours; do not open the oven during this time or the cake will "fall."

6. Serve at room temperature.

*Serves 6*

# PAGNOTTA CALDA DI NATALE
*Christmas Bread*

*This is Borgo a Mozzano's traditional Christmas bread, a wonderful loaf made with dried fruits and nuts and topped with a layer of dark chocolate. Visible in the windows of all the town's food shops from mid-December on, this delicious treat is served on Christmas eve as the culmination of a dinner where the appetizers and the first and second courses consist entirely of fish.*

> 9 tablespoons unsalted butter
> 4 cups unbleached flour, sifted
> 6 ounces sugar
> 3 ounces toasted pine nuts, chopped into fine pieces
> 3 ounces golden raisins, soaked for 30 minutes, drained, and dried
> 2 ounces candied citron, minced
> 2 ounces peanuts, chopped into fine pieces
> 2 ounces dried figs, minced
> Rind of ½ lemon, grated
> ½ cup milk
> ½ cup whiskey
> 4 ounces dark chocolate

1. Melt the butter in a small saucepan.

2. Place the flour in a large bowl; add the melted butter and the sugar. Mix with a fork until all ingredients are well blended.

3. Add the pignoli nuts, raisins, citron, peanuts, figs, and lemon rind and incorporate into the dough; pour the milk and whiskey over the dough and mix by hand until a thick ball is formed.

4. Shape the dough into a large, somewhat flat oval; cut a large cross on the surface of the bread, place on a greased baking sheet, and bake in a preheated 350 degree oven for approximately 1 hour or until a fork inserted into its center comes out dry.

5. Melt the chocolate in a double boiler; pour over the bread while still hot.

6. Cool somewhat before serving.

*Serves 8*

# TORTA DI CIOCCOLATA DI RISO
*Chocolate Rice Cake*

*This cake is prepared during the Christmas season by the people of the Lucchesía. Large numbers of cakes are baked at one time and stored side by side in cool pantries for weeks on end. The crust is a* pasta frolla, *and the filling a rich mixture of semisweet chocolate, rice that has been boiled in milk, raisins, candied fruit, and pine nuts. The distinctive feature of this cake is its scalloped edges whose peaks resemble those of the Apuan Alps.*

> *The filling:*
> ½ cup golden raisins
> ¼ cup sugar
> 4 tablespoons unsalted butter, softened to room temperature, plus butter for greasing cake pan
> 2 eggs plus 1 egg white
> ½ cup unbleached flour, sifted
> ½ cup rice cooked in 1½ cups milk until tender
> ½ cup milk
> 2½ tablespoons unsweetened cocoa powder
> ½ cup toasted pine nuts
> ⅓ cup candied fruit
> ¼ teaspoon nutmeg
> ¼ teaspoon cinnamon
> Salt
> *The crust:*
> 1 recipe Pasta Frolla (page 280)

1. Soak the raisins in warm water for 20 minutes; drain and dry.

2. Put the sugar and 4 tablespoons butter in a bowl; whisk them together to a creamy consistency.

3. Add the eggs, flour, and cooked rice; pour the milk in a steady stream, stirring with a wooden spoon, until all ingredients are thoroughly blended.

4. Add the raisins, cocoa, pine nuts, candied fruit, nutmeg, cinnamon, and salt; mix well.

5. Preheat the oven to 350 degrees.

6. Butter an 8-inch cake pan whose sides are at least 2 inches high.

7. Roll the pasta frolla into 2 rounds, one that is at least 12 inches in diameter; the other at least 8 inches. Both should be approximately ⅛ inch thick.

8. Place the 12-inch round in the pan with its edges overlapping the sides; pour the filling into the pan, tapping the pan on a hard counter-top to create an even surface.

9. Using the overlapped dough, make a rolled crust and pat it firmly against the side of the pan so that it is somewhat flattened; to make the peaks, slice the dough in a continuous "V" pattern, making a series of consistent "peaks" and "valleys."

10. Cut the 8-inch round of dough into strips approximately 1 inch in width, and place on the cake in a crisscross latticework pattern. Beat the egg white with a tablespoon of water; brush the latticework and the peaked crust with the egg mixture.

11. Bake the cake for 70 minutes or until the filling is firm and the dough is a golden color; cool before serving.

*Serves 8 to 10*

# BOMBE AL ZABAGLIONE
*Zabaglione Bombe*

*Bombe—round frozen shells whose insides contain a complementary flavor frozen to a different consistency—are very popular throughout the Lucchesía, as is anything having to do with zabaglione—an egg custard flavored with marsala. This recipe is one that Signora Fontanini calls* una meraviglia!—*a miracle. It consists of a semisweet chocolate lining that is frozen until hard, and a center made of zabaglione whose texture is much like that of mousse. Removed from its mold and sliced into servings, it appears on individual plates as a quarter-moon dark-chocolate outer layer folded around a pale-yellow, creamy, half moon.*

> 4 ounces semisweet chocolate
> 6 egg yolks
> ¼ cup plus 2 tablespoons sugar
> ¼ cup unsalted butter
> 2 egg whites
> 1 cup heavy cream
> ¼ teaspoon vanilla
> ¼ cup marsala

1. Heat the chocolate in the top of a double boiler over boiling water until melted.

2. In a medium bowl, beat 2 of the egg yolks with the ¼ cup sugar until thick and lemon colored; mix in the chocolate.

3. Melt the butter in a small saucepan; fold it into the chocolate mixture. Beat the egg whites until they form soft peaks and fold into the chocolate.

4. Beat the heavy cream until stiff; add half to the chocolate mixture. Add the vanilla.

5. Lightly oil a melon mold and line it with the chocolate mixture, leaving the center hollow.

6. Put the remaining 4 egg yolks in a metal bowl and place the bowl over boiling water. Add the remaining 2 tablespoons sugar and the marsala, and beat rapidly with a whisk until the egg mixture is thick and foamy. Cool to room temperature.

7. Add the remaining heavy cream, spoon the egg mixture into the center of the mold, and place in freezer overnight.

8. To serve, place a hot towel around the outside of the mold until the bombe comes loose; place on a cold plate and keep in freezer until ready to slice.

*Serves 8 to 10*

**Note**: *Salmonella-free eggs should be used—they're expensive but, as Signora Fontanini would say, "meglio essere sicuri"—better to be safe.*

# CROSTATA DI MELE CON CREMA
*Apple Custard Tart*

*Borgo a Mozzano, near where the Signora lives, is known for its crostate, which are rectangular tarts made of fruit. This is the most famous, and it is the one the Signora made for me shortly after I arrived. "Every country has its fruit tarts," she told me, "and I know you probably have tasted them in France and in Germany, but rest assured, you have never tasted one like the one you will eat here." Of course, I knew she would be right even as she was putting it together, but I was not prepared for the wonderfully light and delicately sweet creation that she placed on the table that evening after dinner. From the looks of it, six people could have been served, but we were only three, and by the time she had finished cleaning up the dishes, I had finished the remaining three portions. Heavenly!*

> 4 large apples (slightly on the tart side)
> Juice of ½ lemon
> 2 egg yolks, lightly beaten
> 2 tablespoons unbleached flour
> 1 cup milk
> 1 tablespoon vanilla
> 4 tablespoons sugar
> 1 recipe Pasta Frolla (page 280)
> ¼ cup apricot marmalade

1. Peel the apples and cut them into thin slices; toss them with the lemon juice and set aside.

2. In a saucepan, make the custard by blending together the egg yolks, flour, milk, vanilla, and sugar; cook over medium heat, stirring constantly until all ingredients are well blended and the custard has thickened. Cool to room temperature.

3. Using a rolling pin, shape the dough into a rectangle approximately 8 x 11 inches, leaving enough to overlap the edges; place in pan.

4. Spread the custard over the dough, using a spoon to distribute it evenly over the surface.

5. Roll the edges of the dough into a round cord surrounding the tart.

6. Arrange the apple slices in 3 or 4 rows, overlapping the edges.

7. Heat the marmalade until it "melts"; brush the apple slices with the marmalade, dot with butter, and bake in a preheated 350 degree oven for 40 minutes or until the dough is golden brown.

8. Cool to room temperature before serving.

*Serves 6*

# BRIGADINI
*Aniseed Wafers*

*These wafers are traditionally sold in street stalls throughout Tuscany, and at the local fairs, called sagre, hosted by each town.*

 2 cups unbleached flour, sifted
 1 teaspoon baking powder
 6 tablespoons unsalted butter
 3 tablespoons sugar
 1 teaspoon anise seeds
 2 eggs, lightly beaten
 5 tablespoons milk

1. Mix the flour with the baking powder; cut in the butter and blend thoroughly.

2. Add the sugar, anise seeds, eggs, and milk; mix well with a wooden spoon.

3. Break off small pieces of the dough and roll them into balls no larger than a walnut; press each one into a thin round wafer.

4. Heat a heavy iron skillet over medium heat; cook the wafers for approximately 2 or 3 minutes per side until crisp and golden.

*Makes approximately 30 wafers*

A PANNA COTTA STORY

During my stay, the Signora also made *panna cotta,* baked cream tarts, the recipe for which was given to her by a young woman down the street who acquired it "through nefarious means."

"She went with her husband to have dinner at one of our finest restaurants—I won't say which," the Signora said, "and they served this *panna cotta* which, my friend says, was *so* wonderful that she decided she had to have the recipe. As you may know, it is a very rare occasion when a Tuscan cook gives out a prized recipe. So my friend, who has a very large stomach, told the cook that she was pregnant and that the *panna cotta* was one of the few things she had eaten in a long time with such gusto and could she possibly have the recipe, which she would keep to herself and never reveal to anybody. And so he gave it to her." And here it is.

# PANNA COTTA
*Baked Cream Tarts with Marsala and Pine Nuts*

*The tarts:*
  4 cups half-and-half
  1 cup sugar
  1 tablespoon vanilla
  1 or 2 ounces unflavored gelatin
*The sauce:*
  4 ounces toasted pine nuts
  1 cup honey
  ½ cup marsala

1. Warm the half-and-half; add the sugar, the vanilla, and 1 ounce of the gelatin. Stir constantly over low heat until thickened; add more gelatin, 1 tablespoon at a time, if necessary.

2. Pour into individual custard cups; refrigerate for at least 3 hours before serving.

3. Make the sauce: Mix all sauce ingredients and warm over low heat, stirring constantly; let sit for at least 3 hours before serving.

4. When ready to serve, remove the custard from the cups, place on individual dishes, and top with the sauce.

*Serves 8*

# INDEX

*A*nne Bianchi is a New York City based writer who spends part of every year in Tuscany visiting family and sampling the area's incomparable cuisine. Her previous books include *C. Everett Koop: The Health of a Nation*, *A Music Lover's Guide to Great Britain* and *Introduction to Chile*. Currently she is working on a collection of recipes from Italian women who live in Eritréa. When not writing, Anne Bianchi can be found cooking with friends or working in her upstate garden.